Blowing

One Breath, One Mind

Expanded Edition: Includes Blowing Zen II

Carl Abbott, Santa Cruz, California

First Published as "Shakuhachi Lesson Booklet" 1980

Second Revised Edition 1992

Third Edition 2005

Fourth Expanded Edition 2010, 2012

Acknowledgements

I would like to thank my wife Leslie, Peter Mitracos, Joe Frank, Michael Kanner, Susan Lund, Mary Beth Brooker, Monty Levenson and John Singer. Without their generous help and enthusiasm this book could not have been accomplished.

I am indebted to Kawase (Kansuke then, Junsuke III now) for teaching me San Kyoku. I must also thank him and his father, Junsuke II, for all the help they gave me learning Shakuhachi construction. I am grateful to Goro Yamaguchi for giving me a solid foundation in Hon Kyoku.

I thank Mr. D.C. Lau for his masterful translation of the Tao Te Ching (Penguin Books). To my mind, no translation approaches the essence of this ancient scripture like his. I am grateful for the use of a few excerpts in this book.

Blowing Zen

BACKGROUND

MAKING SOUND

PLAYING INSTRUCTIONS

SHAKUHACHI CONSTRUCTION

THE MUSIC

As Japanese music reads from right to left, the sheet music begins at the back of the Blowing Zen part of the book (about the middle).

Blowing Zen II

A complete Table of Contents for Blowing Zen II begins at the very back of this book. Here, briefly are the main headings

About The Cover

Suizen, or "Blowing Zen", is an old form of Buddhist meditation using music composed for the Shakuhachi. The cover photo is the author playing Shakuhachi in his backyard bamboo grove.

Obtaining A Shakuhachi Flute, Etc.

See the sources listed on page 17 for Shakuhachi flutes, CDs, recordings, etc., The most economical route for the flute is making your own using the instructions given in this book. Those who wish may order this type of flute from us. (See "Other Publications" at the back of this book.)

If you have problems with any of this material, and conscientious attempts to solve them fail, please email at Centertao.org or write. *Enclose a self-addressed stamped envelope* and send to: CenterTao, 406 Lincoln St., Santa Cruz, CA. 95060

Copying The Music

Copy the music so you can read it while referring to the instructions. You can glue the edges of these copies into one long sheet, moving from right to left, and then fold it in an accordion fashion. This will allow you to play the long pieces without having to turn pages.

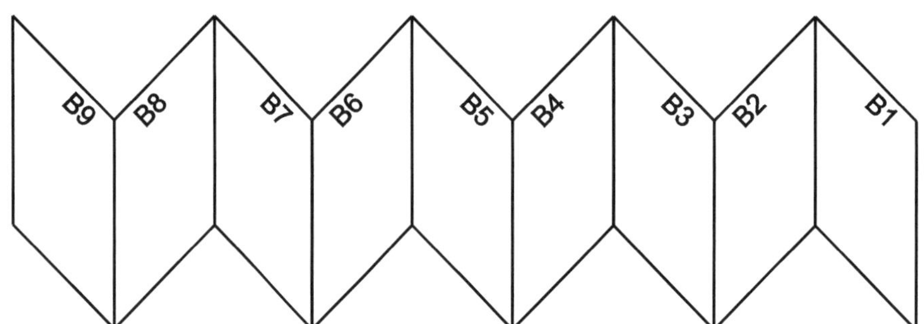

Go On Line

For MP3 sound files, bonus materials, and other information go to:
Centertao.org/learn-zen

INTRODUCTION

Many have fallen in love with the Shakuhachi flute. At first glance, it's just an instrument for playing beautiful music. Yet, hidden in its simplicity is profound possibility. The windy and resonant sound of the Shakuhachi brings deep serenity to sympathetic ears. For the devoted player it is also a spiritual tool for training the mind and breath. For this, Buddhist music plays a vital role.

Buddhist music seems simple. It doesn't use a great range of octaves or impressive musical techniques. In fact, you can begin the first Buddhist piece within a few months. However, you can easily spend the rest of your life perfecting it.

Asymmetry and nuance are the essence of Buddhist music compositions. Their sound has a naturalness like the wind in the trees or the pounding surf. There is no foot stomping beat or melodious aesthetic to heed. These fluid compositions parallel the unaffected qualities of nature. They reach from the "yin" of a trickling mountain stream to the "yang" of a roaring river.

Buddhist music points to the reality only your silent self knows. For the sincere player it offers a way to this mystery within. Listen, and watch its shadowy nature touch your life.

This book enables you to learn the Shakuhachi, with or without a teacher. Interest is the only prerequisite. If you have that, the necessary determination comes naturally. Difficulties along the way are opportunities in disguise; they reflect your expectations. Facing them with surrender helps you follow a more peaceful and perceptive life.

After you learn the basics, seek out a teacher to perfect your playing along formal aesthetic lines. Or just continue on your own. On a journey of self discovery, Buddhist music is an excellent touchstone to help you on your way. When you get discouraged, remember this Taoist saying:

A tree that can fill the span of a man's arms
Grows from a downy tip;
A terrace nine stories high
Rises from hodfuls of earth;
A journey of a thousand miles
Starts from beneath one's feet.
Tao Te Ching

Sparrows sitting on rice stalks, Han Jo-Cho, 12th C.

HISTORY

The origin of the Shakuhachi flute is unknown. Its construction is so basic, it was probably one of man's earliest instruments. Find a reed, blow over the end, and you have it - if all you want is a single tone. Poke a few holes in the side if you want to play a melody.

People around the world play this type of flute. The basic model, like the Ethiopian flute shown here, has a plain blowing edge. The Pygmies in equatorial Africa and the Sherpas in Nepal add a beveled notch to the blowing edge of their flutes. The longer and thinner Egyptian Sabi also has a similar blowing end. The Andean Indians play their hauntingly beautiful music on Shakuhachi-like flutes, the Quena and the Ujusinis. And, of course, the Chinese have their version, the Tung Hsaio.

The Shakuhachi flute entered Japanese life sometime between the stone age and the 6th century AD. Whether it evolved locally or came to Japan from elsewhere is unknown.

Japan remained in Neolithic isolation until the 3rd century BC. This ended with increasing cultural and technological stimulation from China which slowly transformed the Japanese way of life. This influence peaked in the 6th century AD as every aspect of contemporary Chinese culture flowed into Japan: art, calligraphy, medicine, music, metallurgy, textiles and Buddhism.

Ethiopian sheperd with end blown flute

Bolivian Indians with flutes "Ujusisnis"

A six hole Chinese version of the Shakuhachi shows up historically from the 6th century onward as an instrument used in Japanese court music. It flourished until the 10th century, then it gradually lost popularity.

In the 13th century, a guild of wandering Buddhist monks appeared playing a five hole version, the hitoyogiri. Their flute, while closer to the modern Shakuhachi, was still short, narrow, and high pitched.

Legend has it that a Zen monk brought Buddhist music to Japan from China in the 13th century. However, it's more likely that the monks either started from scratch or adapted other forms of music, like Buddhist chants, to meet their spiritual needs.

By the 17th century another guild of itinerant Zen monks had formed. They played the longer "root section" Shakuhachi we know today. These Komuso, or "priests of emptiness", wore large straw hats which symbolized the Buddhist belief in the need to extinguish desire.

Komuso wanderers

The Komuso flourished for several hundred years. They gained official recognition in exchange for informing the government about conditons around the country. In the 18th century, a high ranking Komuso named Kurosawa Kinko collected and compiled pieces of Buddhist music from neighboring temples. He then arranged 36 of them into what is today the standard Kinko school Buddhist Hon Kyoku ("original pieces") repertoire.

By the mid 19th century, the Komuso fell into decline with their remnants evolving into the Meian "school". It was also around this time that the Shakuhachi found increasing use as a secular instrument.

From the mid 19th century on, a growing interest in western music began encroaching on Japanese musical traditions. The Shakuhachi, as an instrument, survived this change best through the Tozan school, because it emphasized modern music.

Thanks to Kurosawa Kinko, the Kinko and Meian schools had a core of 36 compositions to carry on the Buddhist music tradition. These small aristocratic groups are proud of their close relationship to the old traditions.

While the Meian and Kinko schools both retain the original Buddhist pieces (Hon Kyoku), there are differences. The Kinko school has, in addition, a wide repertoire of classical chamber music. This is ensemble music based on the traditional music of two other Japanese instruments, the Koto and the Shamisen. Kinko teachers usually require their students to learn this music well before going on to Buddhist Hon Kyoku music.

On the other hand, students of the Meian school start learning Buddhist pieces almost from the beginning. On the whole, the Meian school adheres more closely to the original Buddhist use of the Shakuhachi.

EFFECTS

The Shakuhachi and its Buddhist music help relieve the ill effects of modern life.

People under stress often breathe with irregular rhythm and shallow depth. The close neurological connection between the brain and respiration causes this loss of natural breathing rhythm and depth. Have you noticed how emotions like anger or excitement effect your breathing?

Happily, it works both ways. For example, the next time you get angry, breath deeply and evenly. You should notice decreased stress and greater self-control. Main-

Fishing in retirement, Ma Yuan, 12th C.

taining natural breathing rhythms in times of stress or emergency increases your calm headedness and endurance under those conditions.

Playing Shakuhachi exercises the diaphragm and chest, and restores natural breathing rhythm . This soothes the nervous system, helping prevent tension build up. A deeper and more even breathing rhythm means the lungs work less and at a pace that quiets the mind.

The regular exercising of the respiratory system also benefits physiological health. Deep breathing, for instance, expels CO_2 and brings oxygen to every corner of the lungs. This is as invigorating as jogging, without all the wear and tear.

Yoga tradition claims healthful breathing increases one's life span. Yogis measure the life span in breaths. Let's say, for instance, that you now breath 14 times a minute. A few years of playing can bring this down to 12, or fewer, breaths a minute. Thus, according to the Yogic formula, you will lengthen your life by 15%.

Modern life isn't the only source of our ills. Part of our stress and sorrow also comes from not noticing the subtle qualities of life. We don't appreciate the small moments which make up most of the day. We yearn to finish our menial tasks quickly to make way for pleasurable activity.

The only alternative is to make the menial pleasureable again. This union of mind and action comes through being watchful in the moment. And Buddhist Hon Kyoku music is a splendid medium for training this watchfulness.

This music embodies a microcosm of life, from the passive "yin", to the active "yang". Sensing and balancing these poles musically helps balance them in daily life. The sound is a mantra directing you towards that silence of watchfulness that lies beyond the "yin" and the "yang". In this reflective awareness, you pass beyond these opposites.

The sound gives you feedback; it mirrors your mind. So, as the mind is, the sound will be. This permits you to search for and use those qualities of mind that you want to develop. Your ears will tell you when you're on track.

What makes playing Buddhist Hon Kyoku different? Aren't the same effects possible playing other music? Hon Kyoku places the emphasis on the instantaneous quality of mind. There are fewer harmonies, frills or emotional lures to distract you. The emphasis is on the quality of one thing - the sound and what it reflects.

Ordinary music evokes an emotional involvement. Melody set to rhythm creates this interest. Rhythm, in turn, requires the illusion of time, i.e., finite reference points of past, present and future. Thus, you have a contrived symmetrical repetition of sound and silence. Buddhist music on the other hand is only very loosely set in time. It's like the rhythm of water trickling down a hillside. You're the creator and observer of an infinite moment - a suspension of time where the mind rests in an eternal present.

Some of what I've tried to explain is impossible to explain. It ends up both exaggerated and understated - not intentionally, mind you. If I've lost you, sit tight. You'll discover these effects, as I did, through playing the Shakuhachi. Be patient though - it takes awhile.

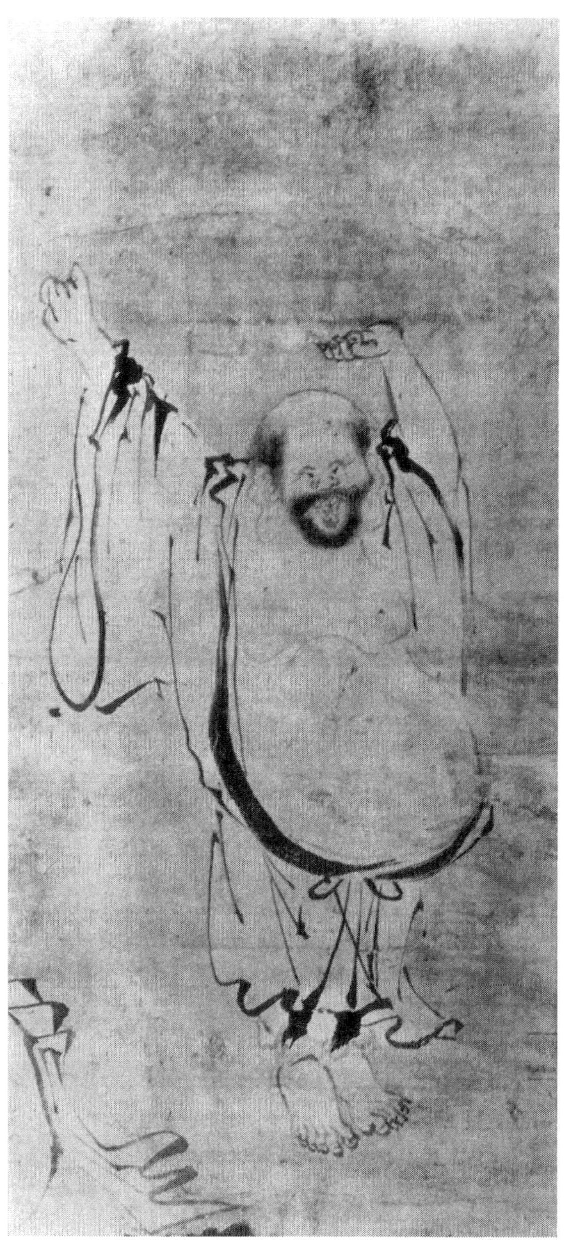

Yawning Hotei, Yamada Doan, 16th C.

PRINCIPLE TECHNIQUES

The more natural and simple the musical instrument is, the more subtle the technique can become. Few instruments are more basic than the Shakuhachi. It's nothing more than a resonant pipe with five holes. Its musical notation and timing are simple enough to learn in a few hours, at most. This simplicity is deceiving; it's a very challenging and rewarding instrument to play.

Holding The Shakuhachi

Some right handed players hold the Shakuhachi with their right hand on the bottom end of the flute. Others hold it with their left hand on the bottom. Try both to find what feels natural for you. Either way, it's important to stabilize the flute with the bottom thumb and middle finger.

Place the thumb and middle fingers between holes #1 and #2 (photo 1), with the thumb directly opposite the middle finger. Always keep this grip firm while playing. You can even keep the thumb a little lower towards the bottom end of the flute. Avoid holding the thumb higher than the middle finger, as this makes the flute unstable. Place a Band-Aid on the flute where your thumb goes to feel the thumb position while playing. Tape your thumb and middle finger onto the flute a few times if you still can't keep them in place.

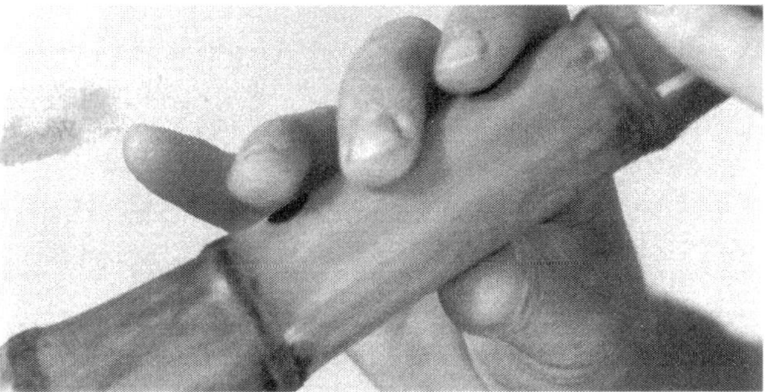

Photo 1

The hands and fingers slant in towards the instrument (photo 2). Place the upper middle finger between holes #3 and #4 and the thumb on the back hole #5. Players usually keep the upper middle finger on the flute to stabilize it. As the photo shows, the forefingers and ring fingers cover the front holes. Take care to use the pads at the end of the fingers for this. Hold the little fingers off the flute or lightly on the flute, but never under it. This restricts mobility of the ring fingers (photo 1, 2, 8).

When removing a finger from a hole, hold it 1/4 inch to 1/2 inch above the hole. It's less than 1/4 inch when playing fast tempo music. Lifting fingers too far above the flute, makes your playing sound choppy.

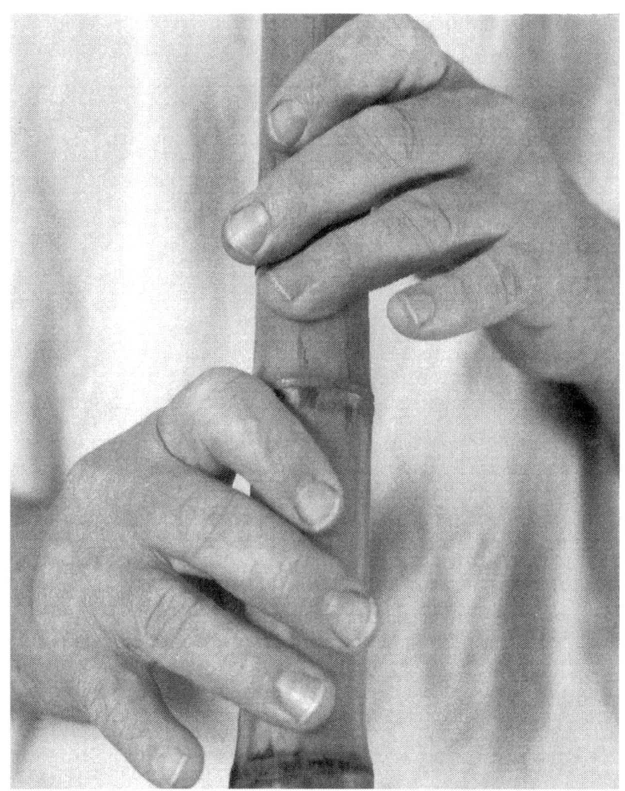

Photo 2

Hold the elbows up, keeping the distance between them equal to the width of the shoulders (photo 3). Many beginners let the flute drop towards the chest, adversely effecting posture and sound quality.

Photo 3

Producing A Sound

The greatest difficulty comes in the beginning - first in getting sound, and then in strengthening and controlling it. Breathing is a problem for a few months until you tone the muscles of the lips and diaphragm.

It helps in the beginning to practice in a room with an echo and a mirror, like a bathroom. Now, using the mirror, hold the flute as described above. Start with the fingers held 1/2 inch off ALL of the holes. Place the blowing end firmly at the pit located between the lower teeth and the chin (photo 4). Now blow!

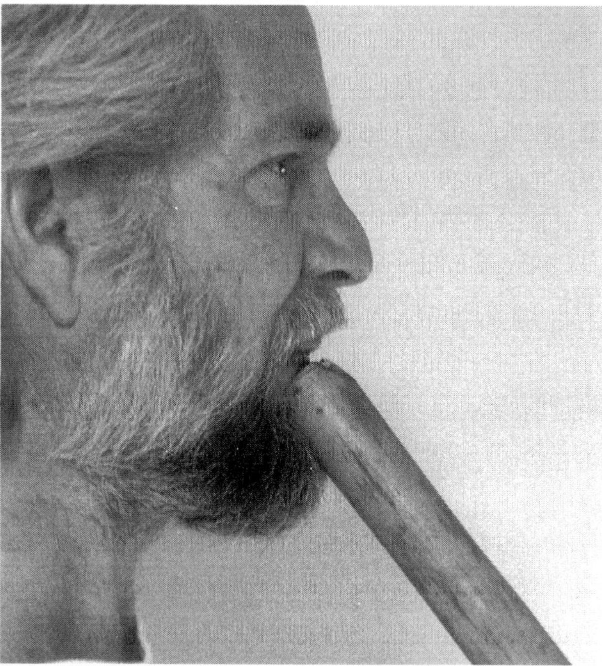

Photo 4

Use the mirror often to compare yourself with the photos. Even after you've been playing awhile, use the mirror occasionally to see what's happening. This helps insure you don't form bad habits.

First try to imitate the lip formation shown in photo 5. With the teeth apart as shown in photo 6, bring the lips down over the teeth. Disregard the tongue position shown here, for now, and rest it on the bottom of the mouth. To achieve this lip formation, pucker the lips slightly as if you are gently blowing on something - and simultaneously stretch them horizontally. *PUCKER AND STRETCH*! Practice this in front of the mirror often to ensure you're getting close to this lip formation.

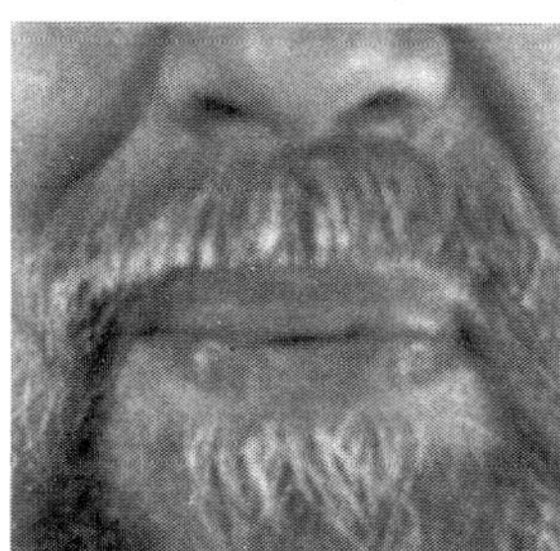

Photo 5

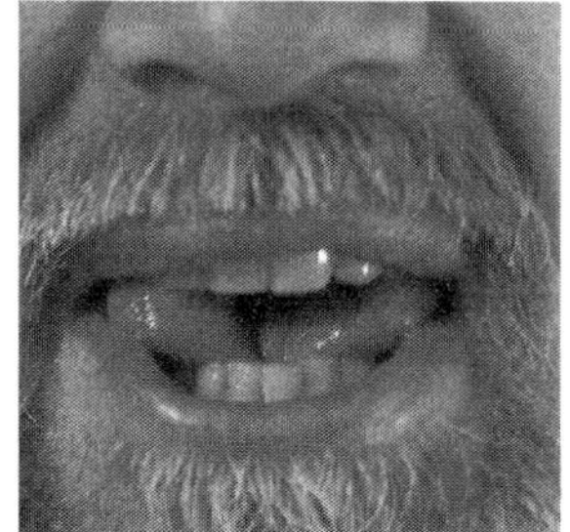

Photo 6

Photo 7

Put some grease (Chapstick) on your lips and place the flute as explained above. **Position the blowing end so it almost touches the crack formed by the upper and lower lips (photo 7)**. The distance between this crack and the blowing edge isn't more than 1/4 inch. It's half that when playing some high octave and MERI (flat) notes.

When everything is in position (photos 3, 4, 5, 7), take a deep breath and blow over the edge with a gentle and prolonged exhalation. Half the air should go into the flute and half over the outside edge. This is like blowing across a pop bottle to produce sound.

To find the correct blowing angle, pivot the flute from the chin. Move its lower end up and down slowly while you exhale. Hunt for the sound by making small changes in the flute's blowing edge position.

Differences of 1/64th inch between your lip opening and the blowing edge can mean the difference between sound and no sound. Beginners often have a large gap between the blowing edge and their lips, making the sound weak and unstable. Careful imitation of the positions shown in the photos saves a lot of frustration.

Breathing And Posture

One benefit of the Shakuhachi is the opportunity to develop healthy natural breathing. Glance over this section now. After learning to play a few melodies, come back and study it thoroughly.

The foundation of breath harmony is good posture, due to the mechanics of respiration. When the posture slumps, the diaphragm pushes the abdomen forcefully and inefficiently. The body must even use the muscles between the ribs to augment breathing, which disrupts respiratory rhythm further.

Full, even breathing comes more naturally if the posture is erect. The main concern is remembering to maintain good posture. If you do this, playing Shakuhachi will help develop your diaphragm's capability; and a capable diaphgram helps you play Shakuhachi.

Full breathing begins deep in the abdominal cavity. Try making fast, yet full, contractions of the diaphragm while playing. This achieves maximum inhalation of air quickly.

Photo 8

Keep the stomach muscles firm, but not tightly contracted. This keeps the stomach from bulging way out as the diaphragm presses downward. Instead of the stomach bulging, you'll feel a pressing sensation in the pelvic area. The fuller the movement of the diaphragm, the more expansion you'll feel there. This is due to the diaphragm pressing down on the abdominal organs, which by the way, benefits the digestive system.

The Japanese play the Shakuhachi seated as shown in photo 8. This position is a variation of the Yoga posture Virasana. Variations of Virasana or other meditation postures are also fine.

If you find these positions too difficult, sit cross legged, sit on a stool or stand. After you establish good playing posture, your playing improves because your breathing improves.

Equally important is the posture's effect on attention. The main influence here is the lower brain stem. This area is lifeless, when the chin tilts up, the jaw sags down and the thoracic cavity caves in. This, in turn, disrupts the vitality of the entire spine.

To correct this, imagine a string connected from the back of your head/lower neck to the sky. Visualize this string lifting you upward. It feels like the string is raising the base of the neck upward and pulling it backward slightly. Also try standing against a wall and press the neck to the wall.

Meditation is most effective when it's continuous, and not just a ritual held at certain times. That means keeping the spine extending upward. Maintaining this spinal lift helps you remember watchfulness and natural breathing. Note: if you have good posture, this lift is only a few tenths of an inch. The more you slump in daily life, the greater the lift.

Another factor in breathing is the air path. Nasal breathing is the natural way to breathe. The Shakuhachi helps develop this, if you bring air into the lungs through the nose as much as possible when playing. The nose and nasal passages warm and filter the air. The fine hairs in these passages filter out 80% of the suspended matter (bacteria, virus, pollution and dust) in the air.

ADDITIONAL TECHNIQUES

Review the following (and preceding) techniques often while learning to play. This is especially important if you're studying without a teacher.

1. Maintain good posture. Don't slump or allow your head to drop forward. This adversely effects playing. Don't let the flute drop down towards your stomach. Instead, hold it out in front so your elbows are in line with the front of the chest (photo 3). Keep the thumb opposite the middle finger (photo 1). Tie it there with a piece of tape.

2. Relaxation of all uninvolved parts of the body is very important. Look for unconscious tensing of the facial muscles around the eyes, in the forehead, temples and throat. Avoid raising the shoulders or gripping the flute too tightly. The body should feel like it's sinking into and rooted in the earth, with only the spine rising upwards. Watch the body while playing to find the parts you habitually tense up, then ease those parts.

3. Many people unknowingly tighten the tongue. Relax your throat area to avoid gravelly vibrations.

4. Never blow softly in order to stretch your air supply. Breathe more often instead. Strive for a solid sound by using lots of air. This also develops your diaphragm.

5. Use lots of air to achieve high octave notes in the beginning. A high velocity airstream helps the flute resonate at high octaves. After you develop a narrow lip opening, you can increase the velocity of the airstream with lower volumes of air.

6. Making high octave notes is difficult in the beginning. Decrease the inner volume of the mouth cavity as you increase the pitch. Accomplish this by making subtle movements of the tongue, lips and cheeks. Increasing the lip pucker brings the lip edge closer to the blowing edge - 1/16th inch apart is about right. The velocity of the airstream is highest at the lip opening. So the closer it is to the blowing edge, the easier it is to produce high octave notes. Try bringing the lips closer to the blowing edge by pushing the flute firmly into your chin. The resulting pressure on the lower gums and chin can cause some temporary discomfort. You can also produce high octave notes easier by raising the lower end of the flute slightly. As it pivots on the chin, its blowing edge comes closer to the lips.

7. After you establish reliable sound and finger control, start paying attention to the small lip muscles around the opening of the lips. These are an important link between the sound and the mind (as is the diaphragm). Later on, try to roll the fleshy moist and smooth part of the inner lip very slightly outward towards the blowing edge.

Do this by that combination of stretching and puckering discussed earlier. When done correctly, the surface of the lip around the opening is shiny and smooth. Compare your lip formation with that shown in photo 5, page 6.

8. If you still have difficulty a few months from now, try a slightly different blowing style. Refer to photo 6, page 6, and form the tongue as shown. It is slightly "U" shaped and rests on the lower teeth. Keep the end of the tongue somewhat square. Bring the lips together and pucker them slightly. Use the "square" end of the tongue to push the lower lip out slightly (especially the moist part). Now, stretch the lips. So, in a way, you are stretching the lips and drawing them over the tongue and teeth. The teeth support the upper lip and the tongue supports the lower lip. Note: keep the "U" shape in the tongue for air to flow out easily.

Whether you play with this tongue support, or without, aim for a relaxed tongue and face. Concentrate on the tiny lip muscles. Avoid tensing your face or tongue to compensate for inattention to the lip muscle.

9. The sound and the mind interconnect in subtle ways. Visualizing the sound you want to produce helps you get that sound. When trying for the high octave, think "high". Also, visualize a solid sound with a deep core. Feel it well up from deep in the abdomen. Feel it come up the throat, out of the mouth, into the flute and out the end into the universe.

10. Clean the flute after playing by drawing a cotton cloth through the bore. Tie a weight to one end of a string and the cloth to the other. Let the weight pull the string through the bore. Then grab the string and pull the cloth through.

11. Occasionly during the first year you'll feel you're getting nowhere. Try to remember that a year or two is a short time when it comes to learning. In fact, the Japanese regard the first three years of practice as just the beginning. Let go of expectations, but let yourself play daily. Mastery will come.

> *Hence always rid yourself of desires in order*
> *to observes its secrets;*
> *But always allow yourself to have desires in*
> *order to observe its manifestations.*
>
> *These two are the same*
> *But diverge in name as they issue forth.*
> *Being the same they are called mysteries,*
> *Mystery upon mystery -*
> *The gateway of the manifold secrets.*
>
> Tao Te Ching

FOLK INSTRUCTION

You can play any kind of music, from classical to jazz, on the Shakuhachi. However, Buddhist music written especially for Shakuhachi suits it best. This music reveals the instrument's capabilities fully. It also awakens deep feelings for the instrument and its quality of sound. This is a valuable asset when playing other kinds of music.

You'll want to study the basics for a few months before beginning Buddhist music. Remember, some Japanese wait up to six years before playing Buddhist music.

The Shakuhachi is a more rewarding experience if approached with patience. It takes a few years to learn to play the flute well, and far longer to master. Why not make it a life long project?

Bamboo in wind, Ku An, 14th C.

Prepare to feel winded after practicing. You'll feel light-headed until you develop awareness of your breath and lip. The high octave notes will screech. Occasionally, the sound will disappear altogether while you are playing. You may also have a combination of sore fingers, mouth, back and legs. Hang in there and these problems will pass before you know it; they're just stages on your road to mastery.

Even if you can't produce a sound yet, go on and study the material in the first tune. This will give you an understanding of the fingering, timing and melody. Then return to the previous sections and find your sound.

Play the lesson CD, beginning to end, to hear what lies ahead. Then listen a few more times to the tunes you'll learn first, i.e., the first 15 minutes of the CD. The more familiar you are with these, the easier they are to learn. If you don't already have this CD, you can order it from the sources listed on page 17, POLISHING YOUR SOUND #11, or from us (see back of this book).

I recommend you Xerox the sheet music at the back of this book. You can then look at the instructions and the music notation simultaneously. Believe it or not, Shakuhachi notation is easier to learn than Western notation. Simply learn a few symbols and sway your body from side to side to keep rhythm.

HI NO MARU NO HATA
Tracks #1, 2, 3, 4, 5 and 6 - Page B2

This title means "Japan Flag". Study the BASIC FINGERING on page B2. Learn the first three fingerings and their pronunciation: TSU (ツ), RE (レ) and CHI (チ) - "tsoo, ray and chee". These are the notes in the first part of this tune: points A through K. Now listen to these three notes on Track #1.

The small symbol RYO (呂) to the right of point A is the low octave symbol. Play all notes following it in low octave unless otherwise indicated. The dots and slashes (/ •) at points B, C, D, E, F, etc., are beat marks. These help you maintain steady rhythm. The dotted line connecting these marks shows you the path your eyes follow. Gently sway your flute or body from side to side tracking the path your eyes follow. Sway 6 to 12 inches until you have a feel for the rhythm. Then reduce this to a few inches or eliminate it altogether.

Sound the note precisely at the beat mark. Continue the sound until you reach the next mark. At this point you either repeat this note or begin a new one. As you sway from side to side, imagine you are striking the beat marks with the end of the flute. Begin the sound at that instant.

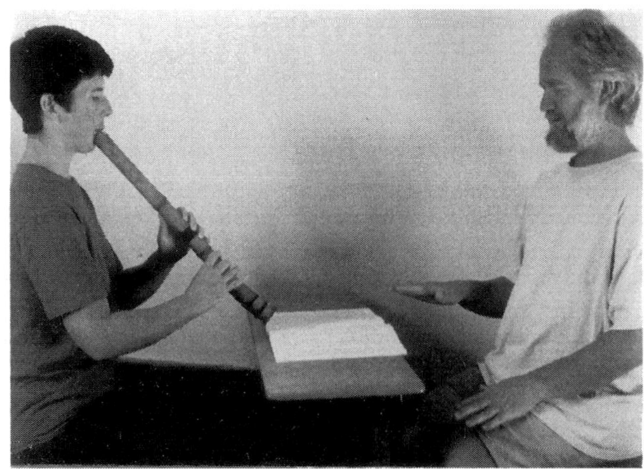

Photo 9

Japanese teachers slap their right and left hands on their knees at the corresponding right and left beat marks. This helps students maintain a steady rhythm while playing (photo 9). Now play Track #2 and listen as I slap out the beat and call out the notes from points B to H.

The symbol at point C is an ATARI (>). It's like a ditto mark telling you to re-articulate (repeat) the preceding note. In this case repeat TSU (ツ). At point E, repeat RE (レ) and at point G, repeat CHI (チ). To re-articulate a note, lift a finger momentarily off a hole; for TSU (point C) lift the forefinger off hole #2. Lift it less than a 1/4" and return it as fast as possible to produce a "chirp" sound. To re-articulate RE and CHI (points E and G), lift the forefinger off hole #4. A small (o) on the SHAKUHACHI FINGER CHART (page B1) shows the proper finger to lift off to re-articulate other notes. Play Track #3 and listen to the re-articulation of these three notes, TSU, RE and CHI. Now play these three notes, points B up to H.

Notice the thin horizontal line between points E and F, and again at point I and point Q. These are measure signs. Use them, in the beginning, to show you where to breathe. Take quick deep inhalations and start the new note on the beat mark. As your capacity increases, play through several of these marks before taking a breath. Don't skimp on air to make it last longer. A solid sound takes lots of air in the beginning. Compensate for this by breathing more often - after every note if needed.

Now let's clear up any confusion that exists about timing. Notes in music occur at different time intervals, or beats. A note played for 2 beats has an uninterrupted sound lasting twice as long as a note played for one beat. A note played for 1/2 beat has a sound 1/2 as long. Therefore, if a beat is 1 second long, then a note played for 2 beats will have 2 seconds of sound. A note played for 1/2 beat will have 1/2 second of sound.

In these first tunes, the beat is about 2 seconds long. One full beat is the time it takes to play from point B through point C and just up to point D. For the first TSU, begin the sound at the right beat mark (point B). Re-articulate it at the left beat mark (point C) and continue playing to the next right beat mark (point D). You played TSU for 1 full beat, but you re-articulated it at point C. So you actually played two 1/2 beat TSU notes, each lasting a second. The same is true for the RE (points D-E-F) and CHI (points F-G-H).

At point H, begin to play RE again. Notice that you play it without re-articulation on the left. Instead, the RE continues, as one unbroken sound, to the next right beat dot at point J. This RE lasts for one full beat or for 2 seconds. As you can see, there isn't a beat slash on the left at points I or Q. In cases like this, imagine there is a beat slash there and swing through it with the same rhythm.

Now I'm going to slap out the rhythm of the first two measures (points B to K) on my knees. I'll alternate from right to left knee while simultaneously calling out the names of the notes. As recorded lessons are more difficult to follow than live ones, I'll do the first few tunes slower.

In the following track, I'll first slap out a rhythm preview to prepare you. You'll hear two slaps, "one and two and", and then the tune will begin on the third slap.

Play Track #4. To start, just listen and slap your knees along with me. Then listen to how it sounds on the Shakuhachi. Practice these few notes, rewind the CD and try to play with the CD as I slap out the beat. Practice and repeat until you can easily play these notes along with the CD.

Now move over to the next column of notes - the complete tune of "Hi No Maru No Hata". You'll have to learn two more fingerings, RI (リ) at point L, and RO (ロ) at point N. Re-articulate these two notes at point M and O, as indicated by the ATARI symbols there. Do this for RI by lifting the thumb off hole #5 (the back hole). For RO, lift the forefinger off hole #2, just like you did for TSU. Remember to raise and lower the finger as fast as possible, and off the hole as little as possible.

THE RI - RO RULE

Whenever RO follows RI, play that RO in high octave. Moreover, play all notes which follow a high octave RO (or other high octave note) in high octave. Keep playing in high octave until either RYO (呂), the low octave symbol, RI or OU appear in the music again. RI and OU are always low octave (except in Buddhist music)

Once the music drops to low octave, play all following notes in low octave. Shift into the high octave when the RI - RO combination or the high octave symbol KAN (㐀) appears.

In this tune, for example, play the RO at point N in high octave. Any confusion about this should clear up after listening to the CD. If you have difficulty making a high octave RO, crack open the thumb hole slightly. Don't remove the thumb from the flute when you do this - just pivot it. This only works on high octave RO.

This is all you need to know for this first tune. On Track #5, I recorded a sample lesson with a student and myself (photo 9). Listen first, then rewind and slap out the beat as you listen again. Hit your right hand on your right thigh and your left hand on your left thigh. Call out the notes along with me. Rewind and repeat until you have a firm grasp of the timing, the melody, and the notes - and their pronunciation. Don't skip this step. It's essential to learn to "slap" and call out the melodies as I do on the CD.

After practicing this tune for a few days, go on to Track #6 and play along with the CD. It's good to practice by yourself 10 times or more for every time you play along with the CD. Simply use the CD to present the melody and clear up misunderstandings. Also, play the CD softly enough so as not to drown out your sound.

After you can play the first tune, go on to the next. Don't spend much time on any of these tunes in the beginning. It's better to move right along and then return later to work on them more. There is only so much you can do with a tune in the beginning. Learning new material, even though you're not ready, gives you useful insight into information already covered.

HARU NO KO GAWA
Track #7 - Page B2

This tune is "Spring Stream". We've covered all you need for this tune, so go for it. Notice the high octave symbol KAN (㐀) next to the TSU at point A. It's difficult for beginners to get a clear high octave sound - or one at all for that matter. Put some grease (Chapstick) on your lips and reread ADDITIONAL TECHNIQUES (page 8, points 5 and 6).

If you have trouble reading the symbols and beat dots, circle them with a red pen or make them bigger with a black pen.

I play the rhythm and then the melody of this tune on Track #7. Listen first, then slap out the beat as you did for Track #5. Practice it alone and then, when ready, play along with the CD. From here on, use the previous tunes as a daily warm up.

YU YAKE KO YAKE
Track #8 and 9 - Page B3

This tune is "Evening Glow". It has some new timing. Play the RE at point A as one continuous sound for 2 full beats. Take a deep breath just before you begin this RE. In cases like this, always sway from the right beat mark to the left hand side of the column as though there was a beat mark there. Then, sway back to the next right beat mark. Play RE (⟵) from point A, to B, to C, to D and up to E, as shown by the dotted line that connects all these points.

Notice the vertical line running straight down through the middle of the notes. This line tells you to play those notes in 1/2 beat segments. The line isn't essential for 1/2 beats because you'll know when to play 1/2 beats by the left hand beat marks present. For example, in "HI NO MARU NO HATA" (the first tune) you played each of the first six notes twice for a 1/2 beat each time.

This type of line is handy when playing notes for 1/4 beat or less. A 1/4 beat note will have two vertical lines running through it. Look, for example, at the next tune "KIMIGAEYO" - points B, to C, to D. A note played for 1/2 beat or less has one or more lines running completely through it, down to the beginning of the next note. Look at the vertical line running through all the 1/2 beat notes of the current tune - "YU YAKE KO YAKE". Notice that this line runs down to, but not through, the RE at point A. Thus, play all the notes before this RE for 1/2 beat, but play RE for 2 full beats.

When a line doesn't run completely through a note, you usually play it for 1, 2 or more beats (like RE at point A). Sometimes, however, you play such a note for 3/4 beat as is the case at point F. Begin playing this TSU (point F) and continue through point G. Halfway between point G and I, play a RE note (point H). Notice that this RE has two vertical lines running from it to TSU at point I. These 2 lines tell you to play this RE for 1/4 beat. In short, play TSU for 3/4 beat and RE for 1/4 beat.

The small triangle symbol (▲) at point G is similar to the beat mark, in that it guides your eye to the left side of the column. It means play the note (TSU) up to and through this triangle, with no articulation, until the next note appears (RE). Careful listening to the CD will clarify this. I play this segment (points F to I) on Track #8. Practice this segment and when you understand the timing, play Track #9.

It's a good idea to review everything now and then, especially when you feel discouraged. After all, you don't have a teacher there to point out any important details you overlooked.

KIMIGAEYO
Track #10 and 11 - Page B3

This tune is the Japanese national anthem. Notice the timing of RI and RO at point B and C. The double line through these two notes means play them for 1/4 beat each. I'll slap the rhythm and play this segment on Track #10 from point A through point E. Rewind and slap along with the CD. Keep the rhythm steady! Note: take a deep breath quickly before starting the RI at point B.

The symbol CHU (中) to the right of TSU at point E means play this TSU as CHU MERI. Study photo 10 and the fingering chart (page B1). The ring finger covers 1/2 or less of the hole. This lowers the pitch of TSU one half tone. Practice CHU MERI in front of the mirror to see how much hole you're covering. Now listen and slap along with Track #11. Practice this tune a while before playing along with the CD.

KAZOE UTA
Track #12 and 13 - Page B3

This tune is "Counting Song". It has two new fingerings to learn. The first is OU (ウ) at point A. Study the fingering chart, page B1. Tilt the chin downward moderately to get the proper pitch. This changes the direction of the airstream which lowers the pitch. The degree of tilt required is between the severe tilt (photo 12) and the regular playing position (photo 4). If this is impossible to do now, play OU at the regular position. Then, over the next month, tilt the chin little by little.

The other new fingering is TSU MERI. The small symbol (メ) next to the note, in this case TSU at point B, represents this variation of TSU. To play TSU MERI, tilt

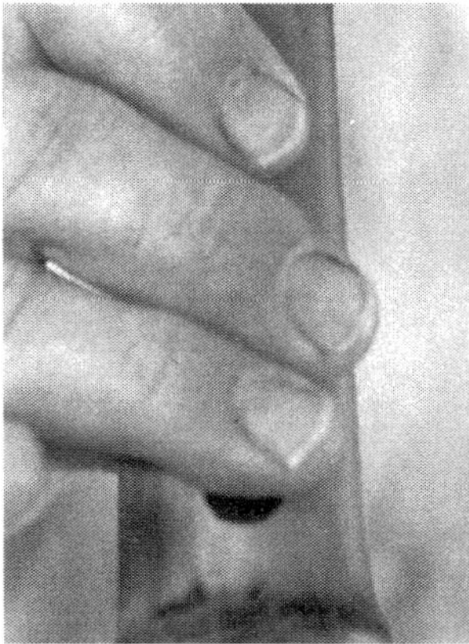
Photo 10

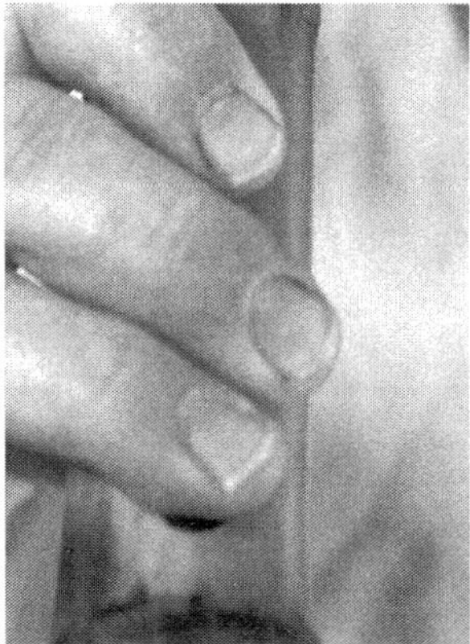
Photo 11

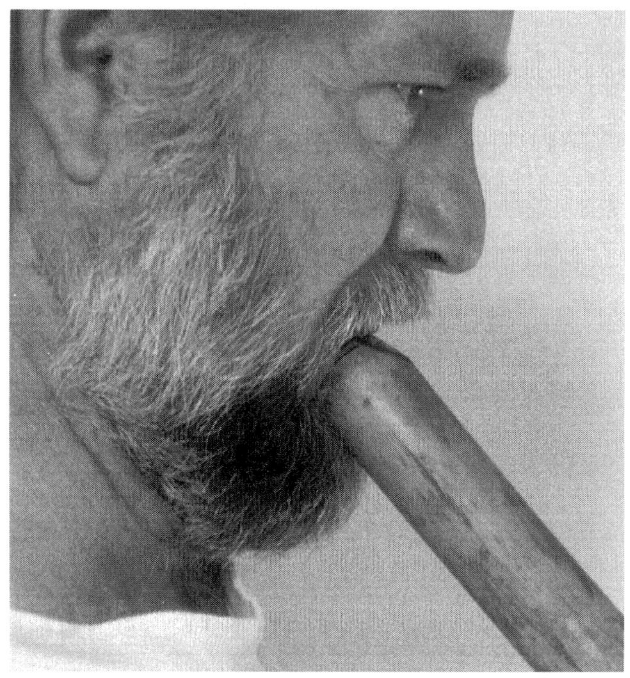
Photo 12

the chin severely (photo 12). Cover Hole #1 about 2/3 (photo 11). Study the fingering chart and then compare photos 10 and 11 (TSU CHU MERI and TSU MERI). The notes requiring severe chin tilt take many months to do correctly, so be patient!

You can cover the hole less and tilt the chin slightly until your lip develops. When playing along with the CD, the difference in pitch on these MERI notes may bother you. Just keep trying to lower your pitch to equal mine and it will come. If all our pitches differ, you're probably not maintaining a correct playing position.

Compare your positions with those shown in the photos. In any case, the more you practice, the more correct your pitch.

On Track #12, listen to the normal pitch of TSU, followed by TSU CHU MERI and then by TSU MERI. Return to this track every 6 months and compare your TSU MERI with what you hear on the CD.

On Track #13, slap out the rhythm and call out the notes simultaneously.

KO JU NO TSUKI
Track #14 - Page B4

This tune is "Moon Over The Castle Ruins". You know all you need for this tune. Listen to it and slap along with it. After practicing, play along with the CD, Track #14.

SAKURA
Track #15 - Page B4

This tune is "Cherry Blossom". You know all you need for this one too, but you may have difficulty with the CHI MERI at point A. At least it doesn't require a severe chin tilt. Study the fingering chart and review the information on playing high octave notes. Slap out the rhythm and call out the notes before playing along with Track #15.

HARU GA KITA
Track #16 - Page B4

This tune is "Spring Has Come". Notice the small symbol KARI (カ) next to the TSU at point A. It's there to remind you to return to the normal playing position after the TSU MERI just played. Move the finger off hole #1 very quickly. Of course, you'll not get as pronounced a separation in pitch as you hear on the CD until you develop the chin tilt and lip muscles.

You'll have a similar problem at point B. Notice the MERI symbol that is inside the RO ( ). Sometimes the MERI symbols are inside or through the notes instead of next to them. Look up RO MERI in the fingering chart. In this tune, play TSU CHU MERI for a little over 1/2 beat. Take a quick breath and start the RO MERI with as much chin tilt as possible. Play this RO MERI for 1/4 beat, then quickly return to the normal playing position to play RO.

HOTARU NO HIKARI
Track #17 - Page B4

This is the last folk tune, "Firefly Glow" and I'm sure you'll recognize it. The Japanese have used it for a university graduation song for years. All its high octave notes make it challenging. In fact, RI is the lowest note in the piece. Don't hold back on air, regardless of how poorly the high octaves sound.

Try improving the sound by subtle changes in the lip and in mouth volume, as explained earlier. In the end, though, nothing substitutes for practice, practice and more practice.

At point A, you sustain the HI GO ( ) for 3 full beats, so get plenty of air.

This concludes the first phase of Shakuhachi training. Go back and review everything covered so far. How are you holding the flute? How are your finger positions? How are you sitting? What is your head position and so on?

WESTERN MELODIES

You know enough now to attempt the Western melodies if you want, pages B18 to B23. You'll recognize most of them, which gives you an advantage. Note: the more asterisks next to a title, the more difficult the tune. Also, go online to download MP3 files of these melodies.

Most of these tunes have a faster tempo than any played so far. This means you have to sway rapidly to play them at the proper tempo. You can do this of course, but there is a simpler way of keeping time in fast tempo music. See 1/2 TIMING on page 16. If this new timing method or the high octaves makes these tunes too difficult, skip them and begin the San Kyoku below.

SAN KYOKU INSTRUCTIONS

These pieces help develop the lip and diaphragm control needed for Buddhist music. Here are a few hints. When playing a piece, don't stop to rest or to correct mistakes. Play from beginning to end without breaking the beat, regardless of how frustrating or exhausting it is. You can, however, work on specific passages by themselves. When playing with proper posture, the flute may obstruct your view of the notation. Try holding the flute a little to the side, out of your line of sight. Finally, take a look at POLISHING YOUR SOUND, page 17.

KURO KAMI
Track #18 and 19 - Page B5

This piece is "Beautiful Black Hair". It begins with a new note, HA ( ) at point A. As the fingering chart shows, play it with the chin in a moderate MERI (tilting) position. The fingers slant off holes #2, #4 and #5, similar to the slant of the upper ring finger shown in the photo on page 26. The closer the fingers are to the flute, the smoother the transition between this HA and the following RO. Note that the HA - RO combination follows the same rule as the RI - RO combination. RO is always high octave when it follows HA.

The RI at point B has two lines through it, so play it for 1/4 beat. Both HI GO and the following RI have three lines through them, so play them for 1/8 beat each. HI GO is customarily a high octave note, but in settings like this, play it in the low octave.

Listen to Track #18 for the rhythm and melody of this section played from HA to RO.

At point C, there is a small circle (○). This is similar to the small triangle which you learned about in "Yu Yake Ko Yake". It shows that the sound continues through that beat point.

At point D, there is a new symbol RU (ﾙ✓). It, like the ATARI (>), tells you to repeat the note just preceding it, but with another kind of re-articulation. For RU, forcefully and quickly tap hole #1 closed with the ring finger for a split second.

There is a new note to learn at point E. This is a high octave version of HA which you just learned. Notice the small symbol GO (五) to the right of HA. This (and other symbols) is either inside HA as shown in the fingering chart, or outside HA as here at point E. These symbols are the Chinese calligraphy for numbers:

1 is 一 ; 2 is 二 ; 3 is 三 ;4 is 四 ; 5 is 五 .

At point F, there is the new symbol SURU (ｽﾙ), which means "to slide". From TSU, gradually slide the finger off hole #2 as you move to the next note, RE. Read about this in POLISHING YOUR SOUND (page 17, #12).

This piece is longer than previous ones. I have divided it into three parts as shown by the double measure lines (▬ ▬). Practice each part separately, then play them together when ready.

SODE KORO
Track #20 - Page B6

This piece is "Kimono Sleeves". If it's too difficult, go to the next piece, and return here later. At point A, play HA for a full beat. Notice the squiggly line between HA and RO. This is a simple YURI, or vibrato, produced by gently rotating the head from side to side. This alters the air stream slightly which raises and lowers the pitch. Note: the head moves only 1/2 to 1 inch side to side horizontally. The Japanese say it takes three years to do this properly.

You'll unconsciously start incorporating this vibrato in other notes before long. Guard against making this a habitual embellishment. For now, do the YURI vibrato only when called for in the music. Keep the other notes as steady and solid as possible. Never do a diaphragm vibrato as done on the western flute. On the contrary, you want the diaphragm to move as smoothly as possible; this soothes the nervous system.

At point C there is a new symbol NAYASHI (▬). This, like the ATARI and RU, means repeat the preceding note - in this case CHI. After playing the preceding note, pause an instant. Then play the MERI of the note just played and gradually slide to the normal pitch of that note. Here for example, after playing the regular CHI, pause and breathe if need be. Then begin playing CHI MERI at the beat mark at point C.

Mother monkey and child, Mu-Chi, 13th C.

Shortly after beginning this CHI MERI, start sliding the ring finger off hole #3. Do this slowly enough to reach the regular pitch of CHI at the second right hand beat mark.

At point D, play RE MERI (ﾚ▬). There are two ways to do this. The following is a variation of that shown on the fingering chart. This method gives the easiest transition to TSU CHU MERI which follows this RE MERI. Close both hole #1 and #2 halfway without any chin tilt.

At point E, notice the SURU. To slide from RI MERI to RE, slide the finger off hole #4 and then quickly go to RE. The double measure line separates this piece into two parts. Work on each part separately and then combine.

Heron (Bittern), Tanan, 15th C.

SHO DAN
Track #21 - Page B7

This piece is "First Step". Notice the many SURUs in it, and a RU towards the end at point A. This RU is for the CHI MERI; do it by tapping hole #1 with the ring finger. Notice how the tempo slows towards the end. This is true for most Japanese tunes.

TSURU NO KOE
Track #22 - Page B7

This piece is "Crane's Cry". It's too difficult for some people. If so, go to the next piece and return here later. Notice the new symbol at point A, above the KARI symbol. It is OH (大), the Chinese character for big. Here, do OH KARI or "big sharp pitch" for CHI. The technique is just the opposite of MERI; thrust your chin upward and outward instead of inward and downward. Another way of obtaining this pitch is to play RI MERI instead, as you'll hear on the CD. Both are the same pitch, but the slide is smoother this way. Gradually lift your finger off hole #4.

At point B there is a string of high octave HA notes. The new one here, HA SAN, is difficult. Try playing HA NI instead, as they both have the same pitch. (See the fingering chart). With HA NI, though, keep a more KARI (sharp) playing position.

Pay close attention to the timing from point B. It's different than anything done so far. Play HA SAN for 1/4 beat, then for 1/2 beat, then for 1/4 beat again before going to HA GO. Point C is another CHI KARI which, like point A, you usually play with a HI MERI, or RI MERI if low octave. Both these high octave notes are difficult in the beginning.

KON GO SEKI
Track #23 - Page B8

This piece is "Diamond". From here on, San Kyoku pieces become longer. This one is fairly easy though. In this piece, play all TSUs as TSU CHU MERI. This piece has four parts, points A, B, C and D.

Review all the pieces learned so far and practice them for a few more weeks. When you're comfortable, start "Hi Fu Mi" - the first Buddhist piece. If "Hi Fu Mi" is too difficult, continue to develop your technique by playing the two additional San Kyoku pieces which follow. It's helpful to play the easier San Kyoku music along with "Hi Fu Mi" during the first year of study. Afterwards, if you like, devote yourself solely to Buddhist music.

ROKU DAN
Track #25 - Page B13

This piece is "Six Steps". It has six parts, points A, B, C, D, F and H. Practice them separately, each for a week or so, and then play them together. Notice the 1/2 sign at point E. If you haven't learned this yet, read 1/2 TIMING METHOD on the next page.

At point G, notice the HA - RO and ATARI which are smaller and thinner, with a vertical line next to them. Either play these notes, as usual, or remain silent. When two people play together, one plays the notes while the other remains silent.

At point I, there is a (2) sign. This means return to the swaying, side to side, method of marking time. This slows the tempo down towards the end of the piece.

CHI DORI
Track #26 - Page B15

This piece is "Plover Rhythm". It begins with a slow tempo, builds to a fast tempo and then returns to a slower one toward the end. This holds true for most San Kyoku pieces. The fast sections of San Kyoku are easier using the 1/2 TIMING METHOD.

At point A, notice the small thin notes like the ones in "Roku Dan", point G. Here again, you can play them or not. Notice the brackets (└─┐) enclosing some RO notes in this column. If two people play this piece, one plays the smaller and thinner notes while the other plays the bolder main notes. You'll find this scattered throughout the piece.

At point B, if two people play, one plays the right column of notes after RO, while the other continues playing down the main column. 5 beats later the person playing the main column remains silent during the thinner notes in his column (TSU, RO and RI). Then he plays the next 3 notes in the main column (TSU, RO and RI), while the other person plays the side column again.

Again, at point C, (and several times later) the two people play different notes. To do this successfully, both players must keep accurate timing. At point C, the player taking the left column begins playing the small thin CHI one beat after the other begins his CHI (just below the brackets).

In other words, the left column player starts his CHI while the other player is still playing his CHI. I hope the dotted lines make this clearer.

1/2 TIMING METHOD

When the tempo speeds up you'll see the 1/2 sign. This begins an easier way to keep fast time. Instead of swaying from the right to left, "bob" the flute up and down evenly. "Bob" downward once for each right hand beat mark.

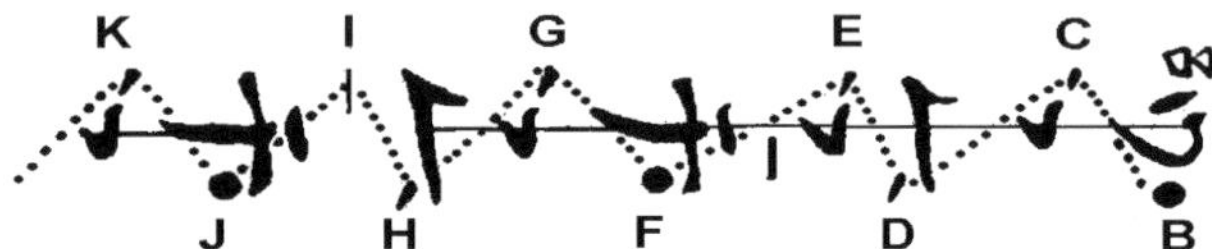

Imagine that the end of the flute is a hammer. Strike each right hand beat mark as if it were a nail. Each left hand beat mark comes at the peak of the upward movement. For example, look at the first tune you learned on page B2. The first section of its notation is rotated sideways (above) to show how to play it by the 1/2 TIMING METHOD. "Slap" out the beats and call out the notes first, using only your right hand and thigh. Practice this slowly at first to see exactly what you're doing.

The notes at the right hand beat marks (point B, D, F, H and J) begin on the "down" beat. Begin calling them out the instant your hand hits your thigh.

Continue to call the note out until your hand reaches the highest point of its upward movement. The notes at the left hand beat marks (points C, E, G, I and K) begin on the "up" beat. Begin calling these out the instant your hand reaches the highest point of its upward movement.

The notes of this section play for 1/2 beat except RE, at point H, which plays for 1 beat. Begin playing the first TSU (point B) the instant your flute reaches the lowest point of its downward "bob". Begin the ATARI of this TSU (point C) the moment your flute reaches the highest point of its upward movement. Then begin RE (point D) when your flute reaches the lowest point of the "bob" again. Continue in this manner until you reach RE at point H. Begin this RE on the lowest point of the downward "bob". Continue playing it up to and through the highest point of your upward "bob", and on until you reach the lowest point of the next downward "bob" at point J. Then begin CHI at point J. Practice this a while, then turn to page B2 and play the whole tune this way.

This method follows the same principle as swaying side to side except that it permits a quicker response. It's similar to Western timing in that you concentrate on the downbeat. It's like the bouncing ball you see in a filmed sing-along.

Examine the section of notes from "Haru Ga Kita" to the right. Play three notes (RE, TSU MERI and TSU KARI) between down beats 1 and 2, and between 3 and 4 (point 1, 2, 3 and 4). At the first down beat (point 1) begin RE, then on the peak of the up beat begin TSU MERI (point A). Now, half way between this upbeat and the next down beat (point 2), begin playing TSU KARI. On the next down beat (point 2) play RE until you reach the upbeat (point B), where you begin CHI.

Then on the next down beat (point 3) begin playing RE again, and continue as described above. Practice this a few times and then turn to page B4. Use this method to play the entire tune of "Haru Ga Kita".

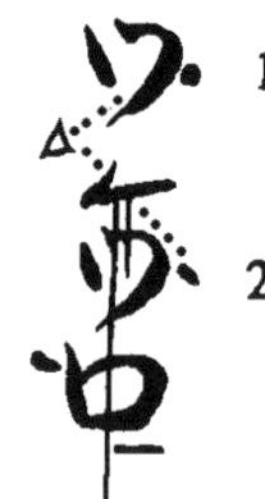

Study the small section of "Yu Yake Ko Yake" (at left). On the first down beat begin playing TSU (point 1). Continue TSU up to and through the upbeat, as shown by the triangle. Then 1/2 way down towards the next down beat (point 2) begin RE and play it for 1/4 beat until you reach the down beat. Practice this section and then turn to page B3 and play the entire tune of "Yu Yake Ko Yake".

To get more experience with the 1/2 timing method play through all the folk tunes and then try the Western melodies. If you don't understand the 1/2 timing method yet, go back and review all the sections concerning timing. Also, you're sure to have problems with timing if you haven't learned to slap out the rhythm and call out the notes. If you only wish to play Buddhist Hon Kyoku,

POLISHING YOUR SOUND

1. Practice daily - if only for a few minutes. It's the quality of practice and regularity that count, not the qunatity. Watch to notice the 'hidden'. Listen for what you have not heard before.

2. Aim for beauty in your finger movements. To play an ATARI, quickly move your finger off the hole. Lift it just enough to make a "chirp" sound. This is especially true for the thumb (RI ATARI). Always make precise movements with your fingers, whether fast or slow.

3. Vary the tension in the fine muscles of the lips to control the sound. Try moving the upper lip slightly beyond the lower lip, keeping both slightly puckered.

4. Remember to breathe. Take quick deep breaths and avoid playing too long on one breath. Plan your breaths ahead of time. Exhale steadily and smoothly. Notice the subtle diaphragm vibrations and jerkiness during the exhalations and try to calm them.

5. Tilt your chin enough to get true MERI pitches. Remember to return to the regular playing position after playing MERI notes. Keep a clear distinction between these.

6. Keep the melody or the phrasing of the piece in mind while playing. Anticipate the notes immediately following the note you are playing. Sense the end of a phrase as you begin it.

7. Be mindful of the sound you're trying to achieve. Project that sound. Feel it start within your abdomen, come up your throat, pass through your lips and down the flute into the surrounding silence. Vary the volume to make the sound more dynamic. Begin phrases with a soft passive sound. Gradually (or rapidly) move into a louder and more vibrant sound. Try going from loud to soft then soft to loud, or soft to loud then loud to soft. Listen for texture.

8. Pause a little at the end of some notes or phrases. Use silence as a part of your "sound". Don't run everything together. Use vibrato (YURI) toward the end of some notes. Don't let the pitch of a note drop towards the end of that note (unless that's your intention). Try tightening and narrowing your lip opening. Also try backing away from the blowing edge slowly until the sound disappears.

9. Aim for a simple and smooth sound. Avoid the ornamentations which cover up the root of the sound. Intricate technique shows skill but can distracts from your mindfulness of sound. When playing Buddhist music, imagine that the sound is like water flowing, sometimes cascading robustly and other times trickling gently.

10. Listen carefully to recorded Shakuhachi music. Develop your attention to detail by trying to imitate exactly what the performer is doing.

Once you can imitate well, you'll have a solid base on which to innovate. Record yourself when imitating another player. Don't try the whole piece though; it's best to record a few phrases at a time.

I recommend the recorded music of Mr. Goro Yamaguchi if you can find it:

"Zen Music", Victor Records (Japan), SJL-2061 through -2066 and SJ-L2094.

"A Bell ringing in the Empty Sky; Japanese Shakuhachi Music", Nonsuch #H72025

Go to the Centertao.org/learn-zen to download MP3 sound files of the songs in this book not in the companion CD, and also for recordings of the Hon Kyoku peices in "Blowing Zen II".

You will also find some of the 'Zen' side of Shakuhachi at Centertao.org. We deal in the flesh and bones of Zen, i.e., Buddhism and Taoism. We toss around each of these sides and in between too. Ponder, post, reflect and then mix and match to make up your own personal Zen.

11. Below are a few excellent sources for Shakuhachi related materials.

Monty H. Levenson's Shakuhachi.com should satisfy all you shakuhachi needs - flutes, instruction materials, teachers, books and recorded music. Monty has developed a unique process of shaping and sizing the Shakuhachi bore to extremely fine tolerances. This results in the superior quality to cost ratio possible with his bamboo Tai Hei Shakuhachi flutes.

Sharaku, 1726 Post St., San Francisco, CA.94115, (415) 929-9084. Japanese musical instruments (including Shakuhachi) and recorded music.

12. To execute the slide (SURU), slide the finger directly forward. Extend it by straightening it out. Do so gradually so the hole starts opening at its side edge first. Play MERI notes by tilting the chin downward and inward towards the throat. Simultaneously pucker and push your upper lip slightly forward, closer to the blowing edge.

This redirects the air stream at a greater downward angle helping lower the pitch further.

13. Review the material covered in this book often to pick up points you may have misunderstood or forgotten. If instruction from a Shakuhachi teacher isn't possible, try a regular flute teacher or other music teacher for a few lessons. They can help open your mind to principles of musical expression, timing and may give you constructive criticism (which you can take or leave).

14. How far can you get without the guidance of a teacher? That depends on what you're really seeking. My life's most meaningful moments have been tangential to the goals I was pursuing at the time.

For example, while studying Shakuhachi with Goro Yamaguchi I found watchfulness. It had nothing to do with my goals of learning Shakuhachi technique:

> One day I <u>really</u> noticed him watchfully remove the cap from his Shakuhachi. (Actually, I can't say whether he was especially watchful or just going through the motions.) I had pondered the importance of watchfulness for years, but at that moment I was finally ready to accept it at the gut level.

Without a teacher, I know this truth would have dawned "in" me through other circumstances, as truth has before and since.

On another occasion, while walking across a bridge, I found compassion. This, of course, had nothing to do with my immediate goals for that day:

> One day while looking at some garbage floating down a river in Tokyo I realized the unity of all things. The garbage was beautiful - as beautiful as anything I had ever seen. I had philosophically recognized the principle of Unity for a long time. At that moment I knew its truth through and through.

Some insist you can't find the way without a teacher - a guru to guide you. It's my experience that the way is within - where no one can help me find it. I must simply mature into it; and that takes time. The role of teachers, from this perspective, is small. So the question of whether you need a teacher or not depends on what you are seeking. (And your point of view).

If you want to perfect a particular style of playing, you need outside help. If you're seeking your spiritual way through Buddhist music, then what you need awaits within you.

15. You can make the Shakuhachi a more explicit spiritual discipline by playing Hon Kyoku in a more Zazen like way.

For example:

a) Keep a more uniform breathing rhythm. Make this a primary objective.
b) Play each phrase the same length, as measured by the breath.
c) Blow your strongest sound at the beginning and let it gradually weaken as you exhale.
d) Eliminate vibrato and other embellishments.
e) Let go of your "performance" desires.
f) Ponder the Japanese expression "Enlightenment in a single sound".
g) Or, just adapt some of these (15 a-f) to the Kinko style taught in this book. For example, keep the stylized approach; begin phrases in serenity, build them to a peak and then return to serenity again. But drop the embellishments and vibrato.

An immortal sage, LiangK'ai, 13th C.

HON KYOKU INSTRUCTION

Hon Kyoku is a loosely metered form of music similar to sounds in nature like rustling leaves or gurgling water. Hon Kyoku compositions don't rely on musical symmetry and contrast, but on asymmetry and nuance. They begin in a low or medium register, build to a high register and then settle back into stillness. It's like the progression of nature: birth, life and death.

Hon Kyoku is deeply enjoyable and meditative when played attentively. This experience is very subjective and doesn't transfer well to an audience.

It's even inaccurate to compare players of this music with each other to see who's playing the "best" Hon Kyoku. No one but the player knows how watchful he is being or whether he's just relying on skill. Watchfulness is the key word in this musical meditation.

Zen priest Choka, Tawaraya Sotatsu, 16th C.

You'll get the most from Hon Kyoku if you let go and allow yourself to remain a beginner. Skill is irrelevant. With a watchful mind you're always a beginner. This beginner mind is your Zen mind. Cultivate it in Hon Kyoku and use it in your daily life.

HI FU MI HACHIGAESHI

Band 24 - Pages B10 - B12

"Hi Fu Mi" means "1, 2, 3" in ancient Chinese. "Hachi gaeshi" means "return the bowl". What does "1,2,3, - return the bowl" mean? Maybe......

> *The way begets one; one begets two; two begets three; three begets the myriad creatures.*
>
> Tao Te Ching

> *Turning back is how the way moves; Weakness is the means the way employs.*
>
> Tao Te Ching

Now to practical matters. Notice the difference in appearance between the notation for the previous music and for Hon Kyoku. See page B10 to clear up any uncertainty. I'll cover this piece in the following pages step by step. This, along with the CD, is enough to teach you basic Hon Kyoku technique. It will be up to you to put this to work.

This piece, Hi Fu Mi, takes years to master. In fact, a life time would not be too much. Remember, this music serves as a mirror to your mind; as your mind goes, so it goes. If you're always growing, it's always growing.

Parts A and C are mostly in the lower register. The high register of Part B is difficult to play initially. For now, learn Part A, then go directly to Part C. Long ago people often played these two parts as a complete whole. When you can play them without much difficulty, go on to Part B.

Spend the first few days playing Part A as shown on page B10. In Hon Kyoku, always play TSU in the MERI position (unless otherwise indicated). In this piece, TSU is always played MERI. Listen to the CD until you're familiar with the notes of Part A. Play without vibrato initially. Once you learn the whole piece, incorporate a little vibrato into some notes. Vibrato in Hon Kyoku is like chili pepper - a little goes a long way.

On pages B10, B11, and B12, I portray the 152 "beats" of this piece graphically, beat by beat. Each frame (rectangular box) represents one beat: right hand beat to the next right hand beat mark. The line that runs from one end of the box to the other plots the relative change in pitch of the note which corresponds to the frame.

You usually breathe every one to two beats. In the beginning, play fast enough so you have enough air to play smoothly. Listen to the CD to learn how and where to breathe. Remember, there are no hard rules. In the end, it's up to you, your needs and how you wish to express yourself.

Practice the first two notes of this piece, TSU (MERI remember) and RO - shown in frame 1 and 2. Learn frame 1 first. Try to duplicate the sound of TSU as well as possible. After you learn this, go on to frame 2 and learn RO. Then play frames 1 and 2 together. Now go on to frame 3, then frame 4, then 5 and so on. Build frame by frame. Don't expect to learn all the subtle detail at once. Take it in steps. Look closely at the pitch graph and then listen carefully to the CD. You can also record yourself playing a note or a phrase and compare your sound with the graph and lesson CD.

PART A

Pitch Frame 1-21

1. The sound of "Hi Fu Mi" begins on the last half of this frame. Listen to the CD. Notice that the graph tells you to play TSU at a MERI pitch a moment before the ATARI (as symbolized on the graph by (↓). Simultaneously the volume builds and there is a slightvibrato. Move this TSU into an extreme MERI, or OH MERI (大メ), before shifting quickly to RO.

2. This frame begins with RO. As soon as you shift from the TSU of the previous frame to this RO, make an ATARI articulation at hole #2. It's very quick as you will hear. Halfway through this second frame, RO starts building in volume and the vibrato comes in. Then the vibrato lessens and the volume decreases near the end of this frame.

3. Both this frame and frame 4 cover the NAYASHI of RO which is two beats long. This frame begins with RO in MERI. Gradually sharpen this pitch so that half way through the third frame you are playing RO at its regular pitch. Then increase the volume and begin the vibrato.

4. At the end of the first half of this frame, the volume starts decreasing and the vibrato tapers off. End RO with a subtle grace tone - represented in the music by a hook symbol (¿). Do this by making a "half" YURI. Move your head to the left (or right) an inch or two, then back and down to the right, with a hint of a hook back to the left again. You can do this better with subtle movements of the lip in place of most of the head movement, but this takes awhile to learn. Play OU in the last half of frame 4. This is done in a similar manner to TSU of frame 1. To play OH MERI of OU, tilt the chin severely and partially cover hole #3.

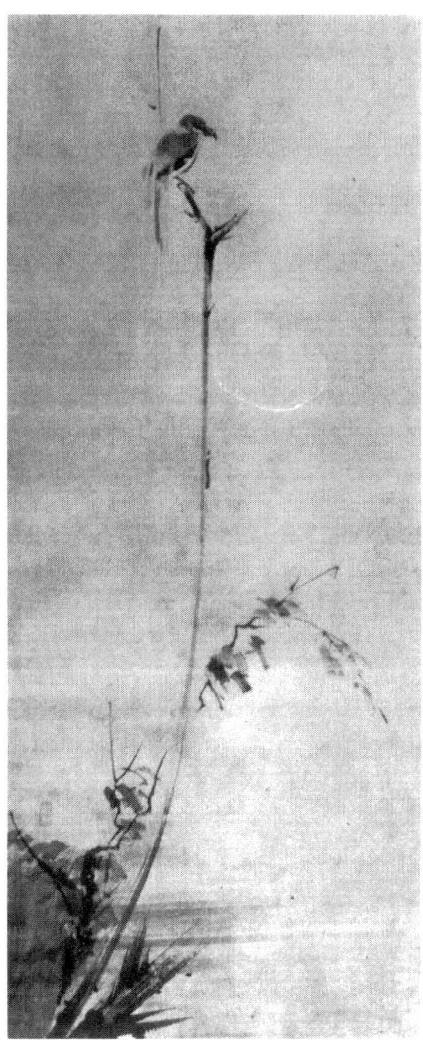

Shrike on a barren tree, Miyamoto Musashi, 16th C.

5. Play RE in this frame. When you shift from OU of the last frame down to this RE, first go to TSU for a moment. Then open hole #2 and play RE. There is a slight vibrato towards the end of RE as the volume decreases.

6. This frame begins with RE MERI, and smoothly rises to the regular pitch of RE. After reaching the regular pitch, increase the volume and bring some vibrato into play. Then, in the last part of this frame, the fingers slide off hole #3 and #4 slightly. Now, almost simultaneously, shift to RO.

7. Play RO in this frame and in the first half of the next one. In the last half of this frame RO starts increasing in volume and vibrato.

8. Both the volume and vibrato of RO taper off in the first half of this frame. Notice the small grace "hook"

symbol. Play HA in the last half of this frame. Its volume and vibrato increase gradually and then taper off quickly. There is a slight pause before the next note begins.

9. This frame begins with a delicate TSU MERI in the high octave. At the end of this frame, lower the pitch of TSU MERI into a TSU OH MERI as much as possible.

10. Continue OH TSU MERI in the first half of this frame with some vibrato. Then decrease the volume, taper off the vibrato and return the pitch to a more moderate MERI. In the last half of this frame begin TSU again. Play it in much the same way as TSU in frame 1, but this time in the high octave.

11. The TSU in the last half of the preceding frame quickly shifts to RO. As soon as you go to RO, make a slight ATARI using the second hole, as you did in frame 2. Towards the end of this frame, decrease the volume and begin a very slight vibrato.

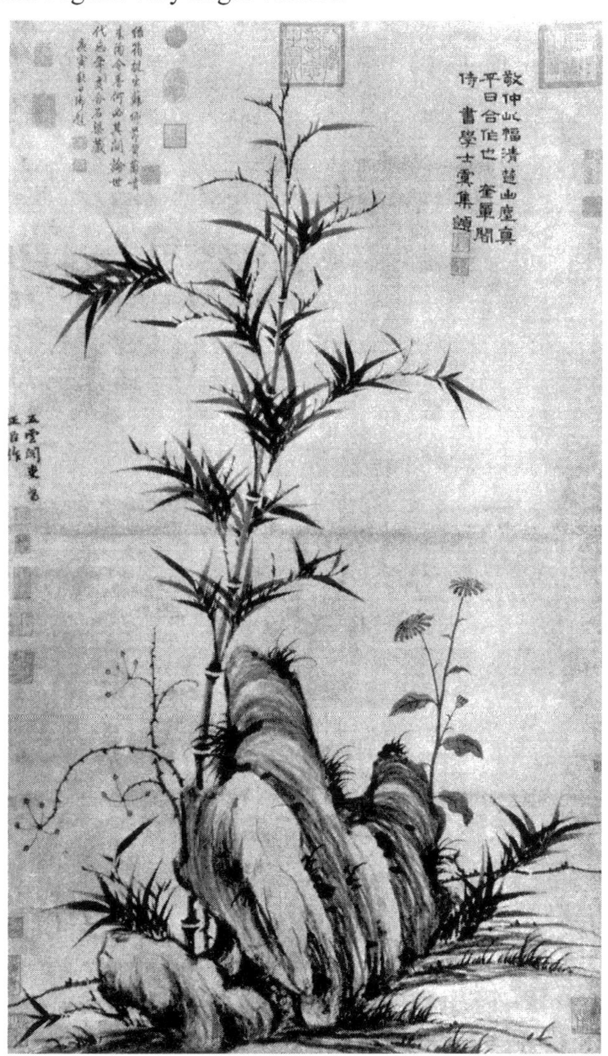

Bamboo and chrysanthemum, K'o Chiu-su, 13th C.

12. Play RO MERI for the first quarter of this frame. Gradually rise to the regular pitch of RO and then increase volume and vibrato.

13. In the first half of this frame the volume and vibrato of RO taper off and end with the grace note. Take a quick deep breath. Notice the small grace note OU SAN ( ) at the beginning. You usually play OU SAN in the high octave, but here you play it as a low octave short duration grace note. Now open hole #4 and play RI with an articulation. The volume increases with a slight vibrato; then it decreases rapidly as you begin the slide into OU of the next frame. Do this by sliding the finger off hole #5.

14. Play OU in the regular pitch for the first half of this frame. Then tilt into OU MERI as much as possible while simultaneously increasing volume and beginning vibrato. Then decrease the volume and return to the normal pitch of OU for an instant. In the last half of this frame, play a grace note for RE. Do this by playing TSU with hole #4 left open. Quickly close hole #4, thus producing the regular pitch for TSU. Then open hole #2 and play the RE of the next frame.

15. In the last half of this frame RE picks up in volume and vibrato for a moment, then decreases. There is a slight slide into RO of the next frame, similar to that done in frame 6.

16. The volume and vibrato begin increasing in the last half of this frame and continue over to the next frame.

17. RO tapers off. Play TSU in the last half of this frame much as you did in the first frame.

18. Play RO the same as in frame 11, but in the low octave.

19. Play RO in the maximum OH MERI position. Very gradually increase its pitch. Then increase volume towards the end of the frame.

20. RO continues increasing in volume and vibrato in this frame.

21. In the first half of this frame RO tapers off and ends with the grace note.

Now consolidate all you have learned so far. Play Part A until you are comfortable with it, then begin Part C below.

PART C
Pitch Frames 106 - 152

106. Part C begins in the last half of this frame. Begin with TSU MERI. Make its articulation and then play as severe a TSU OH MERI as possible. Then quickly lift the finger off the first hole and play a regular TSU for a moment. Now, more slowly, lift the finger off hole #2 and play RE of the next frame. When you play Part A with Part C, go directly from the first half of frame 21 to the last half of this frame.

107. Toward the last half of this frame the volume and vibrato increase a little and then rapidly decrease. At the end of this frame the fingers quickly cover hole #2 and even two thirds of hole #1, and then you begin RE NAYASHI.

108. This NAYASHI is similar to the others except that you play it a little faster, as indicated by the symbols ( ).

109. The last half of this frame is similar to the last half of frame 13.

110. Half way through this frame lower the pitch of OU to OU OH MERI. Then immediately begin a gradual transition by sliding fingers off hole #2 and #4, until by the middle of frame 111 you are playing a low octave HI.

111. Frames 112 though 115 detail a OSHI YURI phrase. It takes a long time to get the right feeling for it. As you reach the regular pitch of HI, increase volume and vibrato. Then towards the end of the frame, taper both off and slide the thumb slightly off its hole. Notice the slight pause at the end.

112. This frame begins with HI OH MERI. It rises to HI with an increase in volume and slight vibrato as the pitch sharpens to HI. There is a slight pause. Then in the last half of this frame, play HI MERI again except this time with less MERI than before. Also, bring the pitch back up to HI more quickly.

113. Repeat frame 112 a few times here. Each repetition is less MERI and of shorter duration than the previous. This whole phrase is similar to a series of NAYASHIs.

114. These NAYASHIs gradually shift into a minor YURI, then to a solid HI just before the next frame begins.

115. This frame begins with an articulation of HI and some vibrato. Then, as the volume decreases, slide the thumb off hole #5. After a very slight pause, play HI again. At the end of this frame lift the thumb off hole #5 for an instant to make a grace note similar to an articulation of HI. Then go quickly to HI GO.

Young crane under Wu-t'ung tree Kao Ch'ip'ei, 18th C.

116. The symbol ( ) is HI GO in Hon Kyoku. The volume and vibrato of HI GO gradually increase in the last half of this frame.

117. HI GO tapers off and the last half of this frame is similar to frame 109 and 13.

118. Notice that OU is very MERI and then sharpens a bit at the end. This frame concludes with a grace note for RE of the next frame. This frame is similar to frame 14.

119. RE tapers off in vibrato and volume as it nears the RU style re-articulation.

Waiting for the ferry,Kuan T'ung, 10th C.

120. This particular re-articulation of RE is done by gently tapping the finger over hole #2 for an instant. After this, increase the volume and vibrato, then decrease them once again as you approach the next frame.

121. This frame begins like frame 120. The vibrato tapers off towards the end of this frame.

122. The end of this frame has a grace note for the HI MERI in the next frame. This is a low octave version of HA GO. At the end of this frame, quickly shift from HA GO to HI MERI.

123. Increase HI MERI in volume and vibrato halfway through this frame. Then pause slightly.

124. Start with HI MERI and then quickly shift to the maximum MERI position while trying to increase volume. In reality, there isn't much increase in real volume and sometimes there is even a decrease. Listen to the nature of the sound. You will hear an increase of "fullness" if not volume. From the OH MERI of HI on, sharpen the pitch until you reach regular HI. Then quickly shift down to CHI in the next frame.

125. As you start decreasing the volume of CHI, begin the vibrato.

126. The first half of this frame is CHI MERI. Then shift to regular CHI. Pay close attention to the relationship between the increasing pitch and volume.

127. Here you have two slides. The volume of CHI decreases just before you slide, and then increases again. After the slide from OU, pause for a moment and breathe if necessary.

128. The volume of TSU MERI begins increasing just before the RU of the next frame. Also lift your finger off hole #1, but keep the MERI pitch of TSU. A severe chin tilt makes this possible. It may take you a few years before you can lift your finger off and maintain the correct MERI pitch.

129. After tapping the first hole, RU, bring the finger down and partly cover this hole again. Toward the end of this frame, attempt an increase in volume as you pull the TSU down into a more severe MERI. Let more air flow.

130. Toward the end of this frame, return to the regular MERI position of TSU.

131. Begin RO with an articulation at hole #2. Gradually increase the volume and vibrato.

132. Here is another OSHI YURI phrase, like in frames 111 to 115. There is one major difference; you always return to RO MERI after each NAYASHI. The movement of the head is a little different from a regular NAYASHI. With NAYASHI, the head moves from MERI to KARI in a fairly vertical line. With this OSHI YURI the head movement is a cross between that needed for NAYASHI and that needed for YURI. The head moves at an oblique angle, up and down 2 to 3 inches. There can also be a slight circular movement as well.

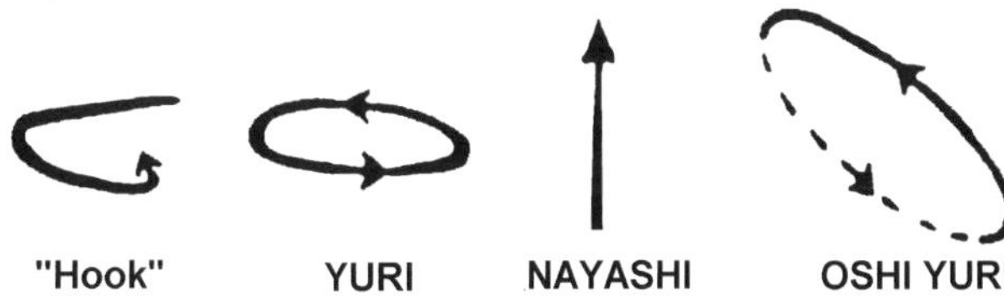

The lines above indicate the movement your lip and the blowing edge make. Note: there is no sound produced during the downward movement of OSHI YURI.

133. The tempo of the OSHI YURI increases as its pitch lowers. By the end you are actually shifting from MERI down to OH MERI. You end the first half of this frame in RO OH MERI with a simple vibrato (YURI). After a slight pause, and breathing if needed, begin a RO NAYASHI. To reach the lowest OH MERI pitch required in Hon Kyoku, try sucking in your stomach a bit.

134. The RO reaches its normal pitch just after the beginning of this frame, then tapers off in volume quickly. Play RI for a moment, then articulate it. At the end of this frame, quickly cover the fourth hole and lift off the third hole.

135. Notice that the vibrato begins only on the end of the OU.

136. Play RE at a lower volume and then taper it off with little or no vibrato.

137. As the pitch of RE rises, the volume and vibrato increase.

138. Play HA in the last half of this frame. Then quickly cover the second hole and move the chin to the regular position for the beginning of the next frame.

139. Three quarters of the way through this frame HA YON GO tapers off. After a slight pause, play a very short and delicate HA NI in low octave.

140. Begin this RE at low volume and increase its volume towards the end of the frame. This gives RE contrast. In general, avoid beginning notes at high volume. Try to notice what happens to the sound within each note.

141. RE gradually tapers off. Then, at the end of this frame play a short HA as a grace note for the HA YON of the next frame.

142. The HA YON of this frame has about the same duration as the one in frame 139, and it ends in a pause.

143. Notice how subtle and delicate RE is at the beginning.

144-146. These frames are a repetition of frames 142 and 143. Play the HA YON progressively shorter and shorter and the RE longer and longer. Also, play these frames at a faster tempo than usual, as indicated by the symbols ( ).

147. This phrase (142-148) ends with a solid RE.

148. The last half of this frame begins the concluding phrase of this piece. Note that you quickly lift the finger off the first hole, then a moment later off the second one.

149. RE starts increasing in volume just towards the end of this frame.

150. After the ATARI, the volume increases and the vibrato begins. Then both taper off.

151. In this NAYASHI, play RE in MERI for over half of the first frame. Then gradually raise it to the regular pitch of RE.

152. RE is at its maximum volume at the beginning of this frame. It then starts to taper off gradually. Notice the ending. It's not the usual "hook" grace note that you played for RE up to now. Here it's more like a "falling" into MERI. Listen to the subtle quality of this drop. Think of it guiding you into the sound of silence, or as a last subtle sound before a concert of silence.

Crane, Mu-Ch'i, 13th C.

Play Parts A and C until you're very familiar with them. This may take a few weeks to months depending on how much you practice and the quality of your practice. Then go on to Part B.

Part B is almost entirely in the high octave. Many of the notes are difficult to do correctly or clearly for quite some time. Practice, practice, practice is all you need.

PART B

Pitch Frames 22 - 106

21. Part B begins in the last half of this frame. The OU in this case is actually OU SAN. Play it momentarily in the low octave and then "push" it into the high octave. Then MERI this OU SAN by tilting the chin and partly covering the hole #3. Then gradually slide the fingers off hole #2 and #4.

Cormorant, Miyamoto Nusashi, 16th C.

Han Shan (Zen monk), Ka-o Ninga, 14th C.

22. Continue this slide gradually enough so you reach HI toward the end of this frame. As you do, increase the volume.

23. After the ATARI, the vibrato increases and the volume begins to taper off.

24. The vibrato tapers off and you play a regular HI (no vibrato). End this HI with a thumb slide off hole #5. Breathe and begin the trill which leads into HI GO of the next frame.

This trill is done by rapidly moving the thumb off and on hole #5. Rapid movement of the thumb is difficult. It can take years to do this smoothly. Try keeping the thumb rigid; move it on and off the hole by pivoting your forearm from the elbow.

25. Notice that the volume of HI GO is soft in the beginning and builds solidly but gently.

26. By this point, HI GO has solid volume and vibrato. End HI GO with a slight push for a sharper pitch (KARI). This is done by extending the chin outward and upward. Notice the grace note, OU SAN, that precedes HI. From HI, quickly slide the thumb off hole #5 and simultaneously place the fingers on hole #3 and #4. Place the finger on hole #3 only partially as this is CHI MERI.

27. The volume for CHI MERI begins increasing just before you lower its pitch further into a CHI OH MERI.

28. Achieve the CHI OH MERI here by partially covering hole #2 as well. When you get the pitch to its lowest point begin the vibrato. Taper off the volume and vibrato and briefly return to regular MERI. Breathe and then play CHI MERI again, increasing its volume just towards the end of this frame.

29. On the ATARI begin a mild vibrato. Halfway through this CHI, taper vibrato off and play CHI at OH MERI by partially covering hole #2 again. As you return to MERI, increase the volume slightly.

30. After this ATARI, play a little more vibrato than in the last frame. In the last half of this frame severely MERI the CHI. Then smoothly slide the fingers off holes #2 and #3, and finally off hole #4.

31. From CHI, slide into this frame and play OU. This OU is a little different from what you have been doing.

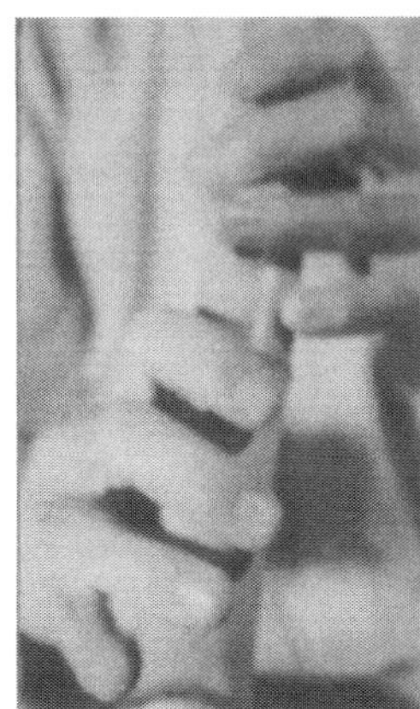

Leave the hole #1 open. It's difficult to do this in the high octave. Notice that at the end of the slide, you quickly place the fingers on hole #2 and #4. Towards the end of this frame, MERI this OU by partially covering hole #1 and #3; this is not the usual MERI. Here, slant your fingers over the side edge of the holes without bending these fingers at the joints. See the upper ring finger shown in the photo at the left.

32. As you start this OH MERI, begin the vibrato. Decrease vibrato and volume as you end this note. Slide your finger slightly off hole #2 just at the end of the OU. Take a deep breath and play HI GO, which serves as a grace note for the HA NI which follows.

33. Hon Kyoku uses HA NI often. Strive to play it at a KARI pitch - which is difficult in the beginning. From HI GO of the last frame, bring your finger quickly and forcefully down onto hole #3. In the last half of this frame, begin a partial covering of hole #2 and #4, and tilt your chin inward to play this HA NI as MERI as possible. Then sharpen the pitch while increasing the volume.

34. At the beginning of this frame, just as the volume peaks, bring your finger down hard on hole #2, and simultaneously make an ATARI on hole #3. You're now playing HA YON. Increase its volume and begin vibrato near the end.

35. Slide your finger slightly off hole #2 at the end of HA YON. At the end of this frame play the grace note for the up coming HI. This is OU SAN in high octave.

36. Notice how HI gradually builds in volume; the vibrato and peak volume occur in the next frame.

37-46. These frames are essentially the same as frames 23 through 32.

46. In the last half of this frame play TSU MERI, then articulate it and for a moment attempt a maximum OH MERI of TSU. Now quickly lift your finger off hole #1 to obtain a regular TSU (no MERI at all). Then a moment later lift your finger off hole #2 and begin the RE of the next frame.

Moumtain's in rain, Kao K'o-kung, 11th C.

Tai Kobo as a recluse, Soga Shohaku, 18th C.

47. Notice that you wait until the end of the frame before beginning to increase the volume of RE. This increase in volume is a build up for the re-articulation in the next frame.

48. After the ATARI, the volume tapers off and the vibrato builds. Then the vibrato tapers off and the volume builds towards the end of this frame.

49. The volume tapers off after the ATARI and the vibrato returns, then both taper off.

50-51. RE NAYASHI can be difficult in the high octave. Concentrate on the lip muscle.

This is especially true near the end of the NAYASHI when the volume tapers off. For this RE, and for other high octave notes, the pitch tends to drop slightly - which of course it shouldn't. To correct this, try narrowing the airstream (lip control) and extending the chin (as you do for OH KARI). A narrow yet high velocity air stream will be soft in volume but of the correct pitch. The grace note at the end of RE is also difficult.

51-54. Play this series of notes, CHI MERI and OU, as in frames 29 through 31. However, at the end of the OU in frame 54, do not lower the pitch but instead increase the volume. Play this OU with the first and third holes open.

55. Articulate this ATARI of OU with a RU. This is done here by tapping hole #3 closed for a split second. After this RU, play a short vibrato and then slant your fingers more and more over hole #1 and #3. After reaching the maximum MERI, gradually slide these fingers off. Then slide your fingers off hole #2 and #4. Notice the slight pause at the end of this frame. Take a breath here if you need it.

56. Begin TSU MERI smoothly and quietly. Then near the end of the frame increase volume and lower pitch simultaneously.

57. The vibrato and volume taper off and then the pitch returns to normal MERI.

57-68. Play these like frames 47 through 57.

68-71. Play these like frames 10 through 13.

Two Birds on an old branch, Li Ti, 12th C.

Bamboo, tree, rock, Chaomeng-Fu, 13th C.

72. RE is soft in volume and tapers off without vibrato.

73-74. Halfway through the NAYASHI, RE increases in volume and vibrato.

75-77. These frames are similar to frames 26 through 28, except that HI is longer and the slide into CHI is more gradual.

78. "Dip" CHI down into OH MERI and then rapidly close hole #3 to go to RE.

79. RE builds in volume and vibrato briefly, and then tapers off. Just at the end, the finger slides off hole #4 slightly and then immediately closes again.

80-81. Tilt the chin sharply and quickly to produce a MERI pitch for RE, but leave hole #1 and #2 uncovered. So, produce this MERI by chin tilt alone, as indicated by the symbol (3|).

82-83. Play these frames at a faster tempo than usual, using the techniques you learned in frames 30 and 31. Here the OU, after "dipping" down into OH MERI slides upward in pitch. Do this by moving your fingers gradually off holes #2 and #4. Notice a slight pause at the end just before dropping into TSU MERI.

84-88. These frames are similar to frames 9 through 13.

88. In the last half of this frame play HA MERI, and after a moment quickly rise into the HA KARI. If you look closely you'll see a KARI symbol hidden in the squiggly line under the HA, i.e., the YURI line.

89. As you reach the KARI of HA, begin vibrato. Then taper the volume off towards the end and gently go to RO. Hold the fingers close to the flute to do this smoothly.

90-91. RO volume increases near the end and then tapers off. Notice the TSU played at the end of frame 91. Here, sustain the "plateau" of TSU (between TSU MERI and RE) longer.

92. Towards the end, RE tapers off and then momentarily increases in volume. At this point, quickly move your finger partially off hole #3 and play CHI MERI.

93. CHI MERI then slides into TSU MERI. Try to feel and play these slide sequences like water in a creek flowing gently downstream.

94-98. These frames are similar to frames 9 through 13.

99-106. These frames are similar to frames 14 through 21.

106. At the end of this frame, play TSU MERI, TSU OH MERI, regular TSU and then RE. Thus you begin Part C.

My congratulations on coming this far! Continue over the years to develop this piece, paying closer and closer attention to the breath and the sound. One mind, one breath, one sound is blowing Zen.

A SIMPLE SHAKUHACHI

Bamboo is the material of choice for the Shakuhachi. Due to the many steps involved in traditional construction, some makers use hardwood or plastic. This lowers the price drastically, often without loss of play-ability. A good traditional bamboo flute can cost many hundreds of dollars. A good wooden flute costs a hundred dollars and a good plastic flute, thirty dollars. While there are differences, it's mostly a matter of economics and aesthetic preference. A well made flute is a joy to play regardless of its material; a poor flute is an agony to play no matter how beautiful and natural its appearance.

For those who sincerely wish to use this instrument as a spiritual tool, the plastic version has much to offer. Today, plastic is a common all purpose building material. In ancient Japan, bamboo and low fired clay were the "plastics" of the time. The Japanese made their Tea Ceremony utensils and Shakuhachi out of these cheap and unpretentious materials. The focus was on the spiritual goal, not the tool.

Many Japanese today place much value on the physical appearance of these tools. We can see the same departure from basics in our own culture. Look at our modern 'Christian' culture. What a difference from the simple non-materialistic life taught and lived by Christ.

The second Chan (Zen) patriarch, Shih K'o, 13th C.

So, after thinking it over, you may decide a plastic flute will do just fine, at least in the beginning. After all, the Buddhist path here is a yielding to breath and sound, not a clinging to the esthetics of the tool.

Plastic pipe is the easiest material to work. A flute made from it is easy to play and possesses a nice vibrant sound. Its smooth uniform bore gives it outstanding resonance, even without a taper. If you want to make your own, the next section details its construction. You can experiment by adding more holes or by making it longer. Don't worry about your construction skill; this is the easiest musical instrument to create, except maybe using two garbage can lids as cymbals. It takes about an hour to put together, and if it doesn't work, you can easily make another and another until you get it right.

Compare the ease of making a plastic flute to the many hours of labor (involving over 100 steps) required for a root bamboo Shakuhachi. Mind you, that labor is a labor of love. Flutes made from wood require less, though still considerable, time and know-how. With interest and perseverance you can succeed with any of these materials by studying the information in this book.

For now though, begin with that modern type of bamboo, plastic! Once you know how to make a Shakuhachi out of plastic, making a traditional one will be easier.

Materials Needed:

1. Two feet of 3/4" Schedule 40 PVC pipe (Figure 1).

2. A 3/4" Schedule 40 PVC coupling (Figure 2).

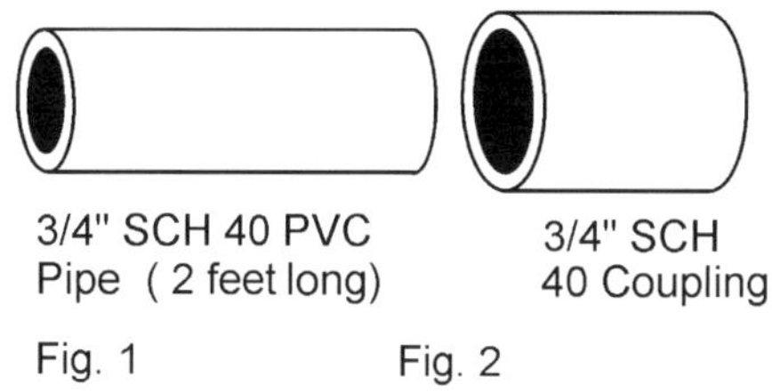

Fig. 1 Fig. 2

3. A can of PVC glue.

4. A fine tooth saw.

5. A drill with a 3/8" and a 13/32" bit (the 13/32" bit is optional).

6. A medium course flat file.

7. Some sand paper, a knife, a pencil and a yardstick.

All of these materials are available for a few dollars at a hardware store. See also page 49, #15 RAW MATERIALS.

Procedure:

1. Clean inside the coupling and outside one end of the pipe. Apply glue and join these two. Strike the end firmly so it goes as far into the coupling as possible. Let dry a few minutes (Figure 3).

Note: If you file away the ridge inside the coupling, it will slide all the way onto the pipe.

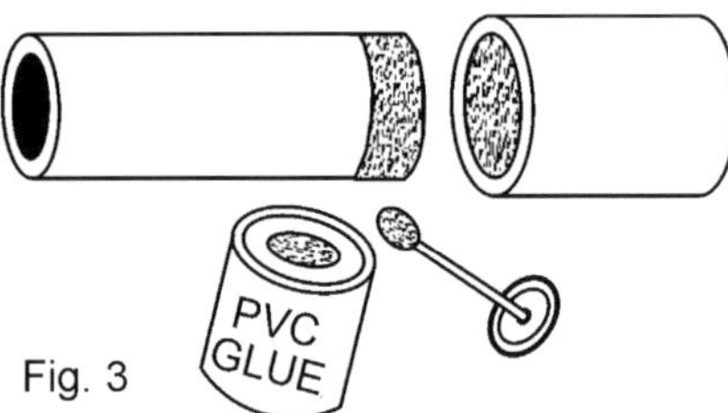

Fig. 3

2. Saw off any part of the coupling that extends beyond the end of the pipe (Figure 4).

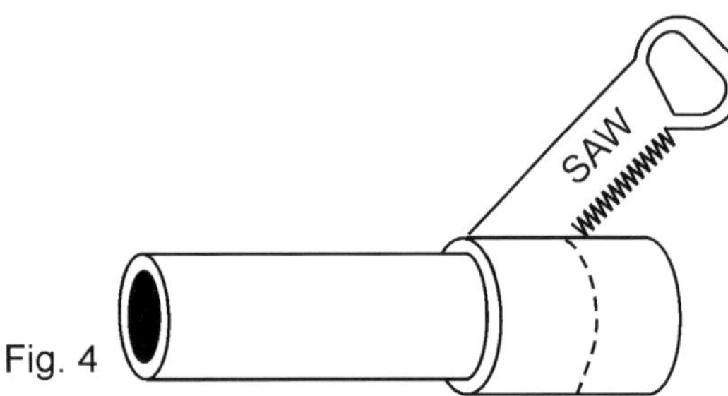

Fig. 4

3. File away any excess coupling that extends beyond the end of the pipe. Then start filing one edge at about a 30° angle. Draw a line to guide you (Figure 5).

4. As you file into the inner bore, a feather edge will form. Lightly carve or sand this away. Go slowly at this stage to get the proper bevel and blowing edge depth (Figure 6).

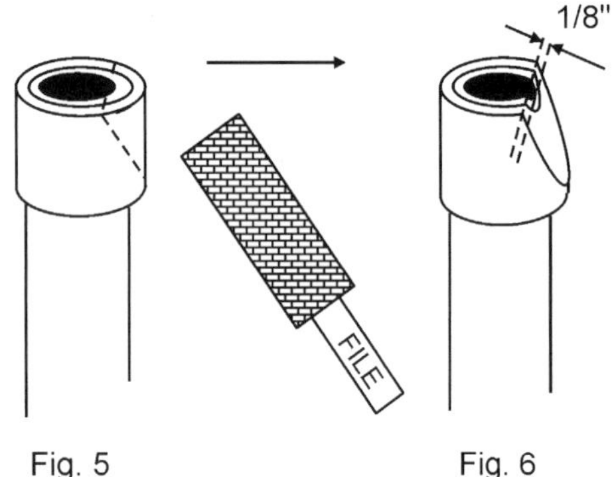

Fig. 5 Fig. 6

5. File the opposite edge round until it looks like Figure 7. The amount you file away is a matter of personal preference.

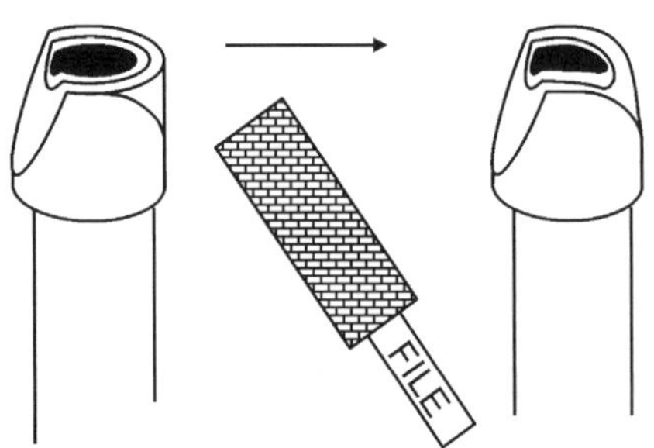

Fig. 7

6. With the blowing edge up, draw a line down the middle of the pipe (Figure 8).

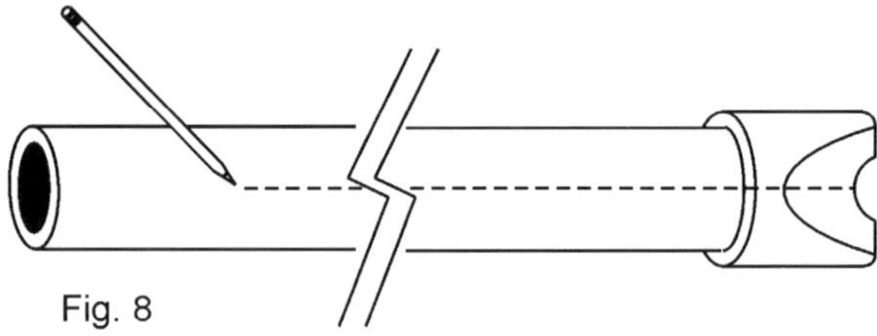
Fig. 8

7. To cut the flute to length, measure 21-1/2" down from the blowing end of the flute and mark. (Figure 9).

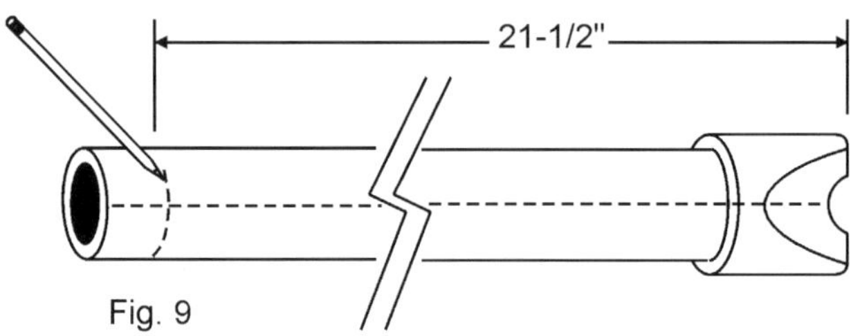

Fig. 9

8. Holding the saw perpendicular, saw off the excess and file smooth.

9. Now mark the finger holes. Measure up from the bottom end 4-3/4" and mark this point on the center line. From this point, measure 2-1/8" and mark the next point. Repeat this until you have the drill points for the four front holes. The back hole is 1-3/8" from the top hole (Figure 10).

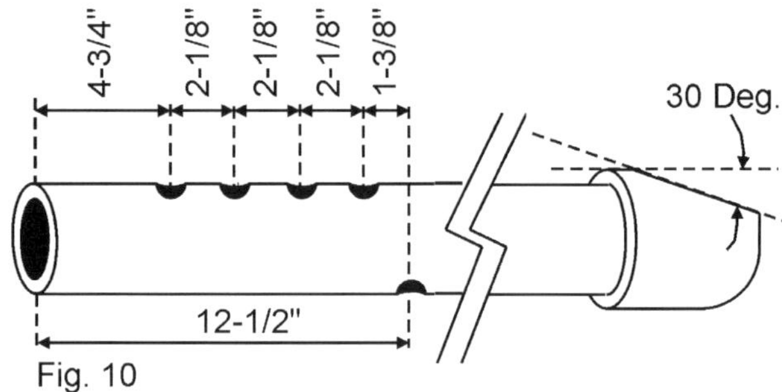

Fig. 10

10. Drill the holes you marked. Use the 3/8" bit for the 3rd hole and the 13/32" bit for the others. If you don't have the 13/32" bit, you can drill all the holes 3/8". You can widen the four holes a little with a sharp knife, if and when the pitch begins to sound a little off to you.

11. Sand the edges around the holes and at both ends until smooth. You can also use sandpaper to clean the outer surface of the flute. Keep sanding to a minimum if you are using clear PVC. Although, high speed buffing will bring the shine back to areas that were filed and sanded.

Your flute is ready to play! If your first attempt fails, try again. Practice makes perfect, and the raw materials couldn't be cheaper.

My tiny workshop in Japan - 1974

A SEVEN HOLE SHAKUHACHI

If you want to play Western music, especially fast tempo pieces, try the seven hole Shakuhachi. Drill a small hole about 1/8 to 3/16 inch in diameter below hole #1 (Figure 11). This enables you to play TSU MERI (E flat) easily. Drill another hole of the same diameter between holes #3 and #4 (Figure 11). This will produce CHI MERI (A flat). To get the exact pitch, drill a smaller hole and gradually enlarge it until the pitch is correct.

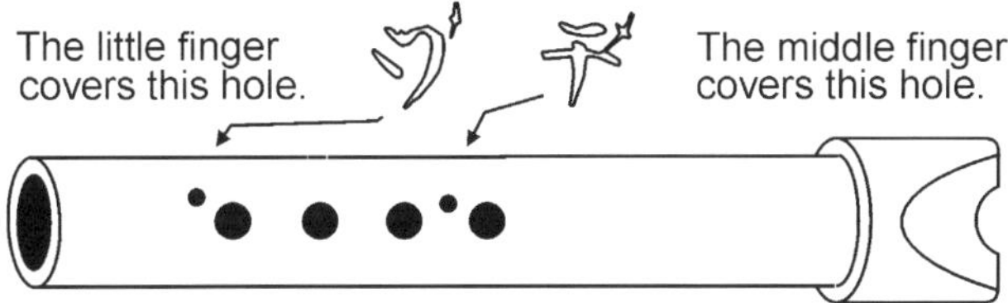

Fig. 11

Experiment with different tunings by placing the holes at other intervals, or by adding more holes, or both. A close look at a recorder shows you that it works on the same principle as the Shakuhachi, except for its artificially guided airstream. In fact, if you saw off the end of a recorder just above the "blow" edge, you'll have a "Shakucorder".

LONGER AND SHORTER FLUTES

Nothing is more pleasant than the deep resonant sound of a long Shakuhachi. It's easy to make a flute of any length because hole spacing is proportional to length. Since it is easier to calculate proportions using the metric system, I'll use centimeters in the formula below. . Note: this works best on flutes with a tapered bore.

$$\text{Bottom end to hole \#1} = \frac{12 \times \text{Flute length}}{54.5 \text{ cm.}}$$

$$\text{Hole to hole distance} = \frac{5.4 \times \text{Flute length}}{54.5 \text{ cm.}}$$

$$\text{Hole \#4 to \#5 distance} = \frac{3.6 \times \text{Flute length}}{54.5 \text{ cm.}}$$

Slender Bamboo, Ku An, 14th C.

TRADITIONAL CONSTRUCTION

Made from the root end of bamboo, the Shakuhachi is solid. So solid that Samurai, after being denied permission to carry weapons, occasionally carried and used the Shakuhachi as a weapon.

Today, the standard Shakuhachi is 1.8 feet long. "Shaku" is an ancient unit of measurement in Japan and coincidentally it is almost exactly 12 inches long. "Hachi" means eight or 8/10ths of a "shaku".

Shakuhachi construction begins with the selection of the raw material. Bamboo is, by far, the most aesthetically pleasing material. Its extremely variable nature also makes working with it challenging and fascinating. Bamboo's cell structure, density and age can all affect a flute's acoustics and appearance. Only a small percentage of bamboo roots harvested will have all the characteristics needed to make a superior Shakuhachi.

A problem in this country is obtaining root end sections of the right bamboo (Phyllostachys, bambusoides - "giant timber bamboo"). Some makers in this country make fine Shakuhachi out of the upper portions of this bamboo, which is imported here from Asia. Search the Yellow Pages for sources near you. Also ask the Agricultural Extension Agent in your county if he knows whether this kind of bamboo is grown in your state. Go where it is grown to obtain root end pieces or buy some rhizome and start your own back yard grove.

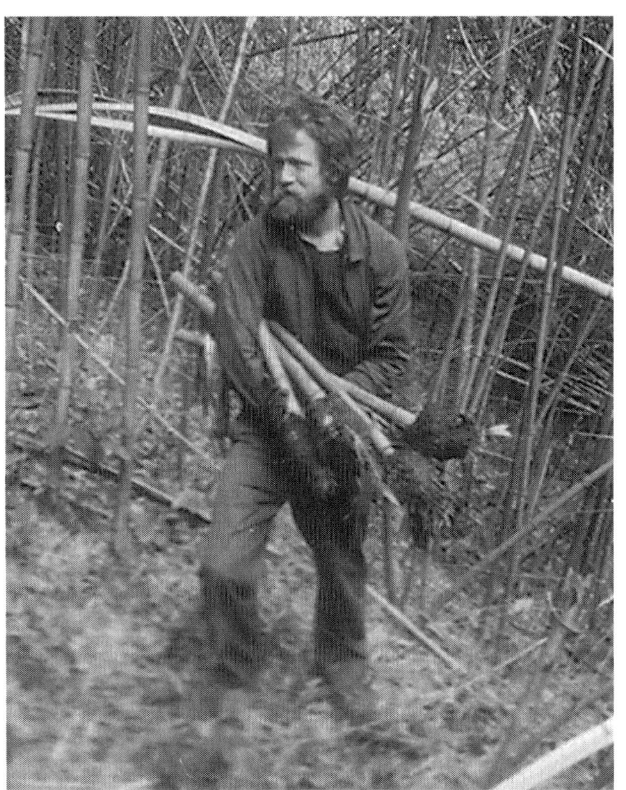

Gathering bamboo, Sado Islands, Japan - 1975

The sixth Ch'an (Zen) patriarch, Liang K'ai, 13th C.

When making a traditional bamboo Shakuhachi, three of the most difficult steps are the joint, the blowing edge inlay, and the tapered bore.

The inlay provides a durable blowing edge. The joint makes it easier to work on the bore taper and allows you to use a wider selection of root end bamboo (by allowing you to remove a part of the middle section of bamboo). And work done to the bore can improve playability. Actually, you can bypass these steps, if you can live without their features.

The next page begins a photographic record of the construction of a Shakuhachi. They contain enough information for you to make a Shakuhachi. However, expect to make several Shakuhachis, and a number of mistakes, before you get the technique down.

Search the grove for bamboo which meet certain standards of age, dimension and character. See ADDITIONAL DETAILS, #1 and #2 on page 44, for more on this.

Because each piece of bamboo is different, each flute will be unique to some degree, of course.

(1) Measure the node spacing (about 11cm, 14cm, and 20cm.) so that blowing end and the holes lay correctly, i.e., See ADDITIONAL DETAILS, #1 and #2.

This inter node spacing is proportional to the flute length.

(2) Measure the bottom node spacing where hole #1 and #2 will go.

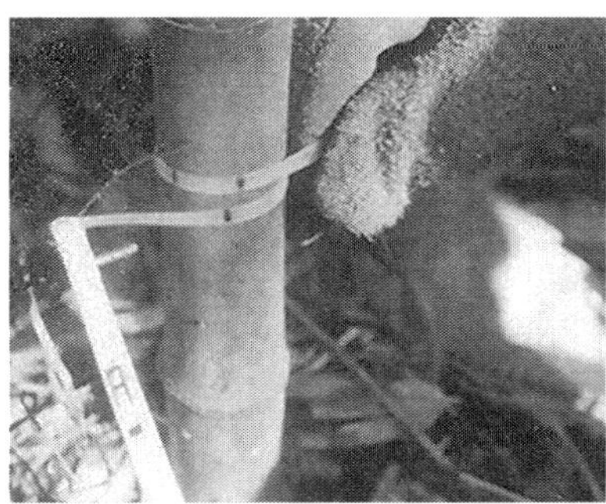

(3) Measure the circumference - about 11 cm.

Mark the desired circumference on a band and wrap it around the bamboo.

(4) After sawing these off waist high, chisel them out of the ground, roots and all.

A <u>sharp</u> steel wedge welded to an iron bar works well. Strike the bar with a sledge hammer.

(5) Bamboo out of the ground.

(6) Chop the soil and the excess roots off.

Be careful not to chop too close to root bell.

(7) Saw off the excess root end.

(8) Trim off the excess root.

Next, select the narrower (2.8 cm diameter) bamboo needed to make the joint cylinders.

(9) Saw the joint bamboo.

(10) Heat and wipe the bamboo.

After hauling everything back, wash the bamboo and "roast" it over a bed of hot coals until the moisture and the resin ooze. See ADDITIONAL DETAILS, #3.

After wiping this off, lay the bamboo out in the sun for a few months to bleach and cure.

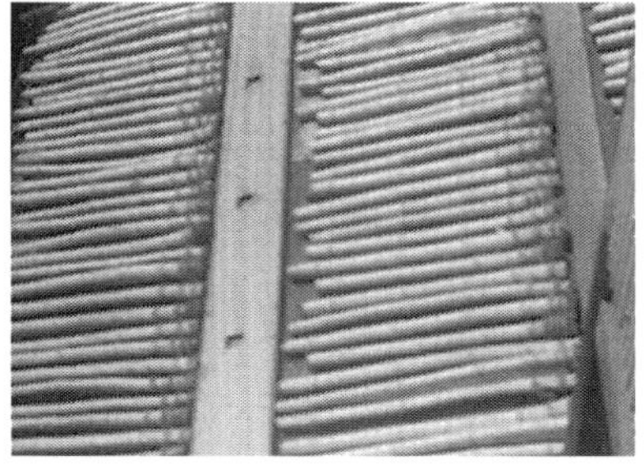

(11) Bamboo bleaching in the sun.

Coat the bleached bamboo with creosote and allow them to cure in a dark place for several years - ideally.

(12) When cured, examine and mark the areas with unwanted bends. See ADDITIONAL DETAILS, #3.

(13) Heat the bamboo over the hot coals.

Wipe it with a wet cloth to keep it from browning or burning.

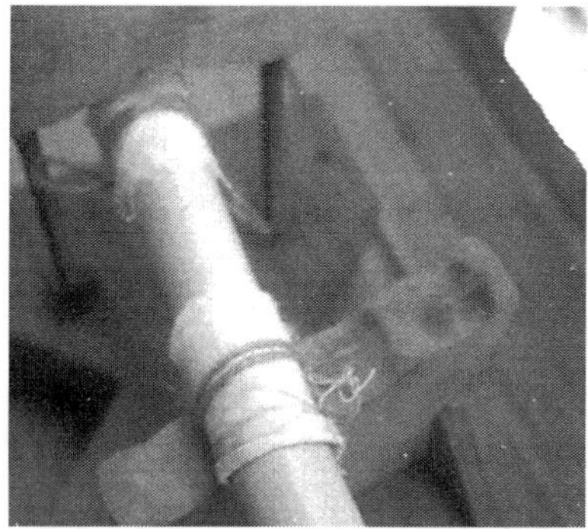

(14) Position it in the bending jig (lever).

Nodes are the strongest areas of the bamboo to place on the fulcrum.

(15) Bending the bamboo - a very tricky job. Apply even downward pressure. Cool it with a wet cloth.

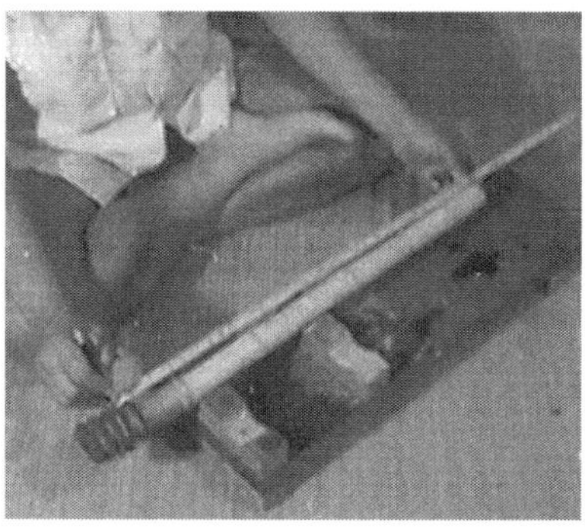

(16) Lay out the dimensions, i.e., total length, center line, hole positions and the joint cut. See ADDITIONAL DETAILS, #1 and #5.

Length is measured from the blowing end node cut line to the joint (28.90 cm.), and from the joint to the bottom (25.60 cm.), for a total of 54.5 cm.

The joint should fall about 2.6 cm up from the center of the 3rd hole.

Making a two-sectioned Shakuhachi allows you to remove enough midsection bamboo to get the exact overall length and yet insure that the blowing-end begins at a node.

A "break apart" mid-joint also makes it easier to work on the bore, especially for l-o-n-g Shakuhachi.

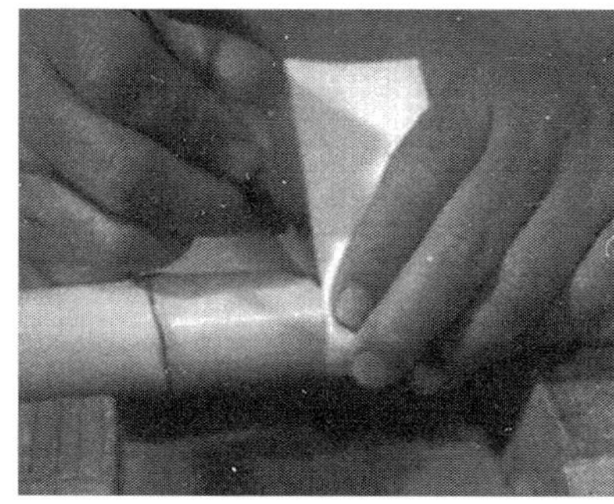

(17) Mark the joint cut-lines.

Wrap a band of paper around the bamboo and use it to draw an even circumference line around the joint.

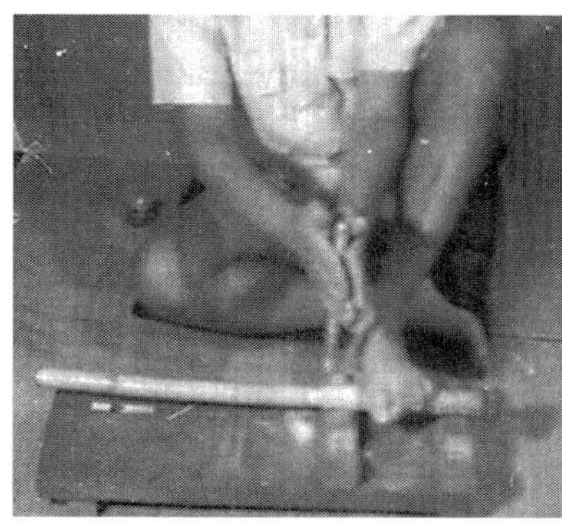

(18) Use an awl to mark the center line at points near each joint end.

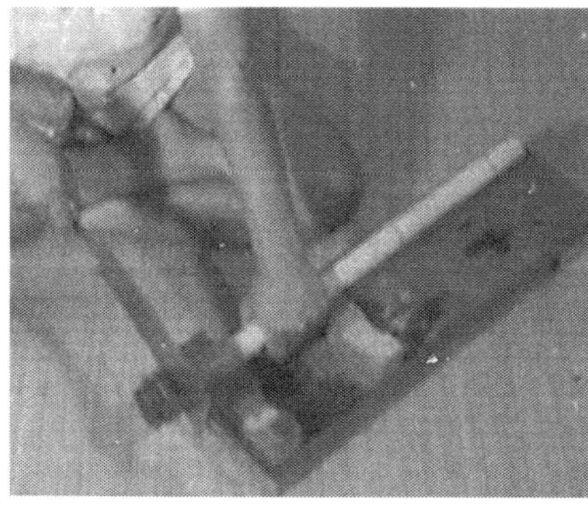

(19) Saw the root to the correct length.

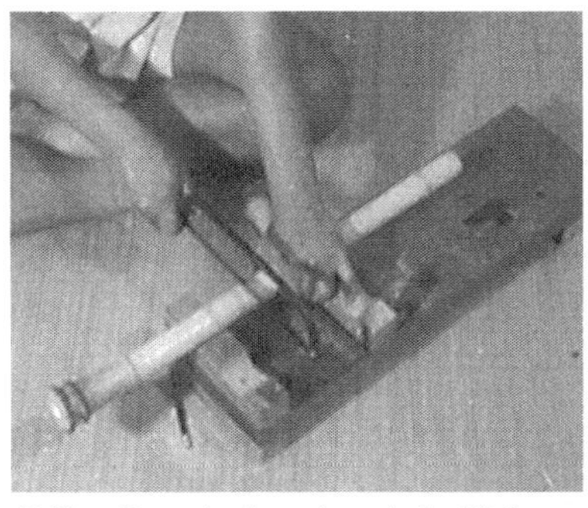

(20) Saw the bamboo in half along the cut-line.

(21) If the bamboo is a little too long, you can cut the excess from the joint end of the upper half.

If the bamboo is too short, you can discard the node above "hole 3" and use the next one up.

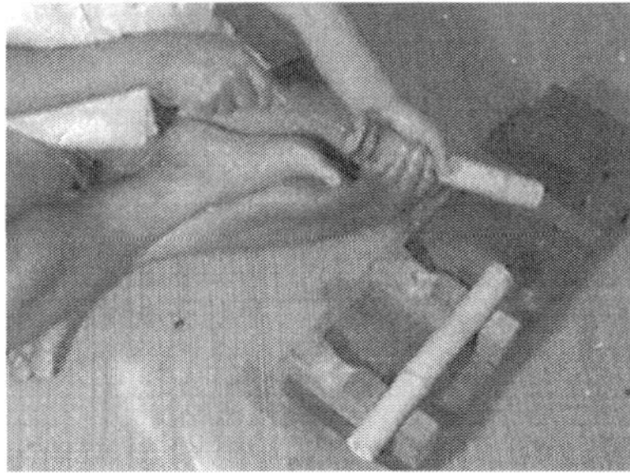

(22) Drill out the node membranes and the bore using a 1/2" hand auger.

(23) Lay out a 6 cm. cut-line on the smaller joint bamboo.

You'll be carving this into a perfect cylinder. You'll then carve matching holes in both halves and glue this joint piece into the lower half.

This may seem harder than it actually is.

Some makers use plastic pipe for this joint instead of bamboo.

(24) Saw a shallow groove, on the 6 cm. cut-line, completely around the joint piece.

Draw the joint circumference line. It should have a 2.5 cm. diameter. See step #29 below.

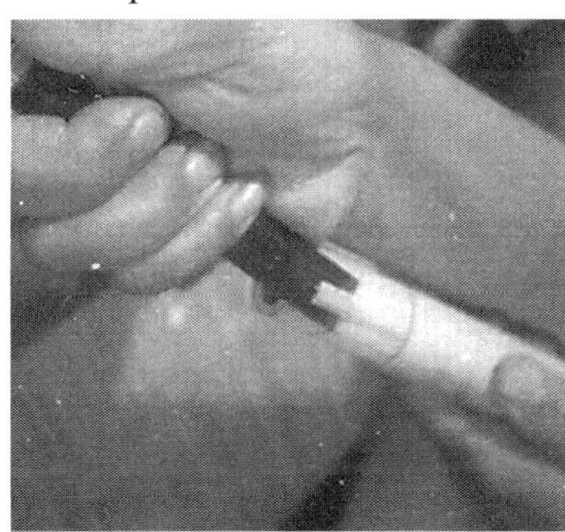

(25) Chisel the joint bamboo along the circumference line.

(26) File the joint smooth.

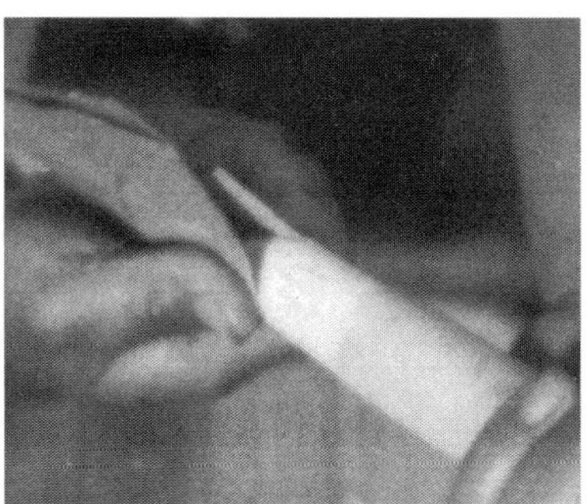

(27) Sand the joint smooth.

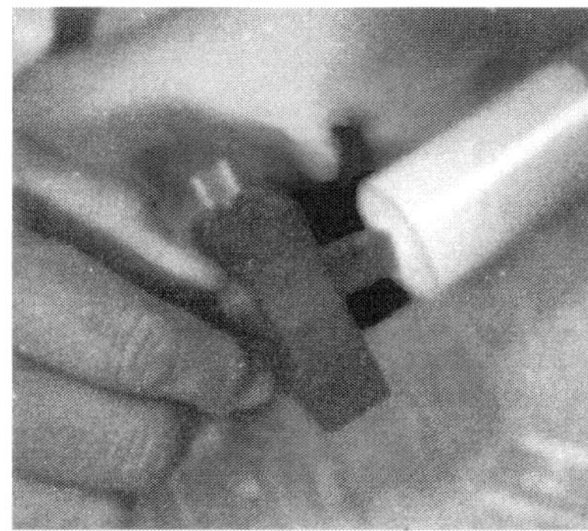

(28) Cut a shallow circular groove, 1.8 cm. down, inside the bore of the lower half.

See ADDITIONAL DETAILS, #4 for more on making the joint and #14 for the tool needed to cut the groove.

Later you'll chisel out a 2.5 cm diameter hole down to this circular groove.

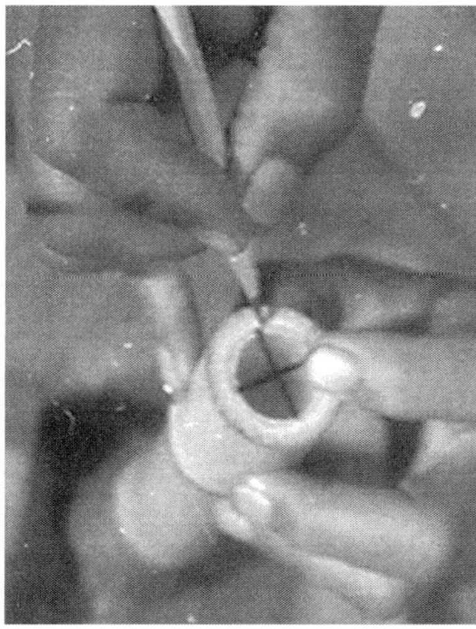

(29) Lay out the inner circumference (2.5 cm. diameter) cut-line on the joint end of the lower half.

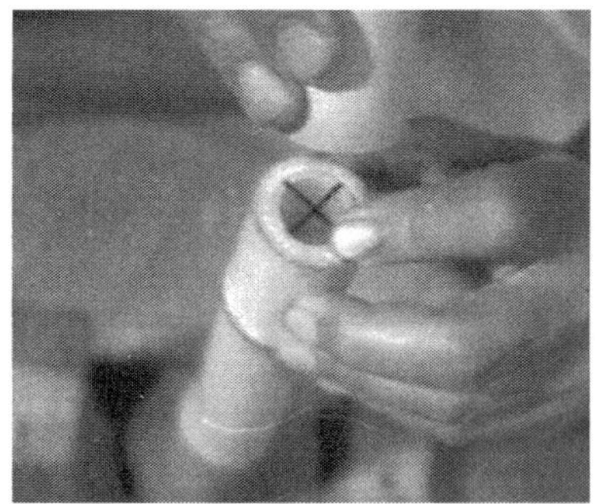

(30) Match up the circular cut-line with the upper half and mark the upper half. Be sure to align the center line marks. See step #18.

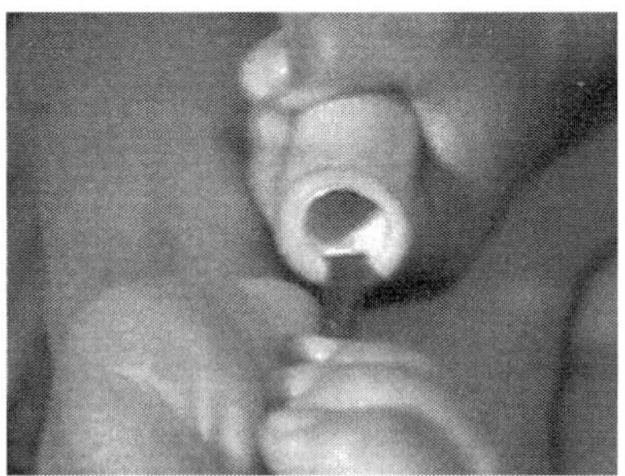

(31) Carefully chisel along the cut-line down to the 1.8 cm. groove.

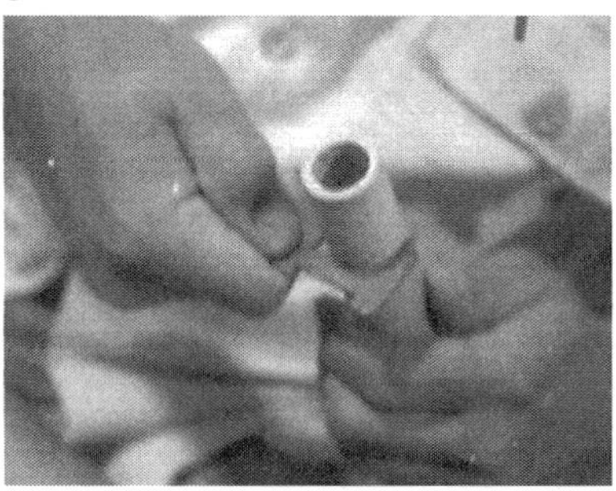

(32) Use a caliper to find high spots on the joint bamboo. File and sand these down.

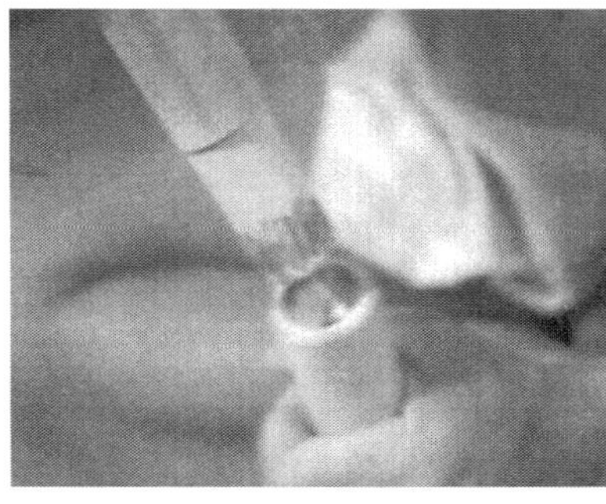

(33) Fit the joint piece into the hole carved into the joint end of the lower half.

Rub a pencil on the joint. The areas where the pencil lead smears show the high spots to sand.

(34) Glue the joint into the hole carved in the lower half.

Drill 2 small holes through this joint opposite each other.

(35) Inset a peg into each hole. This helps lock the joint piece into the lower half.

Lock pegs whittled from scrap bamboo work fine.

Next you'll make a hole in the upper half to fit the joint piece.

Cut a shallow groove 2.3 cm. inside the bore of the upper half.

Chisel out the hole, along the 2.5 cm. diameter cut-line, down to this groove.

Cut this hole as circular as possible and sand it smooth. See steps #28 to #31.

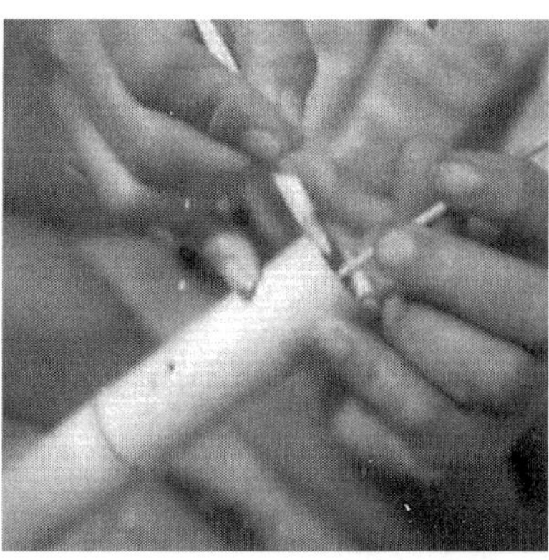

(36) Measure the depth of the hole just chiseled in the upper half.

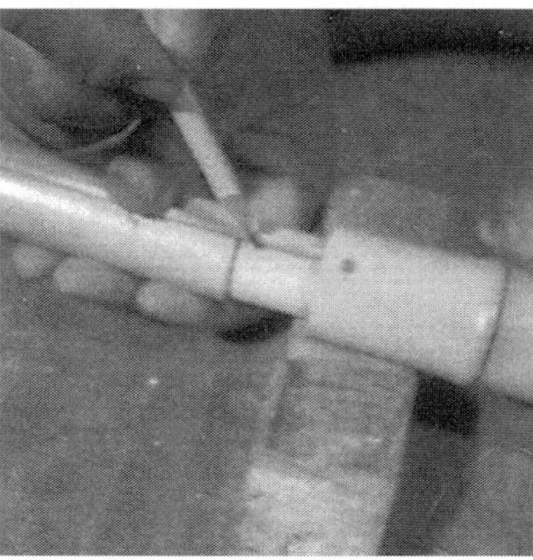

(37) Lay out the depth measured above on the joint (it should be about 2.3 cm.)

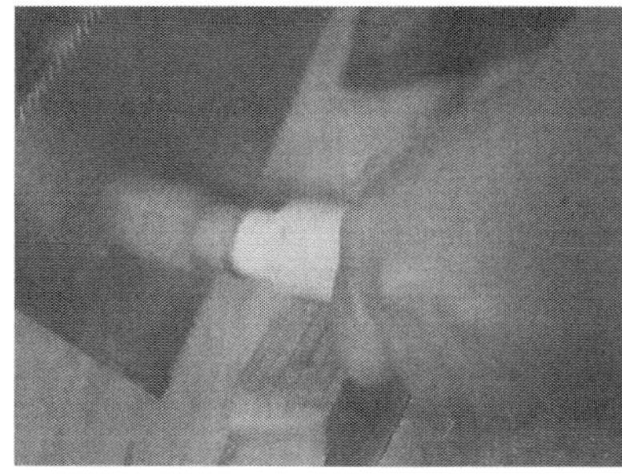

(38) Saw the joint to the hole depth of the top half.

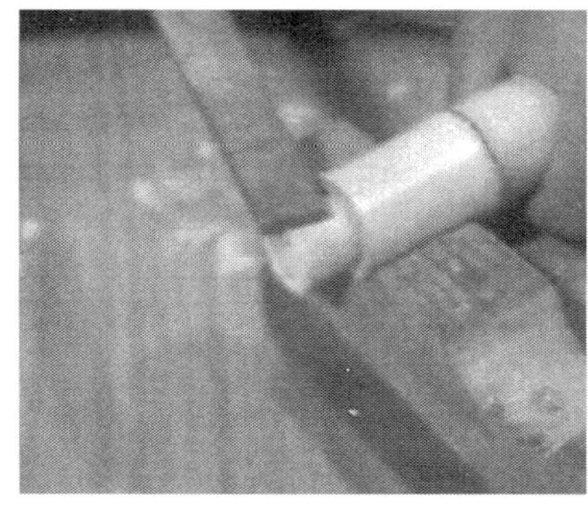

(39) File the joint smooth.

(40) File the female end of the upper half smooth.

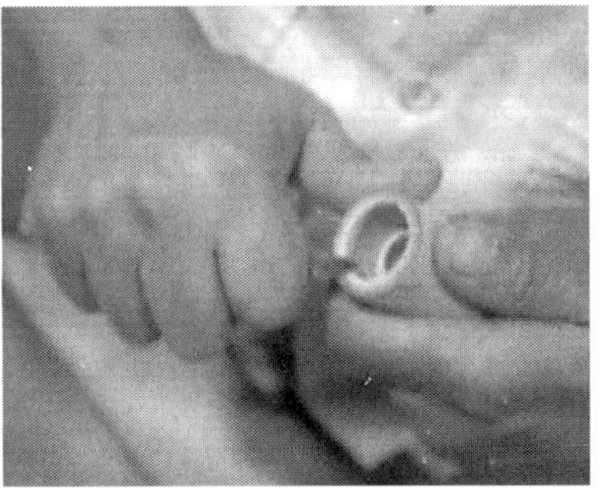

(41) Cut a slightly inward sloping bevel into the female end.

Sand both the male and female ends until they slide together easily. Use pencil to determine the high areas that need sanding.

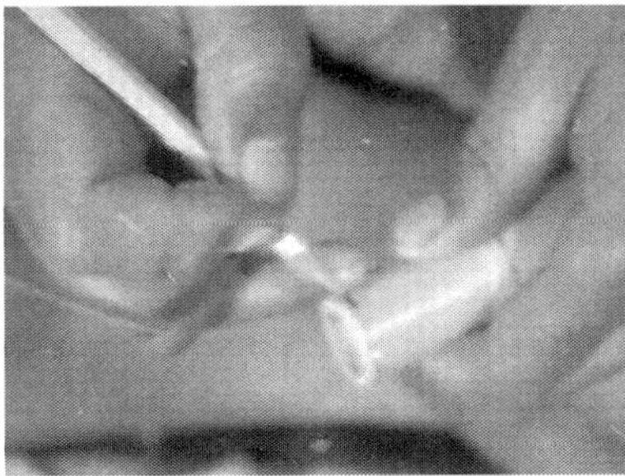

(42) When the fit is good, lay out a 3 mm long "gi" ring insert around the end of the joint.This ring will keep the bore paste out of the joint area.

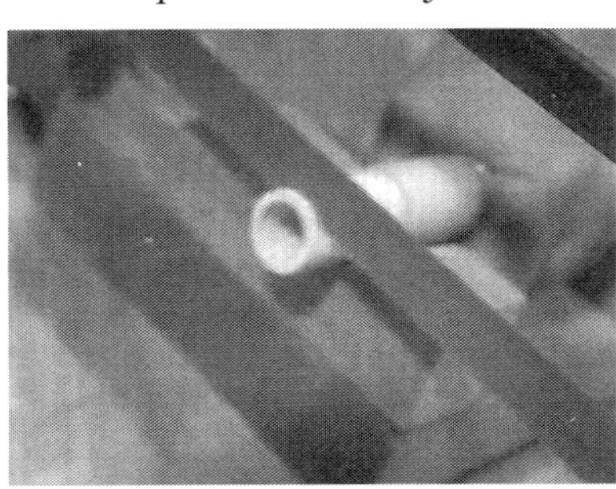

(43) Saw the "gi" ring insert.

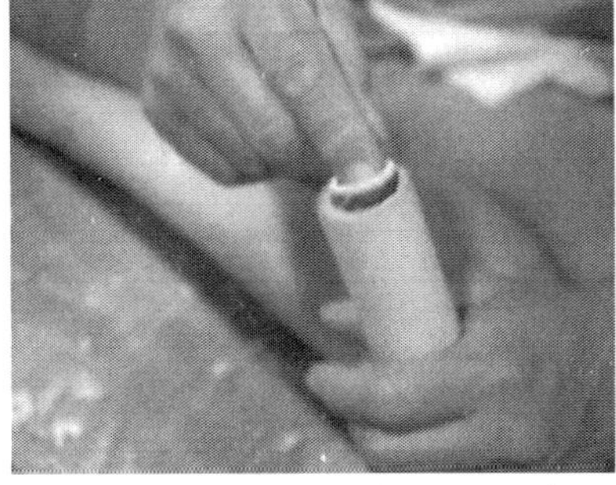

(44) Glue the "gi" ring at the bottom of the hole. (About 1.9 cm. deep.)

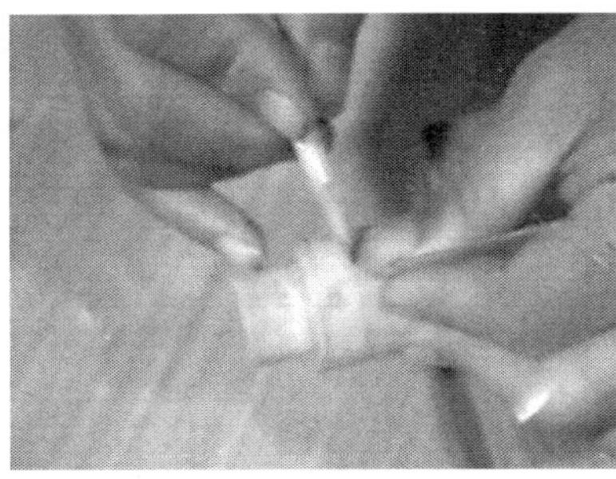

(45) Lay out circumference lines on the upper and lower halves, about 1 cm. apart.

This will be for reinforcing both ends of the joint with a recessed binding to prevent cracking.

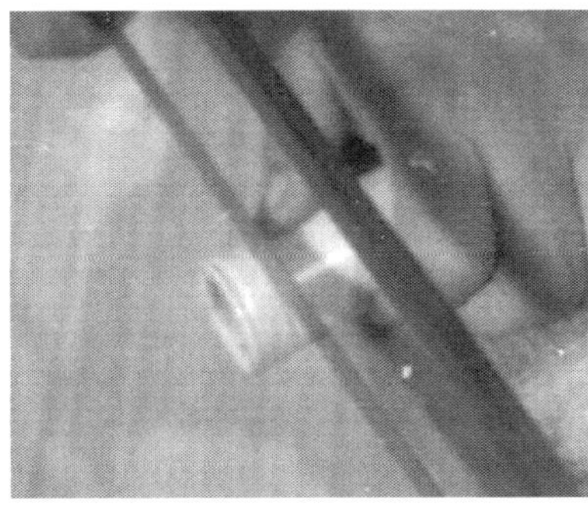

(46) Saw a shallow groove along the circumference lines

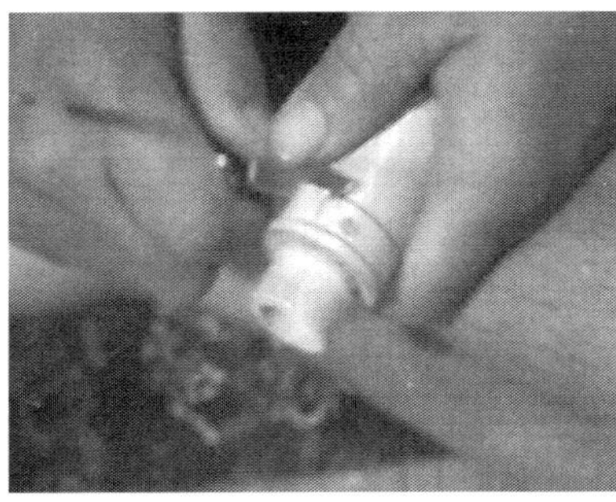

(47) Cut out the wood between the sawn grooves with a knife.

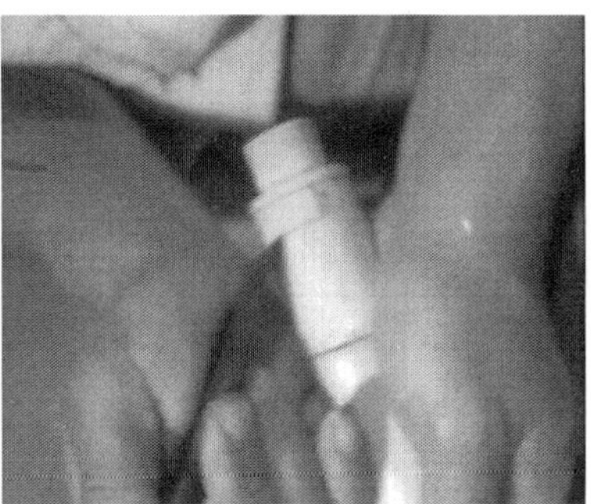

(48) Chisel the recess smooth.

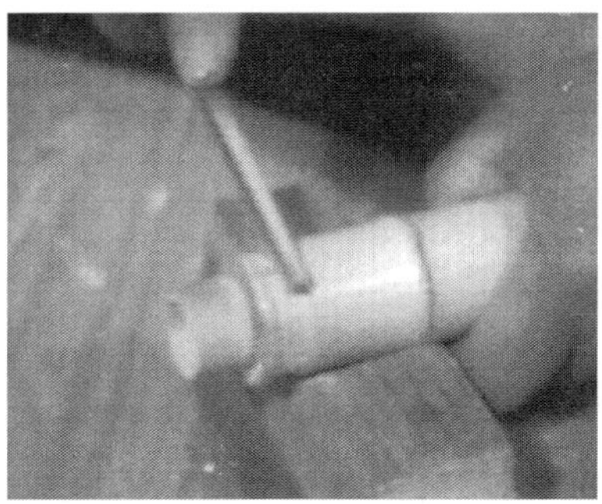

(49) File the recess smooth.

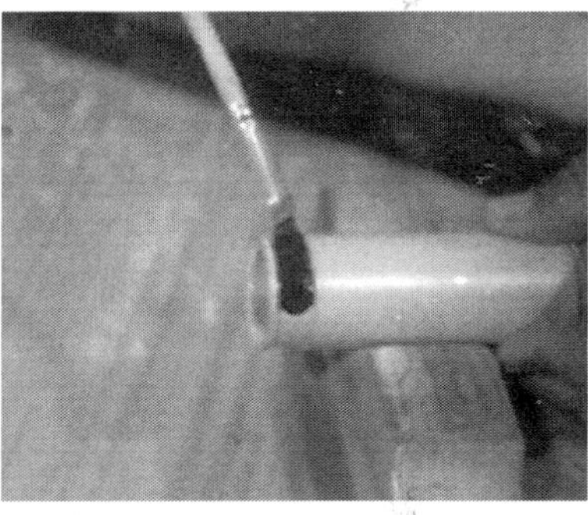

(50) Apply urushi (or a good oil primer paint) to the recess. See ADDITIONAL DETAILS, #10 for information on this unique material.

(51) Wrap the binding string into the recess and wet urushi (or paint). Linen string is traditionally used.

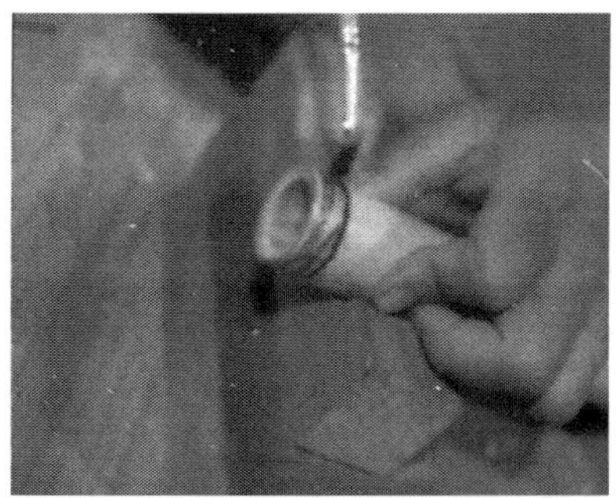

(52) Apply urushi (or paint) to the binding.

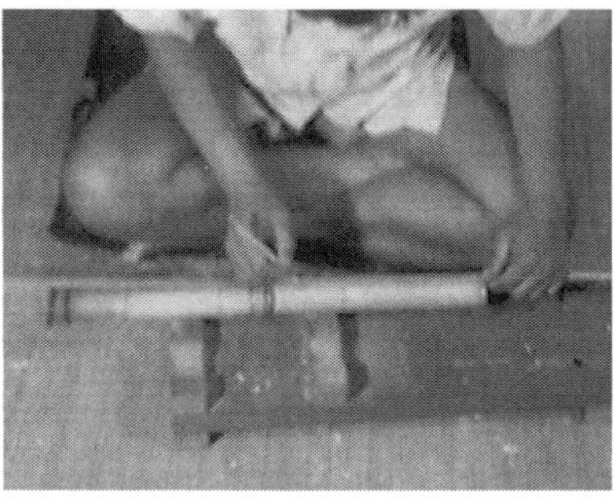

(53) Now, join both ends. Re-sand if needed (the binding can make it too tight). Align the center line marks made above in step 18. Lay out the center line along the bamboo length again.

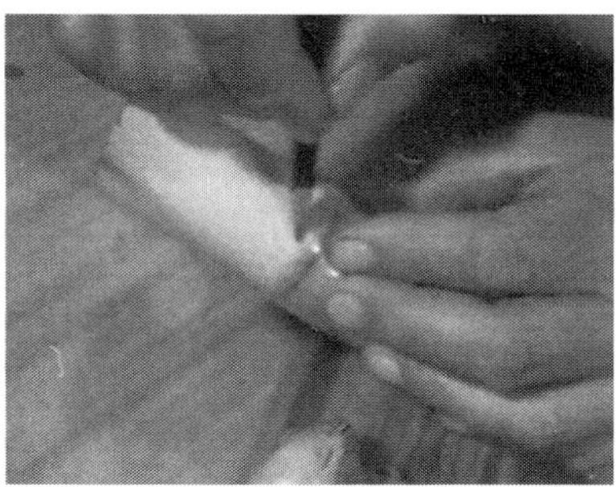

(54) Lay out the blowing end saw line perpendicular to the center line. The blowing end will end at a node (28.9 cm. from the joint).

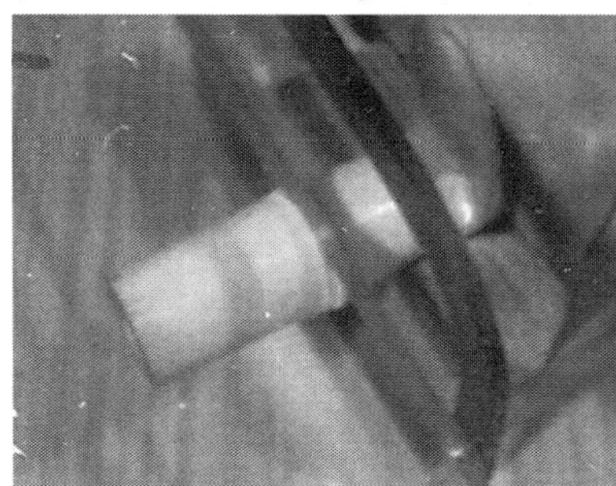

(55) Saw off the excess bamboo beyond the blowing end.

(56) Check the center line - is it straight?

(57) Lay out the hole spacing along the center line.

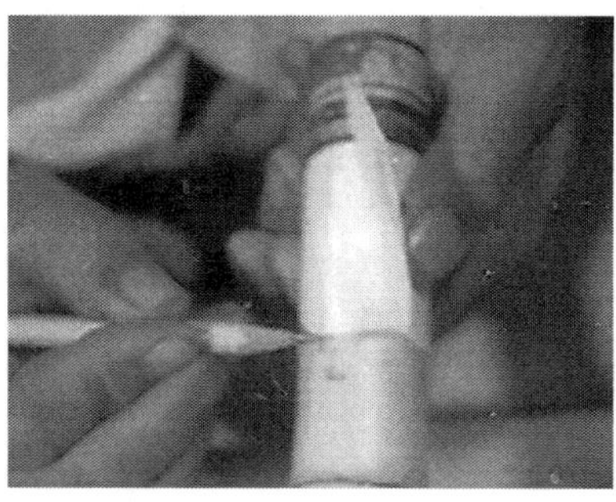

(58) Use a paper strip to determine the back hole position.

Mark the circumference on a paper strip. Now, fold it in half and mark the back hole at the crease, i.e., 1/2 circumference.

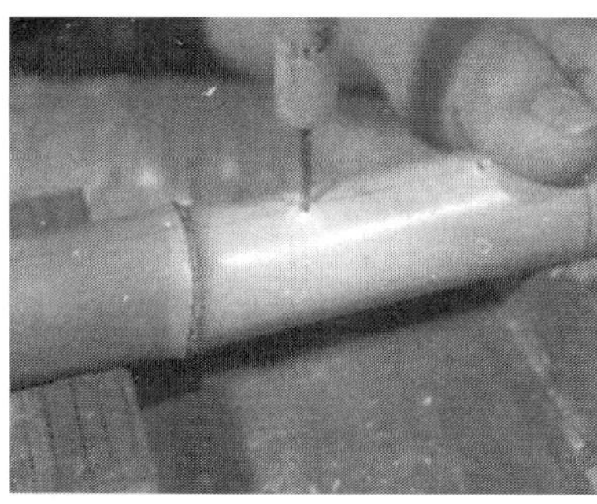

(59) Drill the pilot holes with the awl.

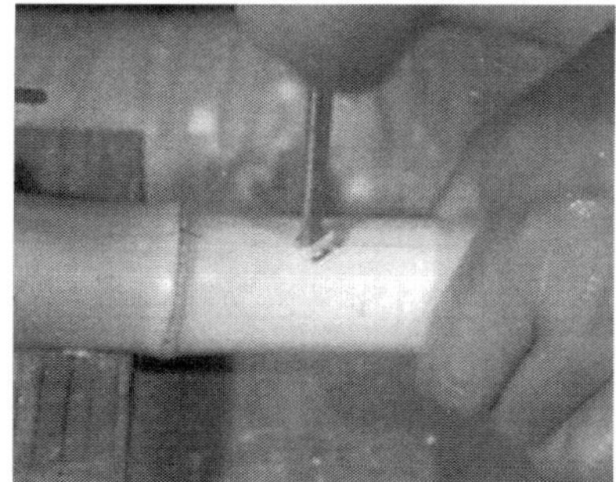

(60) Drill the holes. See ADDITIONAL DETAILS, #6 for more on holes.

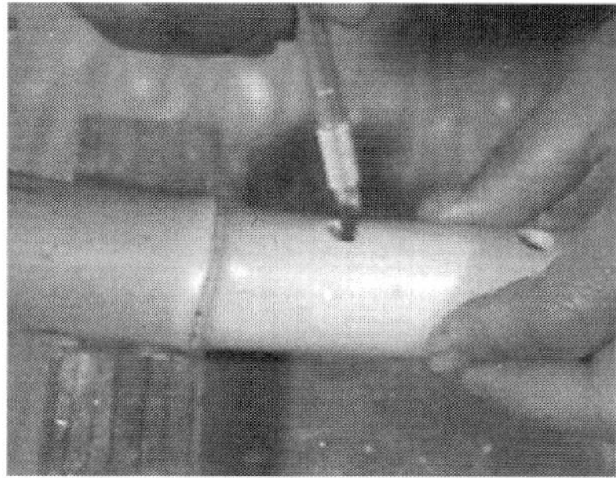

(61) Trim the holes.

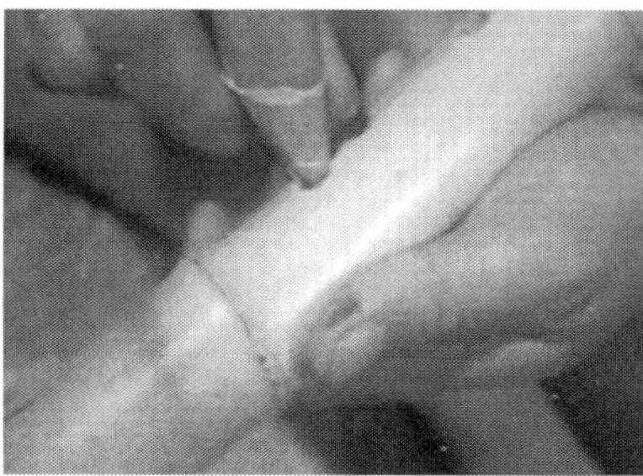

(62) Sand the hole edges smooth.

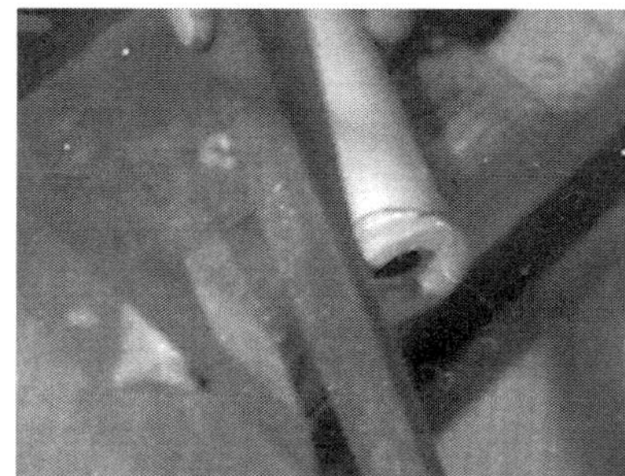

(63) File the chin rest bevel.

Recheck the center line before starting on the chin rest and the blowing edge.

Mark the area on the rear edge of the blowing end for the chin bevel (directly opposite the center line).

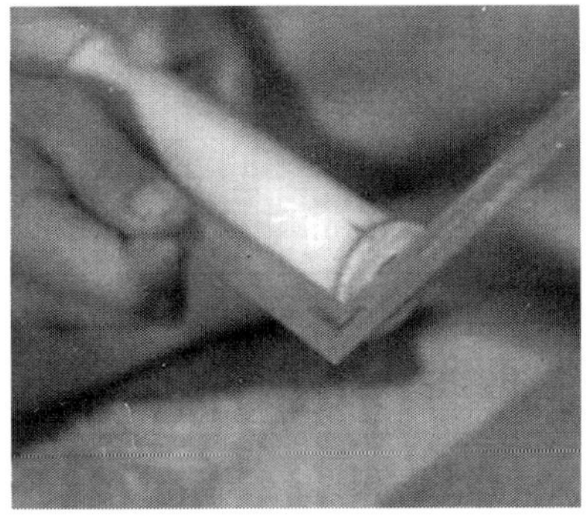

(64) Check the angle of the blowing end to the center line.

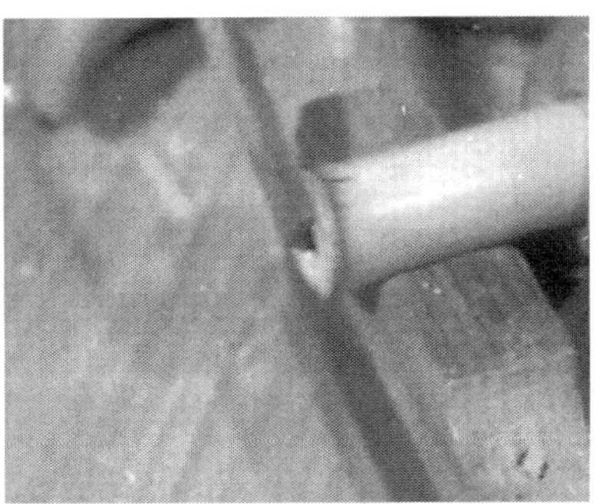

(65) File the blowing end perpendicular to the center line.

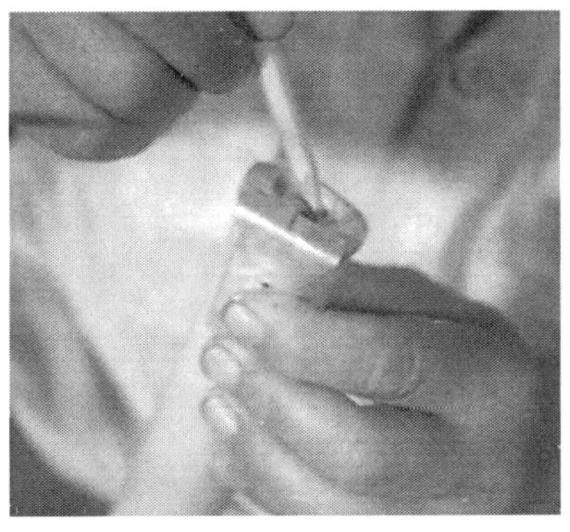

(66) Lay out the blowing edge position and the bevel (30°). A small tin template is shown - handy if you make dozens of flutes.

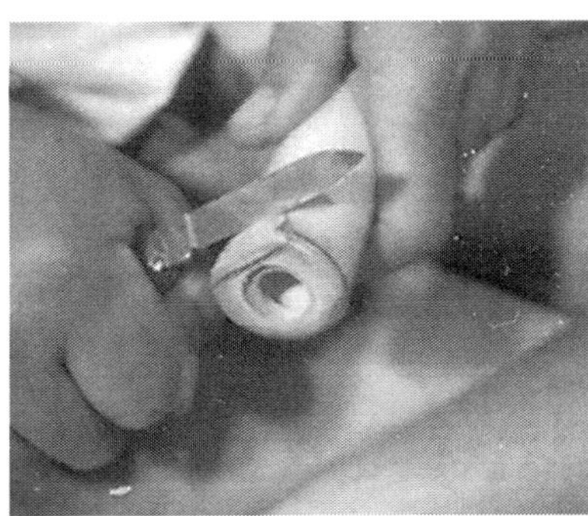

(67) Cut the blowing edge bevel. Use a sharp knife.

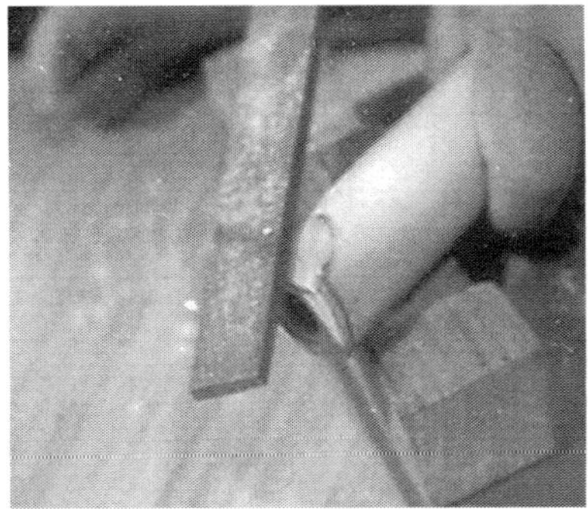

(68) File the blowing edge bevel.

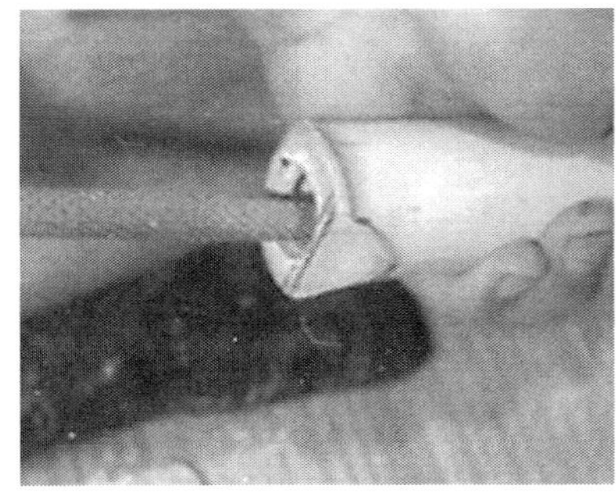

(69) File the inner node to the proper bore size.

See ADDITIONAL DETAILS, #1 for bore sizes.

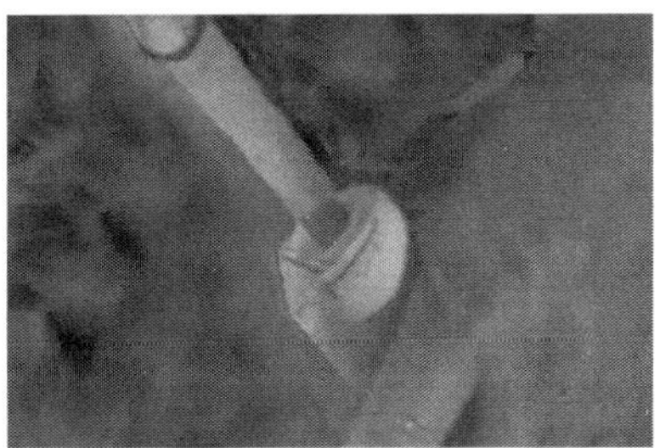

(70) Fine file the bore at the blowing end.

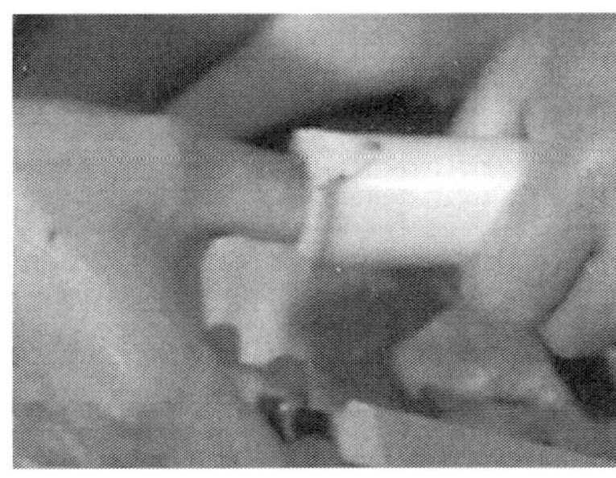

(71) Check the bore size.

Use the thumb as a handy gauge for the mouth end. (1.9 to 2.1 cm.) The middle finger works well for the bottom end (about 1.8 cm.).

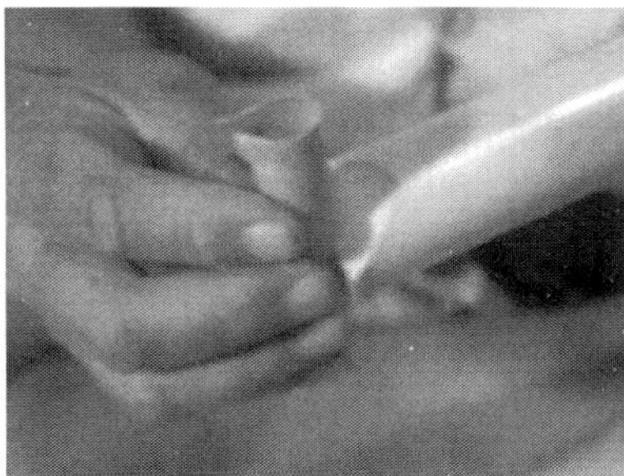

(72) Sand the inner edge smooth.

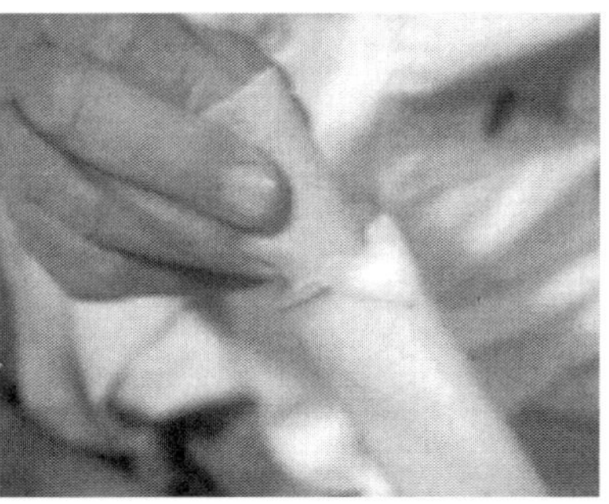

(73) Sand the bore smooth.

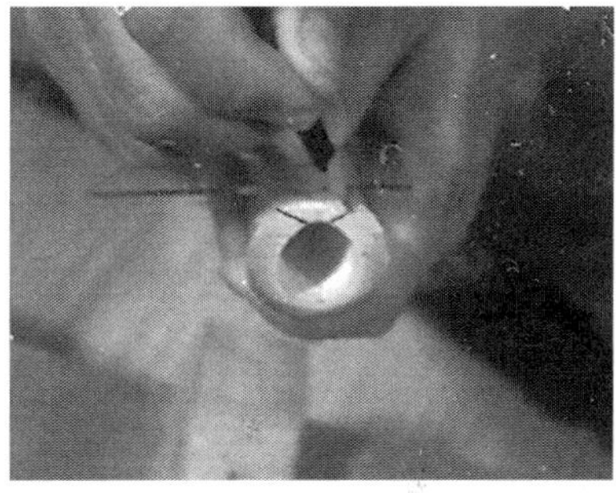

(74) Lay out an "inlay" recess on the bamboo blowing edge.

Later you'll make an inlay from rough ivory or horn and then glue it into this recess which is cut in the blowing end.

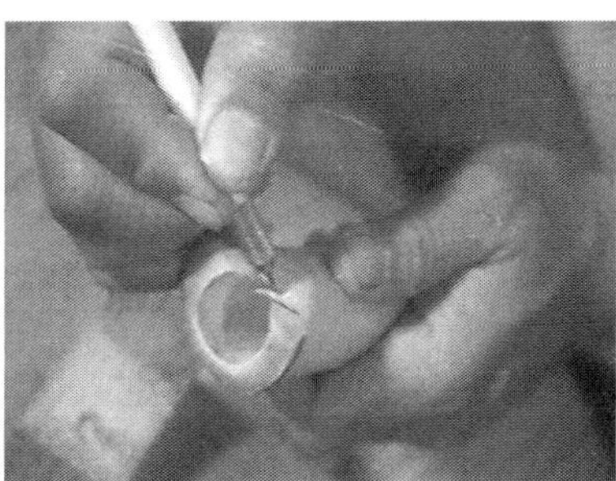

(75) Cut the blowing edge inlay recess. First cut the sides, then the bottom edges. See ADDITIONAL DETAILS, #7.

(76) Shape the blowing edge inlay from a piece of horn.

You can substitute a hardwood (like ebony) or a plastic (like Acrylic) for the horn.

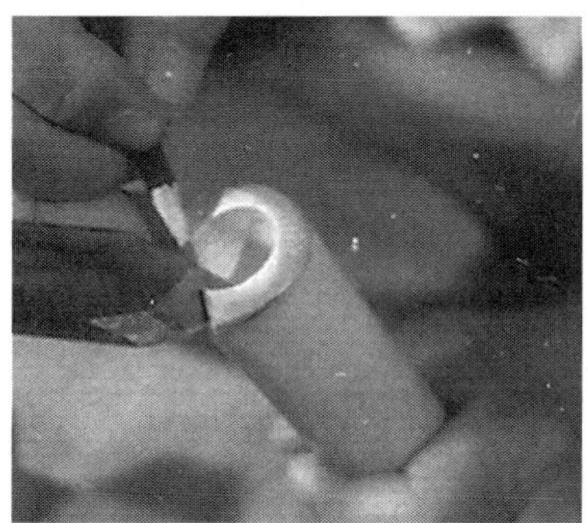

(77) Fit the inlay into the recess and mark the areas to file down. See #76 above.

(78) Glue the inlay and saw off the excess horn.

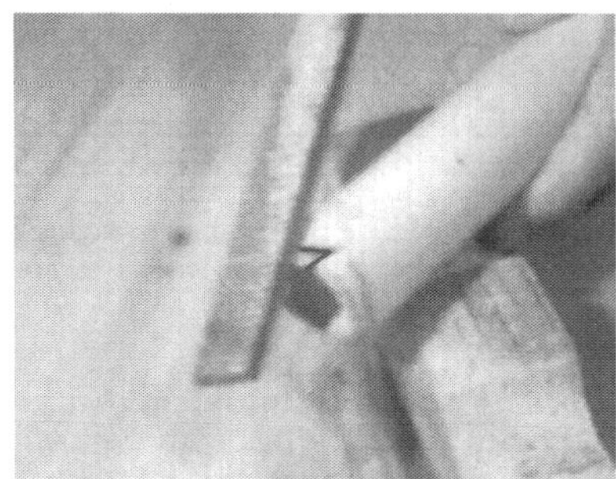

(79) File off the excess horn.

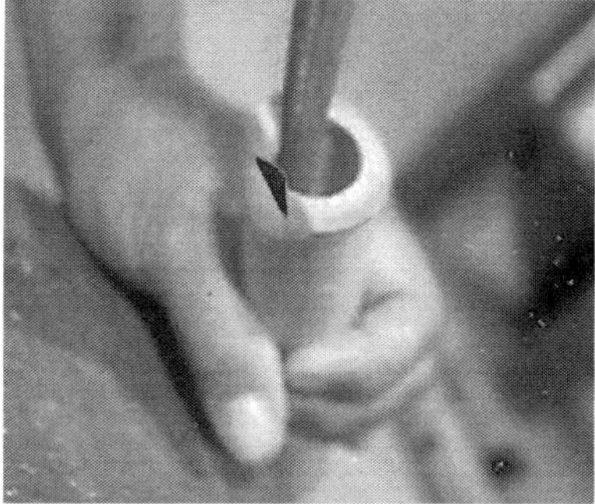

(80) File the excess horn from the inner bore.

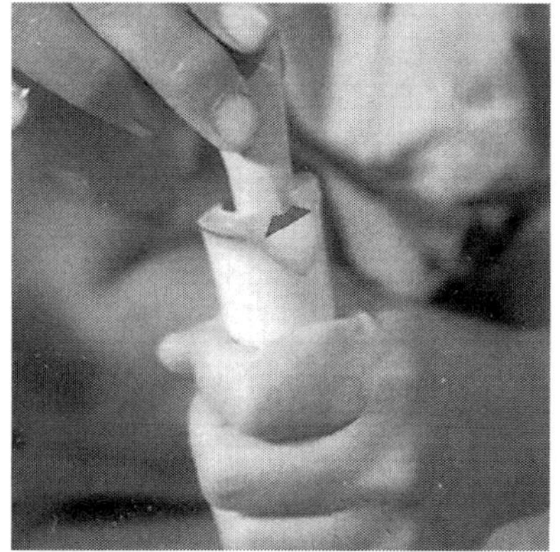

(81) Sand the inner bore smooth.

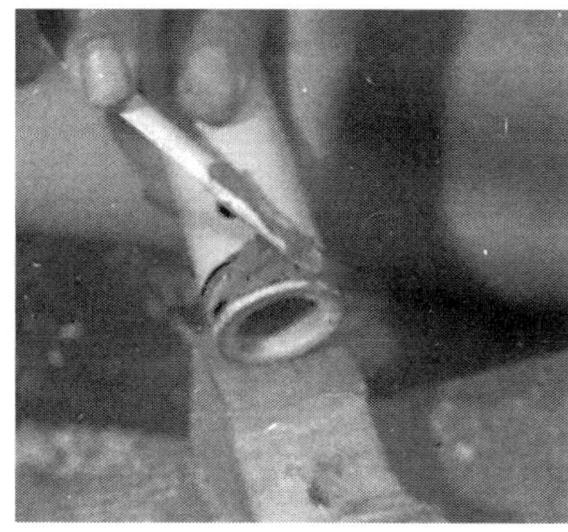

(82) Apply "gi" to the joint binding and set aside to dry for a day or two.

Make "gi" by mixing equal parts of powdered fire clay and urushi. Add water until the mixture has a consistency of thick icing. Use this paste to cover the binding on the joint and, later, to make the bore taper.

Like urushi, "gi" requires moisture to harden. It takes longer to harden than urushi alone. See ADDITIONAL DETAILS, #9 and #10.

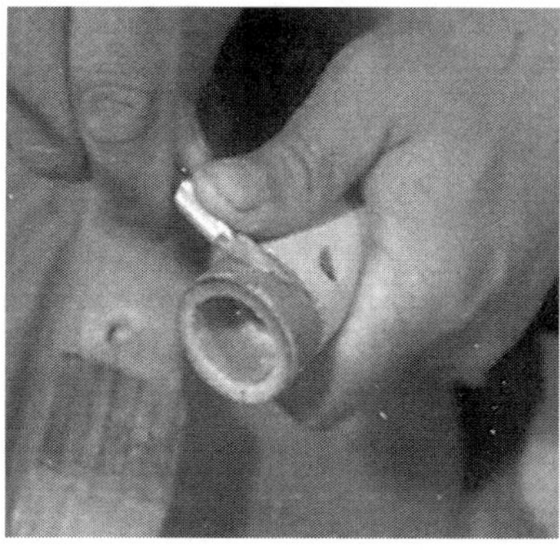

(83) Cut off the excess "gi".

A knife works fine if the "gi" is still soft.

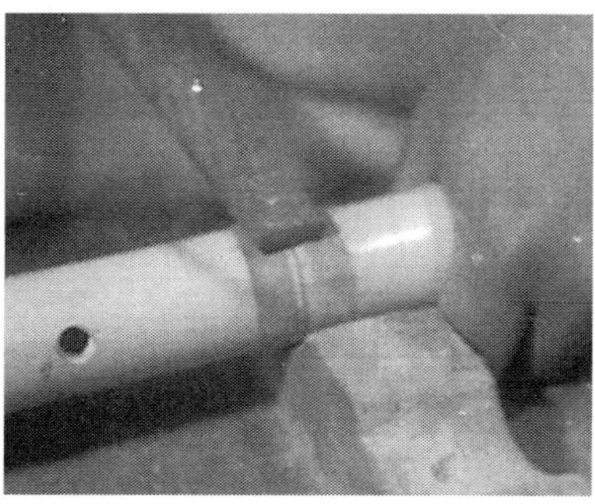

(84) File the joint "gi" until it is even.

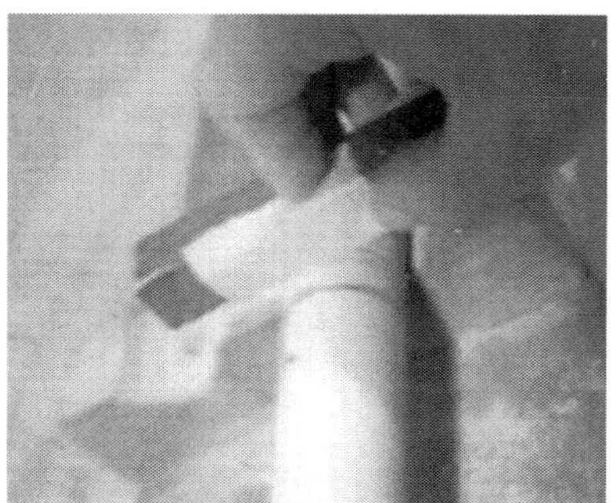

(85) Sand the joint smooth.

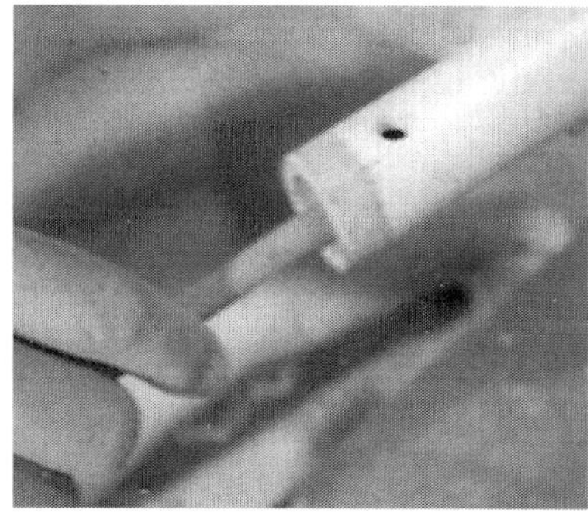

(86) File the node membranes in the bore to the correct diameters. See ADDITIONAL DETAILS, #1.

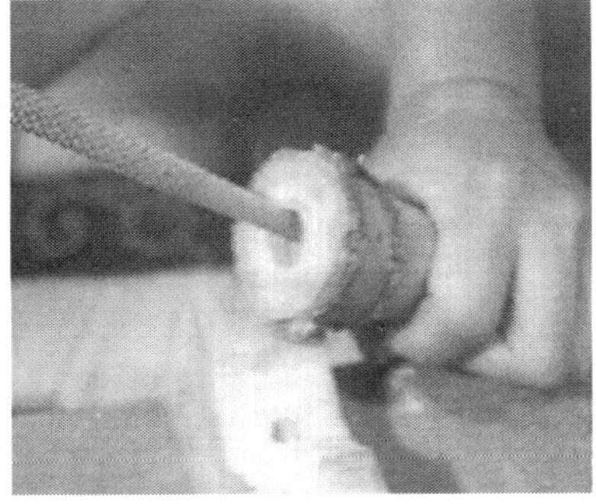

(87) File the root end bore to correct size.

This is about 1.8 cm. at the end and tapers rapidly to 1.45 cm. just below hole #1. See ADDITIONAL DETAILS, #1.

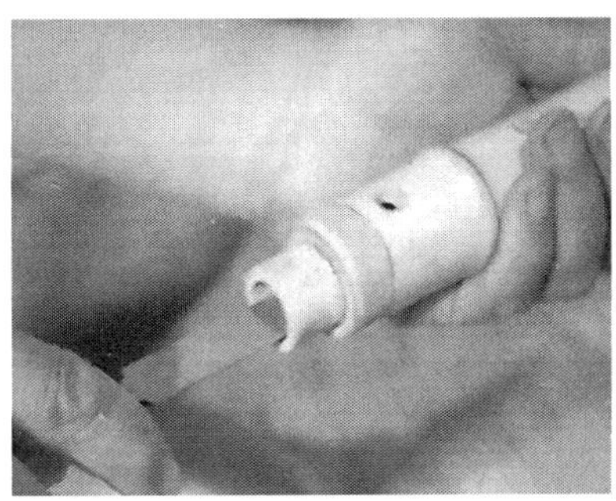

(88) Fine file the inner nodes and the joint.

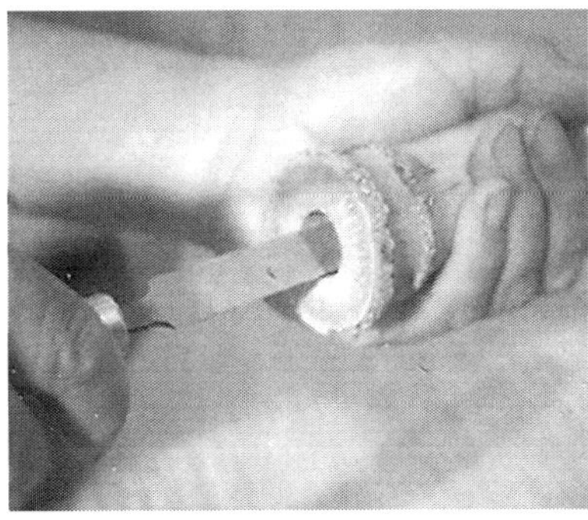

(89) Fine file the bore at the root end.

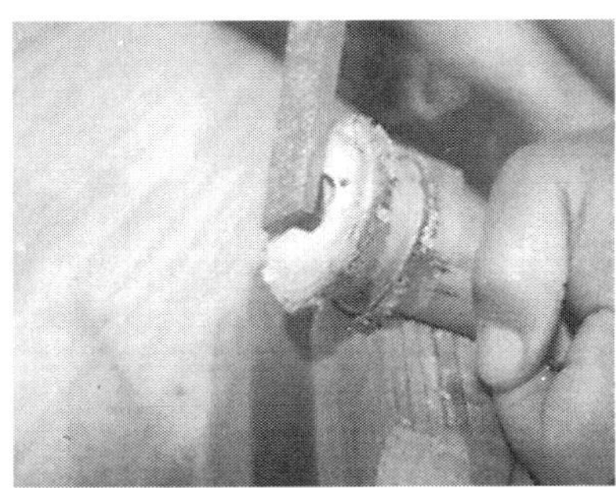

(90) File the root end flat.

(91) File the root bell round.

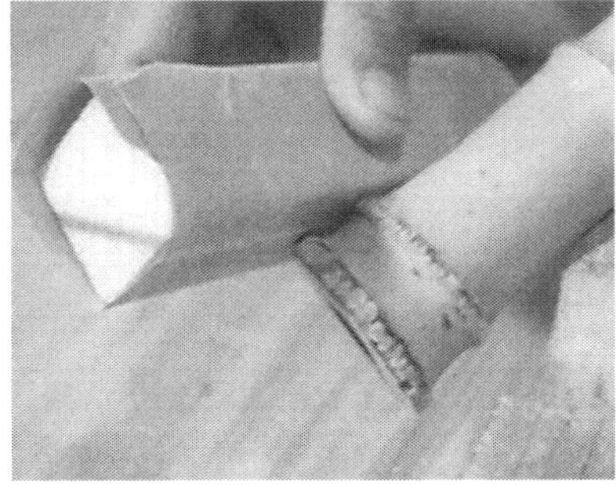

(92) Sand the root bell and the root end smooth.

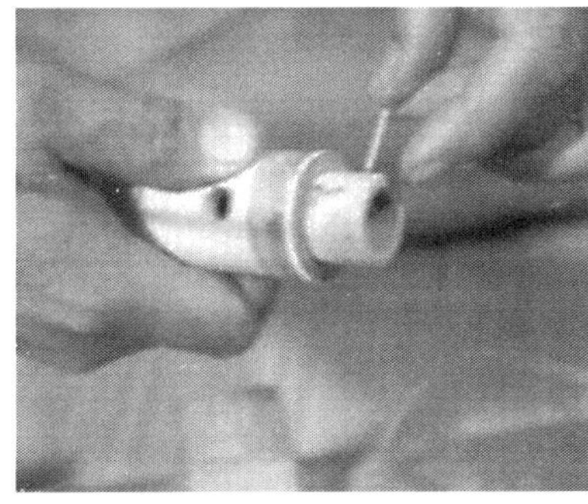

(93) Wrap the rattan binding.

This is an optional covering of the joint. It is usually done with rattan, but can be any other material. The joints of expensive flutes are often done in silver.

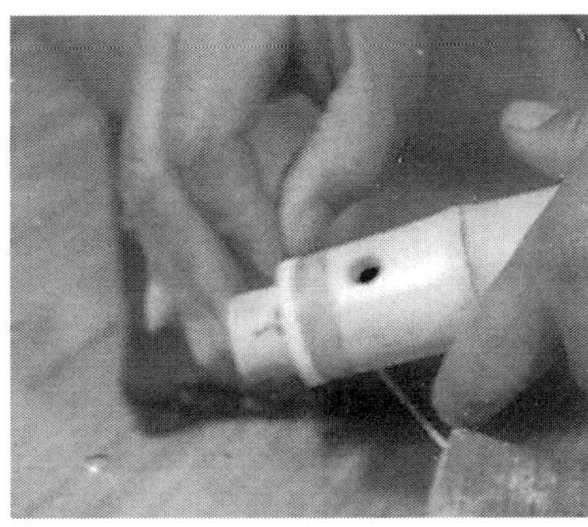

(94) Press the binding together as you wrap.

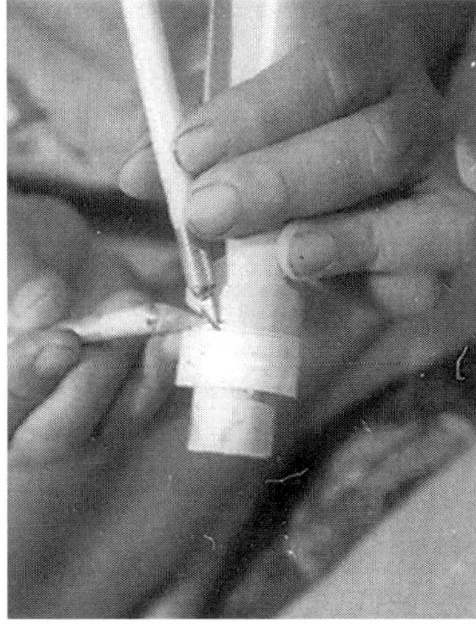

(95) Tie off the rattan strip and glue.

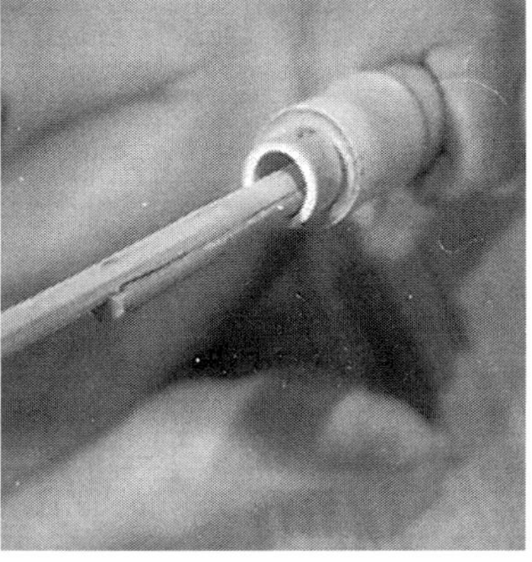

(96) Fine grind the inner bore smooth with a piece of sandstone glued on to a long stick. See ADDITIONAL DETAILS, #14.

This completes the "Shita gu zuri" or primary phase of construction. It's the easiest and takes half a day, or so, to finish - depending on the bamboo. The next stage of construction, the "Choritsu" phase, requires the most care.

First paint the bore and the joint with urushi.

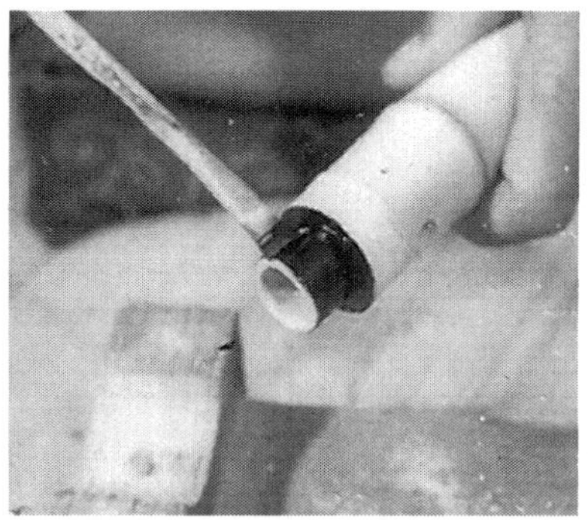

(97) Apply urushi to the joint.

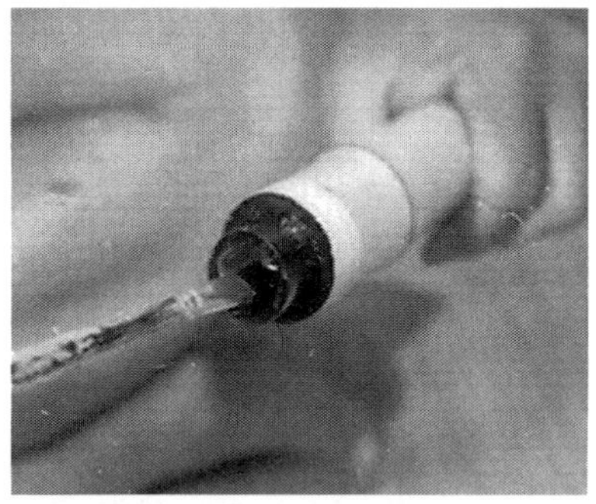

(98) Apply urushi to the bore.

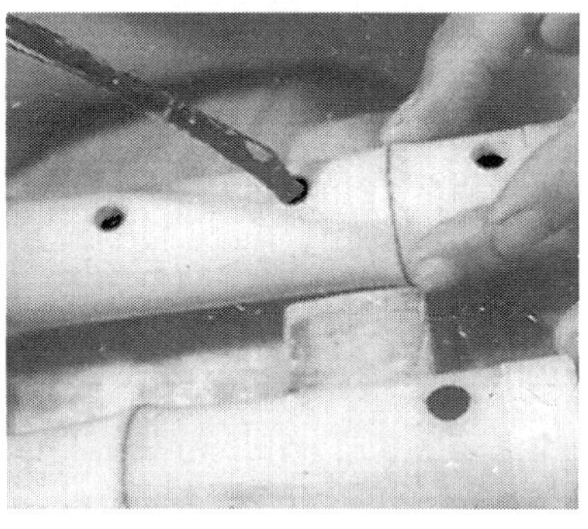

(99) Apply urushi to the holes.

Place the flute in a humid box for a few days to dry.

After the initial coat of urushi dries, apply a pasty mixture of urushi, powdered fire clay and water (as described above in step #82.) in a thin layer along the whole length of the bore.

This first coat of bore "gi" should be on the dry side (somewhat crumbly).

Subsequent coats should be smoother, like icing for a cake. See ADDITIONAL DETAILS, #9.

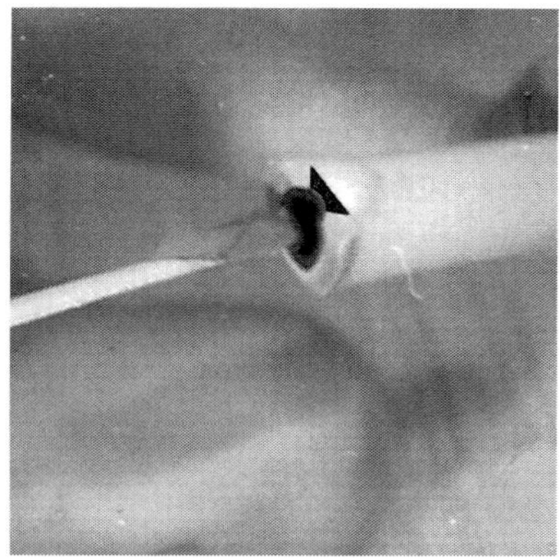

(100) Apply the "gi" to the bore with a long thin spatula.

Press the "gi" firmly, in a circular motion, onto the walls of the bore.

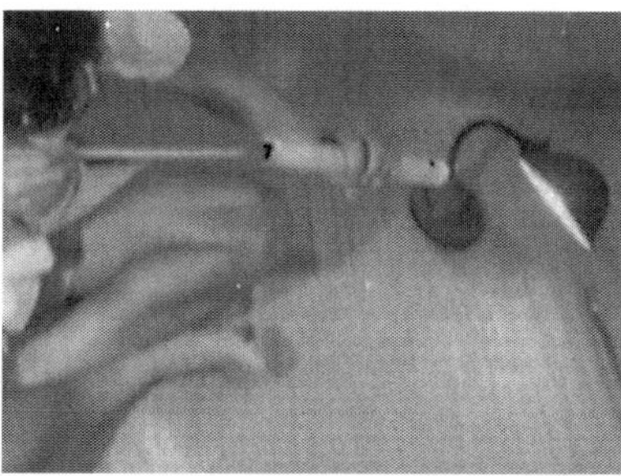

(101) Hold the flute ends up to a light bulb to see inside the bore.

Place in the humid box for a week to harden.

Traditionally, the flute was set aside for a year or more to allow the "gi" to harden and cure thoroughly.

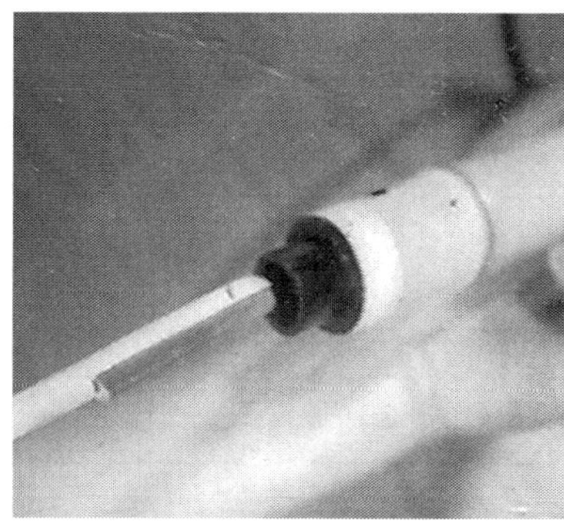

(102) Use a piece of sandstone attached to a long thin stick to grind away the high parts of the hardened paste in the bore. See ADDITIONAL DETAILS, #14.

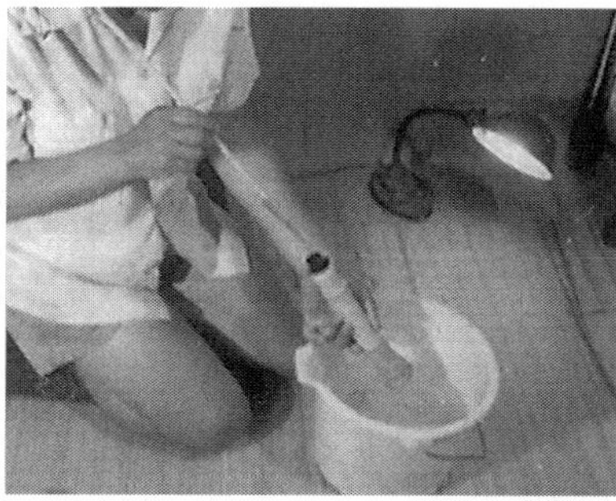

(103) Flush the bore with water while grinding.

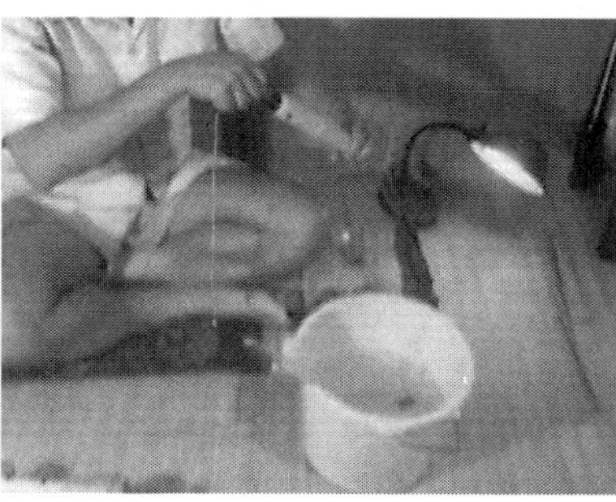

(104) Clean by drawing a cloth tied to a weighted string through the bore.

(105) Visually check the bore.

Give a blowing test. A wet bore will play and sound much like it will after final painting.

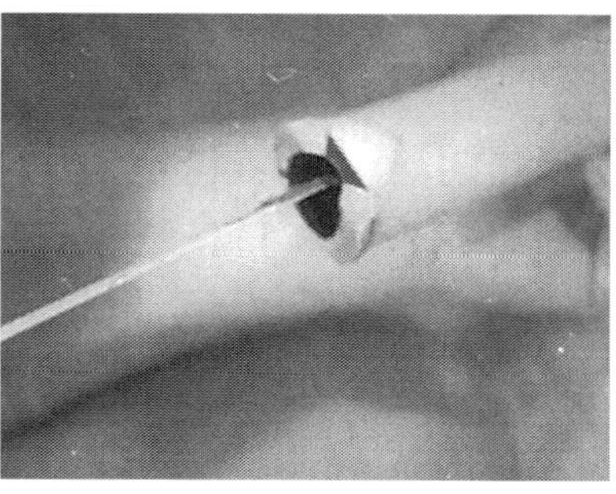

(106) Use a wetter "gi" on a thinner paddle for fine touch up. Fill voids and bring the bore closer to the desired taper.

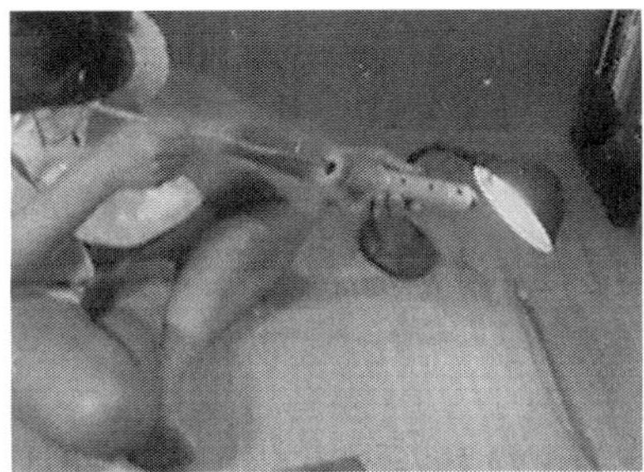

(107) After this dries and cures for a few weeks, re-grind, apply more paste and allow it to harden.

Repeat the process of grinding, testing, applying paste and grinding until you achieve a smooth bore of the correct size. Use gauges as needed. See ADDITIONAL DETAILS, #8.

If you achieve desired results before the taper is smooth and correct, STOP! Good balance can occur without an even taper. See ADDITIONAL DETAILS, #11.

Visually inspect the bore each time for irregularities and blow it to check the pitch, sound quality and ease of playing.

When satisfied with the bore, apply one primer coat of urushi.

When dry, apply several finish coats of a high quality gloss "ro iro" urushi. It dries to a very hard enamel-like finish.

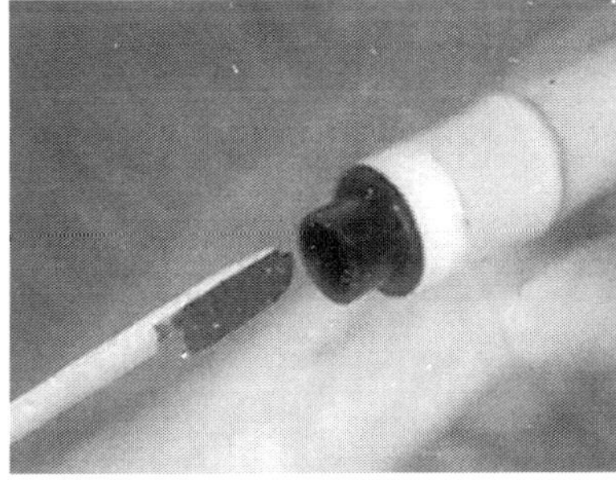

(108) Fine grind the bore with a piece of charcoal glued on a stick.

Fine grind the bore between each coat of "ro iro".

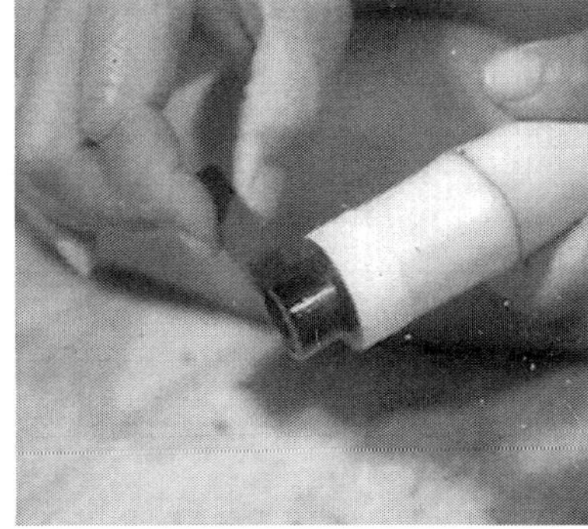

(109) Fine grind the joint with a piece of charcoal.

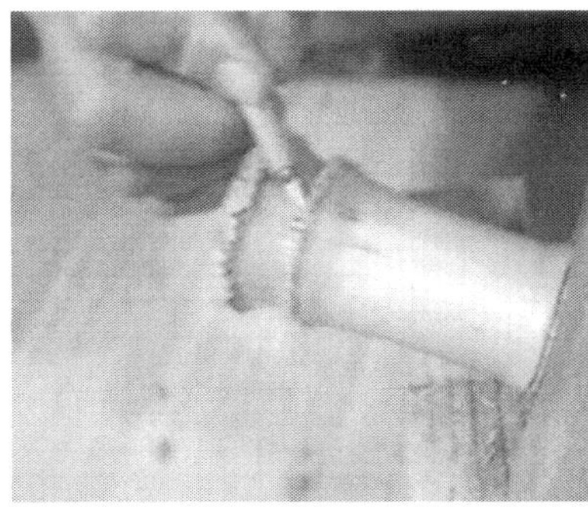

(110) Touch up the root end.

(111) Fine sand the root and the blowing ends.

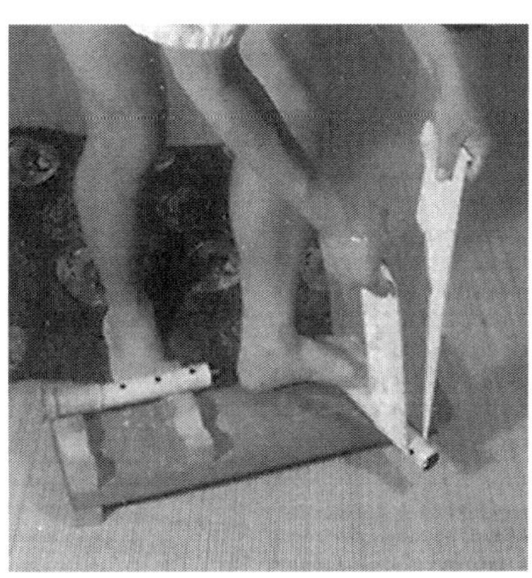

(112) Polish the Shakuhachi.

Congratulations. Now relax and blow Zen. See what the fruits of your labor can do.

Give the flute time to reveal itself. Each one is unique and requires some playing to get to "know".

Each instrument, from harvesting the bamboo to applying the last coat of lacquer, takes many hours of skilled labor.

The amount of time spent on the "Choritsu" stage depends on the quality of the bamboo. Of course, you wouldn't go through all these steps with lower grades of bamboo.

It's still easy to see why even a mediocre flute costs several hundred dollars and a good one can cost thousands. Beauty of form, coloring, feel and the maker's name account for much of the price of the most expensive Shakuhachi.

ADDITIONAL DETAILS

1. Shakuhachi Dimensions

Note: Don't worry about adhering to these dimensions down to the last tenth mil. Bamboo Shakuhachi always vary from one to the next.

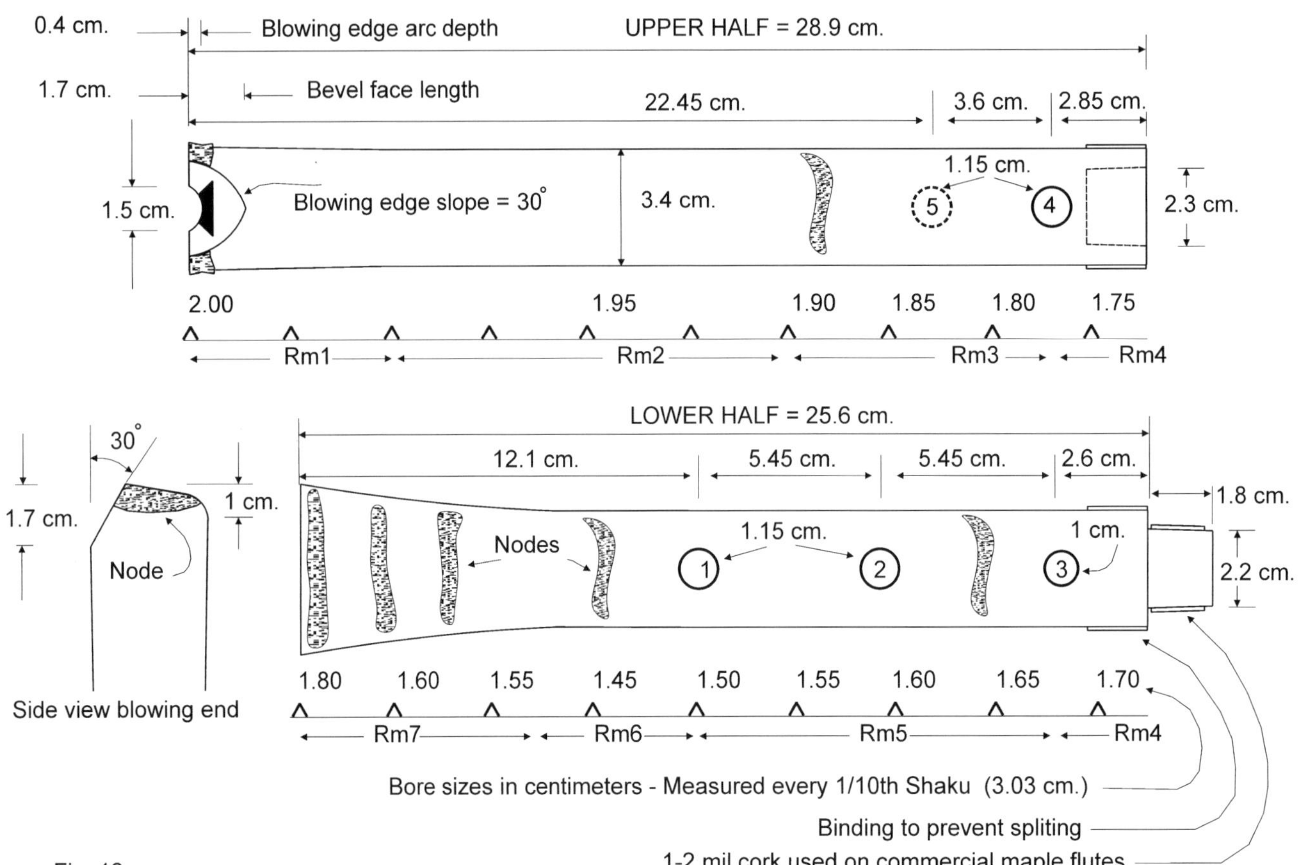

Fig. 12

2. Bamboo: Growing and Selecting

Here are a few sources if you're interested in growing bamboo for making Shakuhachi, i.e., Phyllostachys, bamusoides - "medake timber bamboo". The shoots are also edible when boiled, so you can satisfy the pallet as well as the ear.

American Bamboo Society, P.O.Box 60, Springville, CA 93265

Endangered Species, P.O. Box 1830, Tustin, CA.92681-1830. (714) 544-9505. If you call, leave your address and what you need - they will write.

Tradewinds Bamboo Nursery, P.O. Box 70, Calpella, Ca 95418. (707) 485-0835. They carry bamboo and books on bamboo.

Bamboo Sorcery, 666 Wagon Rd., Sebastopol, Ca. 95472. (707) 829-8106. Send $1.00 for a catalog describing the hundreds of varieties they grow as well as information on cultivation.

"The Book of Bamboo", David Farrelly, contains extensive information on history, types, culture, uses and sources of bamboo. (If unavailable, check the library and used book stores.)

Growing Bamboo:

The best Shakuhachi bamboo is grown in soil that is low in fertility and well drained - even dry. High moisture, fertility and temperature favor rapid and weak bamboo growth. Bamboo grown where winters are cold make the best flutes. Note: Timber bamboo dies below about -10° C. (0° F.)

Choosing bamboo:

Look for culms that look "strong". Are they firmly rooted in the ground, i.e., ones you can't pull up or shake easily? Culms should have a smooth surface. You shouldn't be able to feel any wrinkles on any part of them. Look for culms that have a lot of black sooty dirt on their nodes. This usually means they are old. Culms over 3 years old make better flutes.

The ideal node spacing for bamboo measured from root end is about: 9 cm. to the first node, 11 cm. to the second node, 15 cm. to the third node, 19 cm to the fourth node (blowing end).

Cut the culms in winter. Sweat them over hot charcoal, (see step #10 above). Then let the sun bleach them for a month on a roof top. Cure the best pieces for 3 years, or longer if possible, in a dark place.

3. Heating and Bending Bamboo

Heating:

Put ashes over the coals if the fire becomes too hot and starts burning the bamboo. Begin heating at the root end. Turn the bamboo constantly. When the green fades, it's done. Wipe it as it cools.

Bending:

Hold the bamboo so you're looking at the root end and down the bamboo face. Turn slowly to left and right. Find the side of the first node that has the greatest upward turn (highest arc). This will be the back of the flute. Turn it over and mark the opposite side with a large triangle arrow near the root bell.

Hold the bamboo to find its natural position for playing. Does this coincide with the large triangle marked above? If so, look over the outside of the bamboo to locate all unwanted bends. Start bending from the root end. For reference, mark bamboo on the side opposite where the fulcrum (post) is put.

Place over coals and turn constantly. Make sure there is no flame on coals. Place a wet cloth to cool down areas not to be bent. Keep heat low enough so it doesn't burn the bamboo skin.

To determine when the heat is absorbed into the bamboo, put your thumb and index finger on the bamboo. If you feel abrupt heat, it's ready. If you don't feel the heat in both fingers, it's not ready yet.

When hot, put the bamboo on the fulcrum with the mark facing upward. Place the cool area (on opposite side of the node closest to the area just heated) on the fulcrum post and one end of the bamboo through the arched loop. Press the other end of the bamboo downward. When the desired bend is achieved, place a wet towel on the hot bamboo for a moment. (See steps #13 through #15 above.)

4. Joint

Use a side cutting knife (see Construction Tools, #14 below) to make incisions in the lower halves equal in length to the intended joint recess. When chiselling down, the cut stops at this groove.

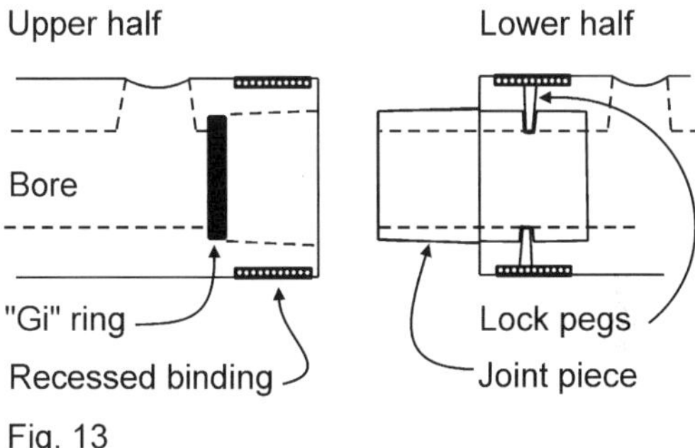

Fig. 13

Refer to steps #29 to #31. Make a round plastic disk with the same diameter as the 6 cm. long joint piece you will insert in the lower half. Place a narrow strip of tape on this disk and center it over the joint end of the lower half. Now, press the tape to the bamboo to hold the disk in place. Using the disk as a template, mark the bore area you must chisel away in order to insert the joint piece.

Next, place the joint end of the upper half over the disk/lower half and align upper and lower halves carefully. Be sure the center line marks (step #18) are aligned. Peel the tape off the lower half and stick it to the upper half to hold the disk steady while you lay out the bore area to chisel away from the upper half.

In the final fitting of the joint, sand the male end until it slips half way into the female. Then enlarge the female end until the male fits all the way.

Use the joint male end to push the "gi" ring, step #44, to the correct depth.

5. Nobetake

"Nobetake" is a piece of bamboo that is the exact size, when harvested, for the flute you're going to make.

For Nobetake bamboo, you can shape the blowing edge, drill the holes, and file out the nodes slowly. Flush with water and test it, then remove more of the node. If you get it to play exceptionally well, keep it "natural", i.e., do as little as possible to it. That can mean no joint and no (or little) bore "gi". Each piece is different. Set it aside for months or even years. The more time you take the better.

6. Finger holes

Make a little sand paper cone for sanding holes.

You can taper holes to change the pitch. Start cutting the area nearest the blowing edge and closest to the bore, i.e., make the taper narrowest at the surface of the flute. Do one hole at a time beginning with the lowest.

Placing tape on the bamboo before drilling the holes helps prevent splitting. (See below, #14 CONSTRUCTION TOOLS)

7. Blowing edge

Using a razor sharp knife, cut the recess sides straight down to the bottom edge. Then cut the side angles and extend the bottom edge. Cut the bottom edge at an inward sloping angle (about a 45° angle to the bore). This steep angle makes a strong blowing edge.

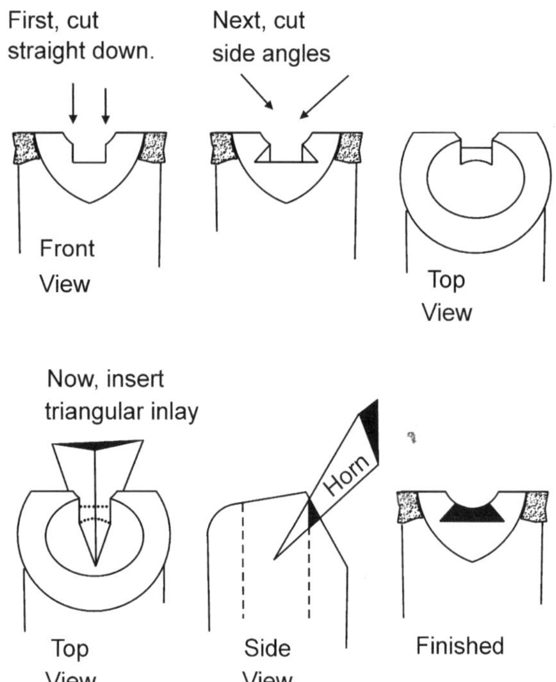

Fig. 14

Smaller bore flutes pivot higher on the chin and so require less filing.

Seal the blowing edge with hot bee's wax, lanoline or even glue. Then buff to a sheen.

8. The Tapered Bore

Making a flute with a tapered bore isn't difficult. However, it does require attention to detail and a little manual dexterity. And, of course, you must train your eyes and ears by the old and tested method - practice!

There are two methods of making a tapered bore. When making a wooden flute you remove material from the inner walls. With a bamboo flute you remove material from the root end and node, and apply a pasty material to the bore to build up its walls where needed.

The goal is to get the bore to taper smoothly from a larger diameter to a smaller one and then back to a larger one according to precise dimensions. (See above, #1 Shakuhachi Dimensions.)

A skillfully fashioned bore with several coats of gloss urushi (or enamel lacquer) is dazzling to look through. Ironically, though, some of the finest Shakuhachi have atrocious looking bores. Acoustic balance is the name of the game here. So STOP if it plays well, or at least slow down! Don't let the taper be the goal per se. It's the sound and feel you're after.

You can use a set of gauges to measure the bore as you make it. Make these by cutting circles from tin or plastic in diameters from 1.4 cm. to 2.0 cm, in 0.5 mm. increments. Attach each gauge to a long thin hardwood dowel. Mark the bore depth for each gauge on its dowel rod. Lower the gauges into the bore starting with the smallest ones first. Shakuhachi Dimensions #1, above, shows the dimensions for a standard bore taper used by many makers in Japan.

You can also make a set of bore gauges out of an old pool cue. Use a caliper to locate the areas of the pool cue which match the bore dimensions. Saw these off in 1/2" lengths and attach rods.

Hold the flute firmly in the palm of the hand and sand evenly, keeping the sandstone rod centered in the bore. Any wobble causes unwanted curves in the bore.

9. "GI" bore paste

It usually takes three applications of "gi" and subsequent grinding to get desired results.

Use a thin flexible paddle stick to apply the 2nd and 3rd coats of "gi". Use pressing and turning motions, then patting and sliding motions. The "gi" for these applications is quite wet as opposed to the crumbly mixture used for the initial application.

Regular "gi": mix 1 part seshime urushi + 1- 4 parts tonoko (fire clay) + water to suit (about 2 parts)

Seko "Gi": 1 part seshime urushi + 3 parts seko (plaster of Paris) + 2 parts water.

Seshime urushi is just straight urushi. It is used for the first coat like a primer and for making "gi". I haven't looked into making "gi" without urushi. Powdered fired clay and plaster of Paris are readily available here. What to substitute for urushi?

10. Urushi

Urushi is the condensed sap from a tree of the Sumac family (the same family as poison oak and ivy). When dry it's extremely hard and long lasting, and no longer toxic. Unfortunately, when wet, it amounts to painting with liquid poison oak - hard to do without dripping some on yourself occasionally.

When finished applying the urushi, you put the flute into a humid box to dry. Urushi cures through a chemical reaction between its resin and high humidity into an extremely hard surface. An essential characturistic of any urushi substitute should be hardness.

If you wish to make your own urushi, collect it in the early fall. Choose the oldest plants (poison oak) and make a series of cuts. Cut only the bark, not the inner ring. Evaporate the collected sap in the sun or with charcoal heat.

Strain "ro iro" (enamel) to remove any small particles suspended in the liquid. Sand lightly between coats (with very fine sandpaper or charcoal on a stick).

Use turpentine to thin and clean.

11. Tuning

The following method is for improving particular notes. If a flute is weak in one area, you can correct that area without adding "gi" blindly to the whole bore. This allows you to balance the bore without making it exactly tapered, thereby using a minimum of "gi" - which is preferable!.

The bore is divided into 7 areas, or "rooms" - Rm1 through Rm7. See Shakuhachi Dimensions #1, above, for their locations. You work on one or more "rooms" to correct a certain note. Be careful though; what is done to improve one note can adversely effect another. Always remember that balance is your goal.

You can insert moist strips of paper into the bore to see what additional "gi" in a particular area ("room") of the flute will do. If this doesn't work, then grinding away is the next step.

When you tune a Shakuhachi using this method, you can end up with a bore which only roughly resembles a taper. This method takes longer to master, but is worth the effort.

If the low octave notes are good, the high ones will usually be good too. RO is the exception.

RO doesn't sound: Rm1 & Rm6 are either too wide or too narrow. Try adding paper first, then grind. Last, check Rm4.

RO difficult: Rm4 is usually too wide.

RO slips to Kan: Rm2 is too wide (add paper here first), or Rm5 is too narrow (so grind away).

RO is high pitched: The volume of the upper and lower halves is unbalanced. Add paper to Rm1 through Rm4.

RO is low pitched: The volume of the upper and lower halves is unbalanced. Add paper to Rm4 through Rm7.

RO is weak: Grind Rm6.

RO KAN is difficult: Add paper to Rm7. If it is unchanged, or worsens, try adding to Rm5. Last, check Rm6.

RO is bubbly: Check Rm5 and Rm3.

TSU is thin & unclear: Add paper to Rm1, then grind Rm3 (careful, RE is easily effected). Lastly, check Rm5.

TSU is too high: Grind Rm1 (stop if this effects other notes) or narrow hole #1 by adding "gi" to its upper wall.

TSU is too low: Add paper to Rm1. If other notes are effected, enlarge hole #1.

RE is thin & unclear: Add paper to Rm1 first. If no effect, grind Rm3 (slowly). Lastly, check Rm6 and Rm4.

RE goes KAN: (When blown hard) Add paper to Rm3.

RE is too high: Grind Rm1 or narrow hole #1 and #2 by adding "gi" to the upper walls.

RE is too low: Add paper to Rm1, or enlarge inside hole #1 and #2.

CHI is thin & unclear: Grind Rm2. Lastly, check Rm3 and Rm6.

CHI is too high: Grind Rm1 or narrow hole #3.

CHI is too low: Add paper to Rm1 or enlarge inside of hole #3.

RE, TSU & RO are bad: (No sound in the low octave.) Check Rm5.

HA is thin & unclear: Grind Rm2. HA is relatively easy to tune. It has a close connection to HI.

HA goes KAN: (When blown hard) Add paper to Rm2.

HA is too high: Grind Rm1. If other notes change, put "gi" inside holes #3 and #4 to narrow.

HA is too low: Add paper to Rm1, or enlarge holes #3 and #4.

HI is thin & unclear: (In low octave.) Grind Rm2.

HI goes KAN: (When blown hard) Add paper to Rm2.

HI is too high: Grind Rm1, or narrow hole #5.

Hi is too low: Add paper to Rm1, or enlarge hole #5.

And:

Sensitivity in the upper octaves varies inversely to bore size. Therefore, small bore flutes are a little easier to tune and balance.

The better you can play the Shakuhachi, the better you can make one.

12. Cracked Shakuhachi

Cracking is caused by dry conditions. Avoid direct sun light and central (or electric) heating. Store the flute in a moist environment if you live in an especially dry one. Plastic bags work.
Repair cracks in bamboo flutes by wrapping them in a moist towel for 24 hours. Small cracks can be glued and clamped. Make a recessed binding for the large ones. (See steps #45 to #52.)

13. Working With Wood And Clay

Wood is a good alternative to bamboo. Because wood grows at a slower pace than bamboo, it has less variation and so provides more predictable results. The challenge with wood is finding a variety that resonates well - something you can't know until the flute is finished. I'm still searching for the best wood. Let me know if you find it. Maple and Rosewood (both used commercially) are a safe beginning.

The lathes and tapered reamers used commercially aren't available to low budget makers, but that isn't a problem. The exterior can easily be shaped by hand using a draw knife. The bore is trickier. I use long hand augers (1.4 cm. and 1.7 cm.) and bore in from both ends. Hold the wood and auger "true" with a jig while drilling. You need to drill as perpendicular to the wood as possible to make both bores meet. Then use a long coarse rasp to remove wood from the bore sides until it tapers correctly. In other respects, construction is the same as bamboo.

A high fired ceramic Shakuhachi has a distinct sound and feel, quite different from flutes made out of bamboo, wood or plastic. Clay also presents its own set of unique problems. Clay shrinks when fired and you must compensate for this shrinkage. This takes some experimentation.

First whittle a bore form out of wood. Use calipers and the bore dimension given in #1 above. Roll out the clay and wrap it around the form. When the clay is firm, carefully slice through it lengthwise, down to the wood form. Next repeat this cut on the opposite side. After the clay dries remove each half from the form. "Glue" the halves together by wetting their edges and pressing them together. Use wet clay to fill any gaps. Now complete the holes and the blowing edge. When it's dry, glaze as desired. When the glaze is dry, it's ready for the kiln.

14. Construction Tools

If you have trouble finding the best tool or technique to accomplish a task, go to a good hardware store in your area. Ask their advice.

The tool used to cut the shallow circular groove (step #28) is the "Kebiki", a Japanese marking gauge. You can buy one for $20 from Hida Tool Inc., 1333 San Pablo Ave., Berkeley, CA.94702. (510) 524-3700. You can make a Mortise and Tenon Gauge (available everywhere) into this kind of tool.

Cut the joint hole with a "reverse bevel" gouge, i.e., bevel on the inside. If the bevel is on the outside, grind it to an inside bevel.

Drill the finger holes with a bit suitable for doweling, like a Brad Point bit or a Forstner bit. You can spot grind the outer cutting edges until they cut the bamboo cleanly.

Open all the nodes in the bore with a 18" long 1/2" drill bit. Use a long rasp to enlarge these to the desired dimensions. Make one by welding a 4" piece of a large round bastard file to a steel rod.

Make the bore sanders with sandstone. Make shallow grooves in a slab of sandstone and snap pieces off, a few inches long. Shape them by grinding each one on a large piece of sandstone, using water as a lubricant/flush. When finished, glue to a stick.

15. Raw Materials

There is adventure in selecting a raw material and then discovering how a flute made from it turns out. It's exciting. Here are a few ideas and sources:

PLASTIC:
Clear PVC is better than regular PVC. It's more expensive and harder to find than regular PVC, but worth it. It produces a superior sound and is much more attractive. Look in the Yellow Pages under PIPE. You may have to order it. Inquire about other types of plastic pipe, too, if you want to have fun experimenting. Let me know if you find something better than clear PVC. I'd like to try making one out of Acrylic.

Ryan Herco, 1819 Junction Ave., San Jose, CA. (408) 436-1141 carries the clear PVC and will ship COD via UPS. You have to order a minimum of 10', which they cut into two 5' lengths for shipping. That's enough to make 4 flutes, so order 4 clear couplings as well. Ask for:

3/4" clear PVC pipe
Size Code# 4000-007 @ $14.20 for 10'

3/4" clear PVC slip coupling
Size Code# 4029-007 @ $1.68 each

Pipe diameters vary so ask them to be sure the pipe fits snugly into the coupling.

METAL:
Type M 3/4" copper pipe and a no stop coupling make a good beginning on a search into metal Shakuhachi. A CxC drop ear might make a better blow end than a coupling because it's bulkier. There is also the heavier gauge type K and type L pipe to try. Keep in mind that a certain size pipe may be more suited to longer (or shorter) Shakuhachi than the standard 54cm. version. Go to your hardware store or look in the Yellow Pages for metal pipe dealers.

I'd like to try making one out of 1" soft copper pipe. I'd cut it length wise and unroll it. Then I'd lay out the bore dimensions, trim the excess off the edges, roll it into a tapered tube, braze it together, and anneal it.

BAMBOO:
While little root bamboo is available commercially, upper section timber bamboo is. It's used in making fences, poles for gardens and decorations, and in making rattan and wicker furniture. You can make a fine Shakuhachi by using the lowest nodes of this bamboo. Look under Bamboo, Wicker or Rattan in the Yellow Pages of big cities near you. These are some folks who carry bamboo in California:

Mr. E's Inc., 12758 E. Lakeland Rd., Santa Fe Springs, CA 90670, 944-8979

Monty Levenson (P.O. Box 294, Willits, CA. 95490) now sells cleaned and cured "root end" and "upper section" bamboo.

WOOD:
Look in the Yellow Pages under Hardwoods or Lumber. Also, go into the forest and look for branches of the right size. I believe a flute made from a branch would be superior to one made from sawn lumber. Let me know.

American Indians made flutes by cutting branch wood lengthwise, carving out the bore on each half and then gluing and binding the halves together. It's worth a try on a Shakuhachi.

And last but not least....

> *Lay plans for the accomplishment of the difficult before it becomes difficult; make something big by starting with it when small.*
>
> *Difficult things in the world must needs have their beginnings in the easy; big things must needs have their beginnings in the small.*

Tao Te Ching

Carl and his sons gathering bamboo.

About The Author

Carl Abbott began Yoga in 1960 at the age of 17. At 19 he emigrated to Australia. Pursuing a deep inner quest he spent the next 15 years wandering and working in mostly in Asia, studying Yoga, Taoist and Buddhist philosophies and related disciplines: Hatha Yoga, Tai Chi, Karate, Zen and Shakuhachi.

In Japan, he studied Shakuhachi construction and playing with Kawase Junsuke II, Kawase Junsuke III, and Mr. Goro Yamaguchi, three respected masters of the Shakuhachi.

He returned to the United States and settled in California, where he lives with his wife and two sons. He is currently spokesman for CenterTao in Santa Cruz.

About CenterTao

The Center For Taoist Thought And Fellowship (a.k.a. CenterTao), founded in 1982, is a California non-profit religious (Taoist) corporation. It is located at 406 Lincoln St., Santa Cruz, CA 95060.

A Taoist meeting is held the first Sunday of every month at 10 a.m. The general public is welcome. The hour long meeting is divided into 3 parts, each divided by the ringing of a bell.

The service begins with a short silent period, followed by a reading from the Tao Te Ching. Those who wish discuss the verse and what it means to them personally. The service concludes with another short silent period.

The first verse of the Tao Te Ching illustrates the humility we endeavor to bring to the service:

> *The way that can be told, is not the constant way;*
> *The name that can be named, is not the constant name.*

Other Offerings

Blowing Zen After covering basic information and history background you'll be guided step-by-step from producing sound and playing simple folk tunes to playing Buddhist Meditation music.

This book combined with the free online video lessons at Centertao.org/learn-zen will take you from absolute zero to Honkyoku (Zen Buddhist meditation through the shakuhachi flute).

There is also detailed information on making two types of Shakuhachi: a simple plastic pipe version and the traditional tapered bore root bamboo version. Preview this book at, Centertao.org/zen-book. Listen to samples at Centertao.org/hear-zen

The **Yuu Shakuhachi** is made from high quality plastic. This flute while lacking the genuine look and feel of bamboo, comes very close. Most importantly, it plays and sound better than bamboo flutes costing much more. Perfect for seeing if the Shakuhachi is right for you. Another important advantage, it won't crack! Take it to the mountains; taket it to the beach; take it to work. Go to Toneway.com/products/blowing-zen for more information.

Hatha Yoga: The Essential Dynamics guides you step by step from beginning through advanced Yoga using vectorial information for 138 postures as taught by B.K.S. Iyengar.

The full page, large print format enables you to learn (or *remember*) at a glance, what you need to be doing while your are doing it. You can preview this book at Centertao.org/yoga-book

Tao Te Ching, Word for Word is a more literal translation of this Taoist classic. First, I give a poetic rendering of the chapter. This is followed by a word-for-word, line-by-line translation of the Chinese.

Using these to cross check frequently with one's favorite English translation can deepen one's understanding. Translations invariably lose some degree of the ancient 'original intention' due to the modern cultural context we bring to our language's words… our 'education'. The word-for-word section provides the many related synonym-like meaning with which the reader can use to piece together something closer to the original.

The second half of the book includes extensive commentary that relates each chapter to various aspects of life. Preview this book at Centertao.org/tao-book.

Shamisen of Japan teaches you how to professionally play and make the Tsugaru Shamisen, simply and enjoyably! It's really two books in one:

Included are step-by-step instructions for building your own shamisen, and a learning guide for playing shamisen, including notation for 16 traditional shamisen pieces. It is a valuable resource for both the beginner and the shamisen enthusiast! Learn about shamisen, watch the free shamisen crash course, and join the growing shamisen community at Bachido.com!

• • • • • •

If you have any questions e-mail us at Centertao.org or write CenterTao, 406 Lincoln St., Santa Cruz, CA. 95060 for more information.

SHAKUHACHI FINGERING CHART

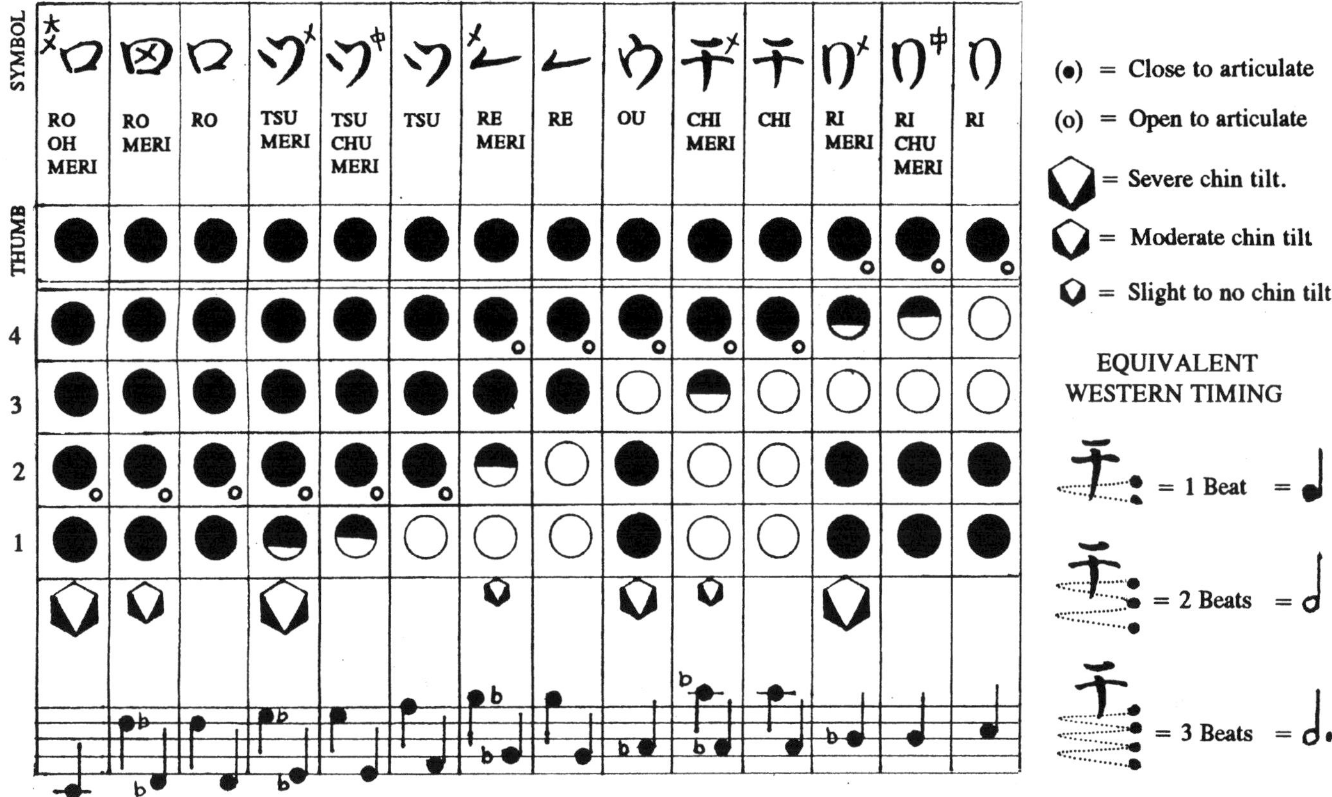

HA	OU SAN	HI MERI	HI CHU MERI	HI	HI GO MERI	HI GO	HA GO	HA NI	HA SAN	HA YON	HA YON GO

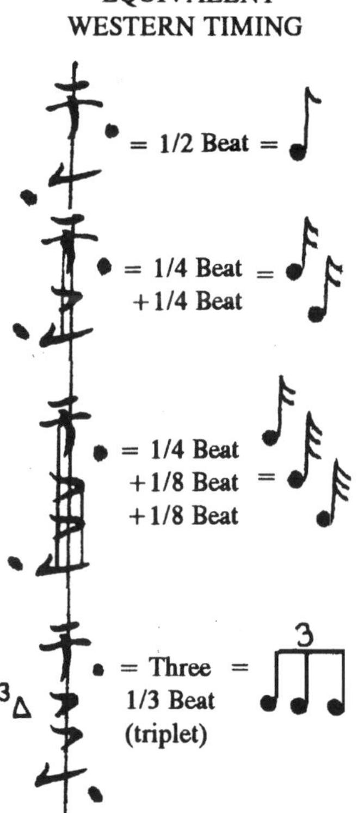

NOTE: The notes from OU SAN thru HA YON GO are played high octave only, except occasionally in Buddhist Hon Kyoku.

HARU NO
KO GAWA - Track 7

HI NO MARU
NO HATA - Track 1,2,3,4,5,6

SHEET MUSIC

THE BASIC SYMBOLS

(呂)	=play low octave
(:)	=beat marks
(>)	=repeat previous note
(甲)	=play high octave
(中)	=cover 1/2 of hole
(メ)	=cover 3/4 of hole with chin tilt
(ル)	=tap the open hole
(ス)	=slide finger off hole
(カ)	=raise and extend chin
(o)	=beat mark where the sound continues on
(ヨ)	=shake head
(︵)	=chin tilt rises to normal position during note

THE BASIC FINGERINGS

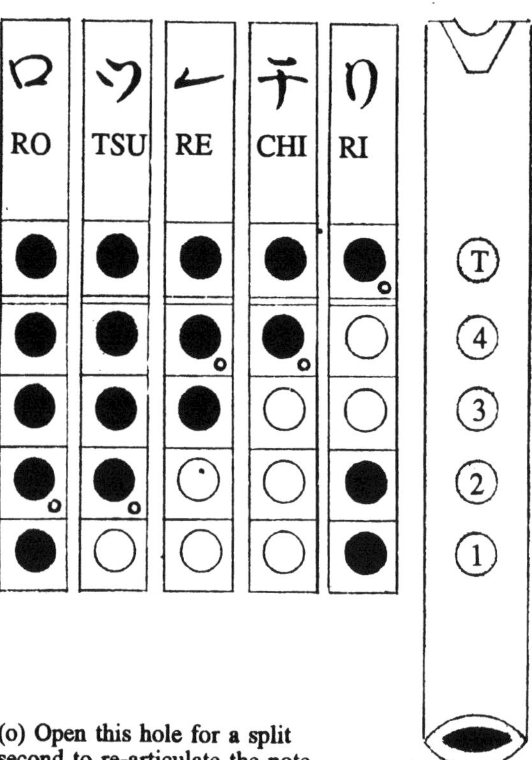

(o) Open this hole for a split second to re-articulate the note.

NOTE: Shakuhachi notation is played from right to left. Begin playing down the far right hand column to the top of the next column to the left.

TSU
CHU
MERI
OU
TSU
MERI
KAZOE UTA
Track 12, 13
KIMIGAEYO
Track 10, 11
YU YAKE
KO YAKE
Track 8, 9

KO JU NO TSUKI
Track 14

SAKURA
Track 15

A

CHI MERI

HARU GA KITA - Track 16

A

B

HI

HOTARU NO HIKARI
Track 17

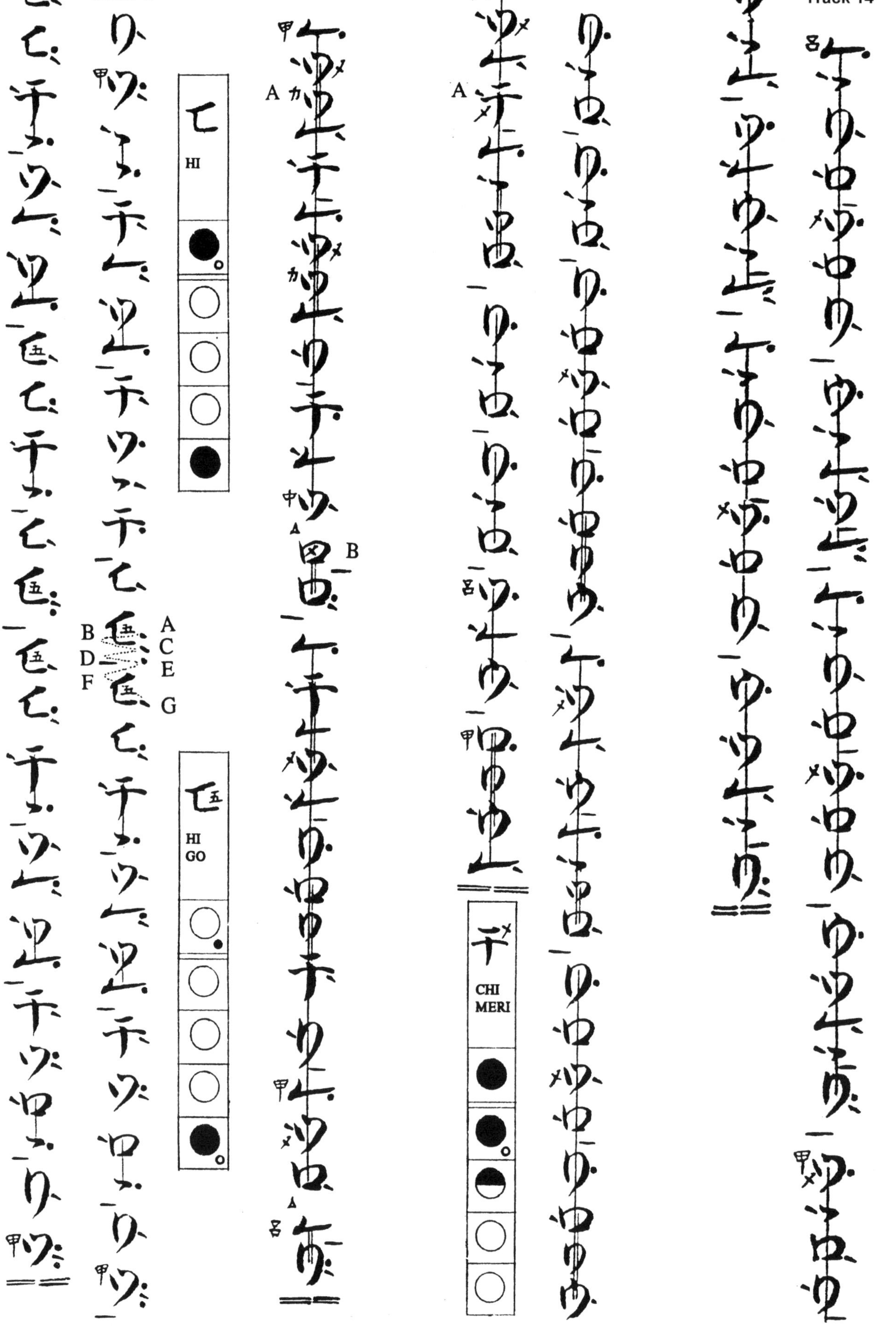

B D F

A C E G

HI GO

KURO
KAMI
Track
18, 19

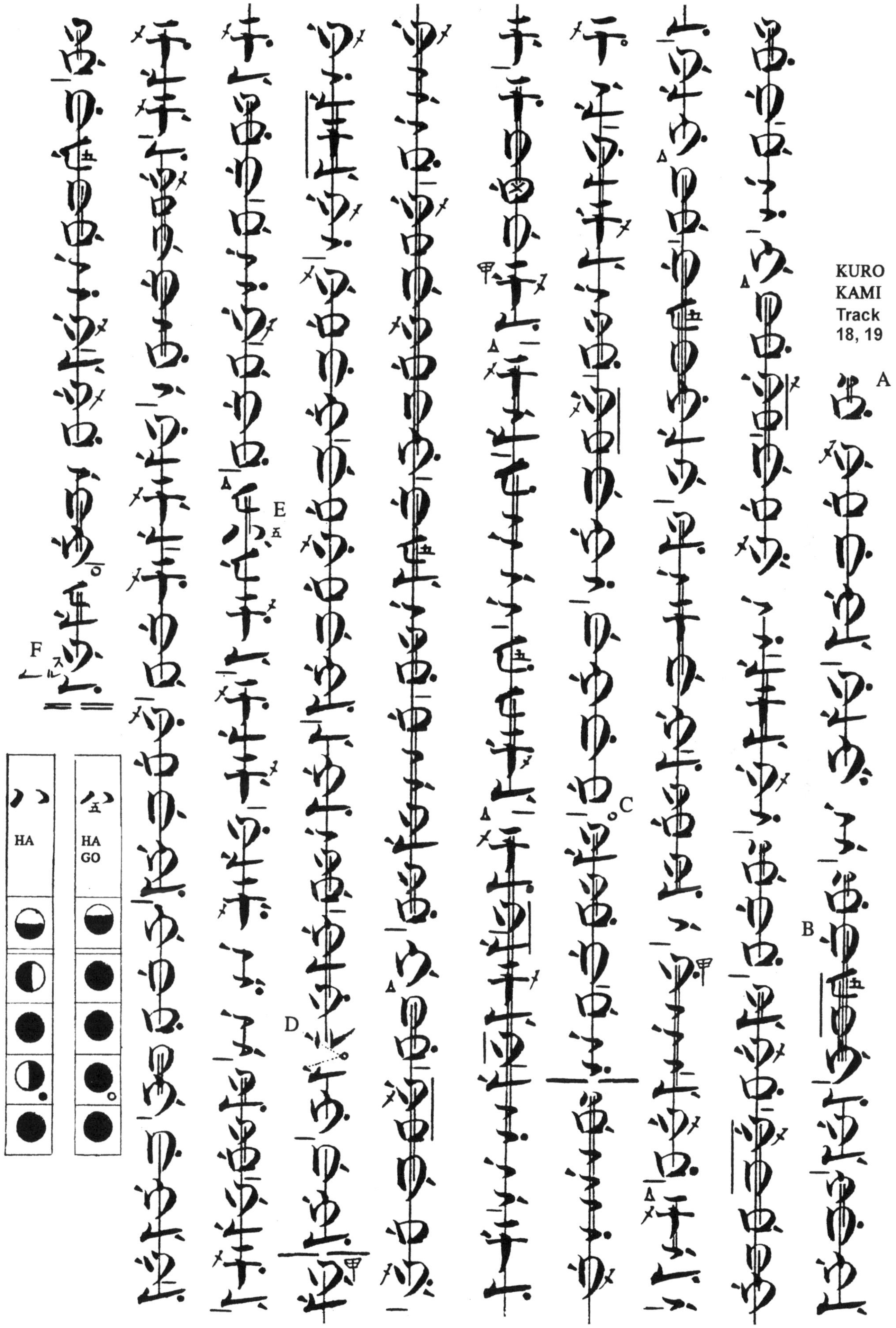

A

B

C

D

E

F

HA

HA
GO

SODE
KORO
Track 20

A

B

C

D

E

RE
MERI

HI
MERI

RI
MERI

SHO DAN
Track 21

A

HA SAN

TSURU NO KOE
Track 22

A

B

C

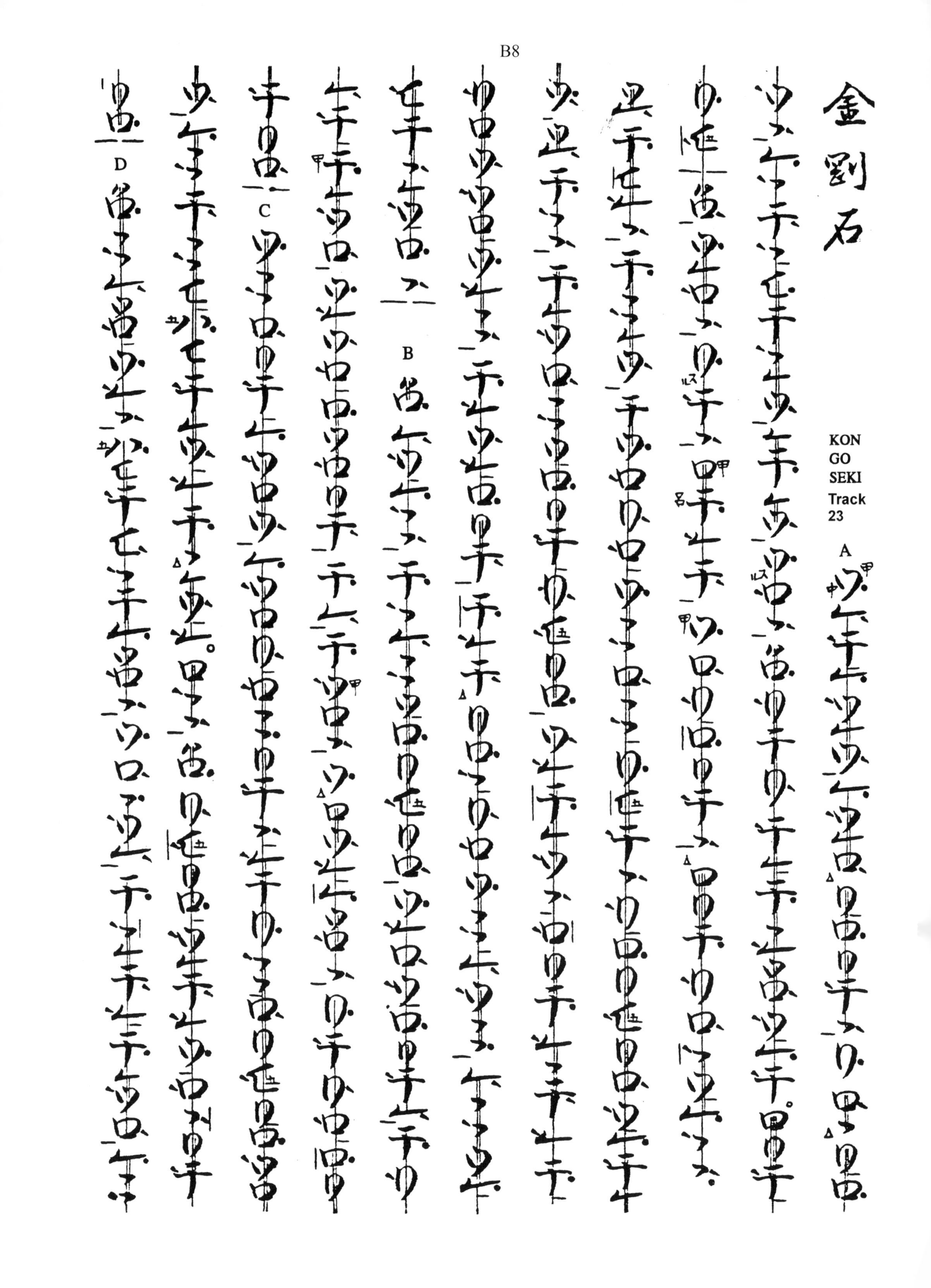

金剛石

KON
GO
SEKI
Track
23

A

B

C

D

HI
FU
MI
Track
24

一二三鉢返壽調

A

B

C

トメ

ハニ
HA NI
○
○
●。
○
●

ハ五
HA YON GO
○
○
●
●
●

HI FU MI

PITCH GRAPH SYMBOLS:

( ) = the line indicates relative pitch change.

(1,2, etc.)= indicates hole/finger number to use.

( ) = atari - re-articulation
(メ, 大メ) = meri/oh meri - tilt
( ) = ru - tap hole
(ス) = suru - slide
(△) = quick transition to the next note

numbers by these symbols indicate the finger to use.

(<) = volume intensifies
(>) = volume diminishes
(ｏ) = slight pause

(カ)= kari - standard pitch
(中)= chu meri - half meri
(メ)= meri - low pitch

( ) = simple yuri by slight horizontal shaking of the head.

( ) = tempo of notes between these symbols is increased.

NEW NOTATION FOUND IN "HI FU MI":

(ｏ) = similar to the measure marks.
( ) = pitch variation for that note.
( ) = low octave
( ) = naiashi
( ) = open the thumb hole of HI, thus producing GO HI.
( ) = repeat previous note with a meri chin tilt, but no half holing.
( ) = repeat the phrase.
( ) = the end.
( ) = a major yuri vibrato: go from meri to kari at an increasing rate.

( )=RO, (ツ)=TSU, ( )=RE, (ウ)=OU,
(チ)=CHI, (リ)=RI, ( )=HI, ( )=GO HI,
( )=HA,

(A)

1.
2.
3.
4.
5.
6.
7.
8.
9.
10.
11.
12.
13.
14.
15.
16.
17.
18.
19.
20.
21.

(B)

22.
23.
24.
25.
26.
27.
28.
29.
30.

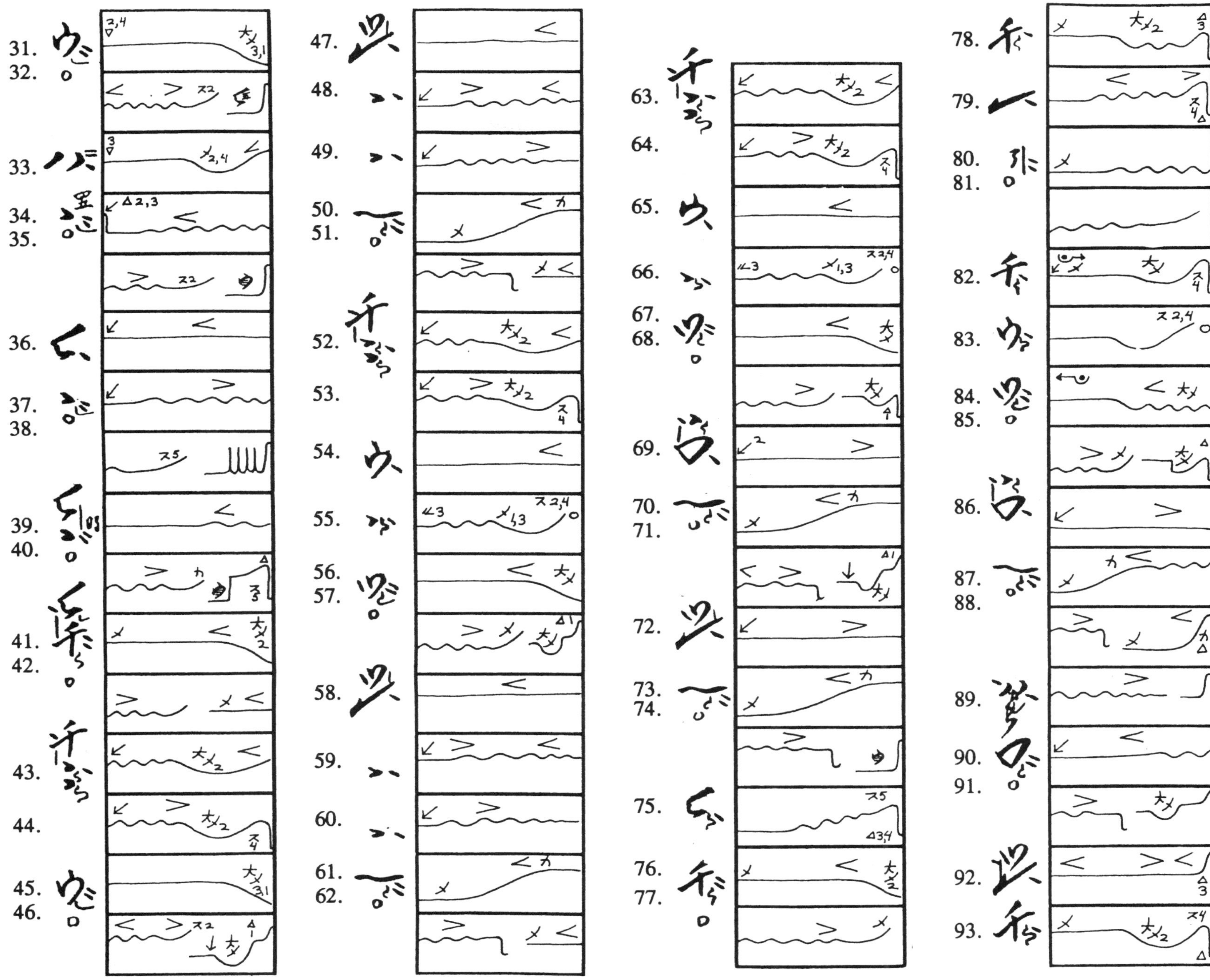
31. 32. 33. 34. 35. 36. 37. 38. 39. 40. 41. 42. 43. 44. 45. 46.
47. 48. 49. 50. 51. 52. 53. 54. 55. 56. 57. 58. 59. 60. 61. 62.
63. 64. 65. 66. 67. 68. 69. 70. 71. 72. 73. 74. 75. 76. 77.
78. 79. 80. 81. 82. 83. 84. 85. 86. 87. 88. 89. 90. 91. 92. 93.

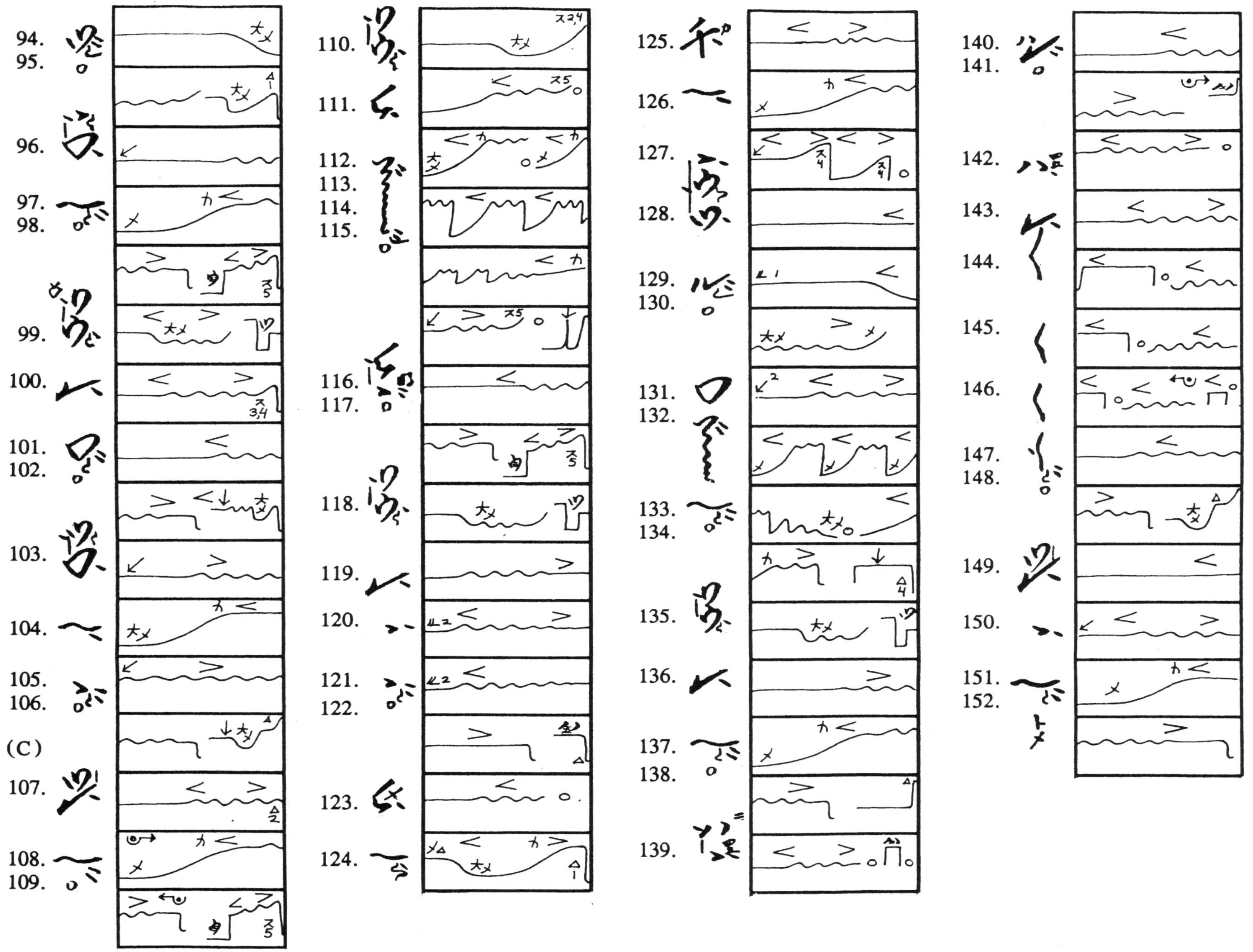
94.
95.
96.
97.
98.
99.
100.
101.
102.
103.
104.
105.
106.
(C)
107.
108.
109.
110.
111.
112.
113.
114.
115.
116.
117.
118.
119.
120.
121.
122.
123.
124.
125.
126.
127.
128.
129.
130.
131.
132.
133.
134.
135.
136.
137.
138.
139.
140.
141.
142.
143.
144.
145.
146.
147.
148.
149.
150.
151.
152.

六段之調

ROKU DAN
Track 25

A

B

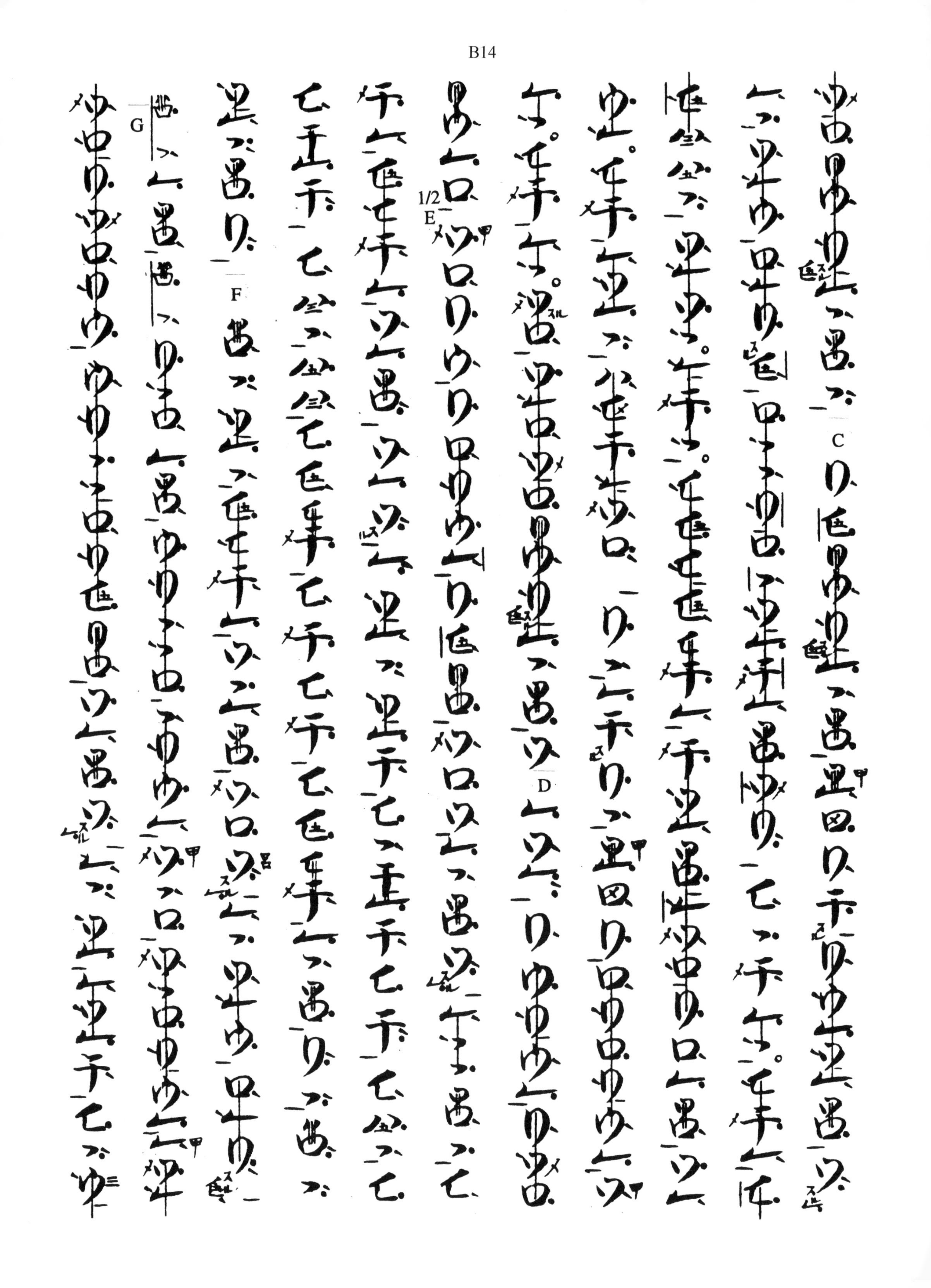

C

D

1/2
E

F

G

H

I

2

千鳥之曲

CHI
DORI
Track 26

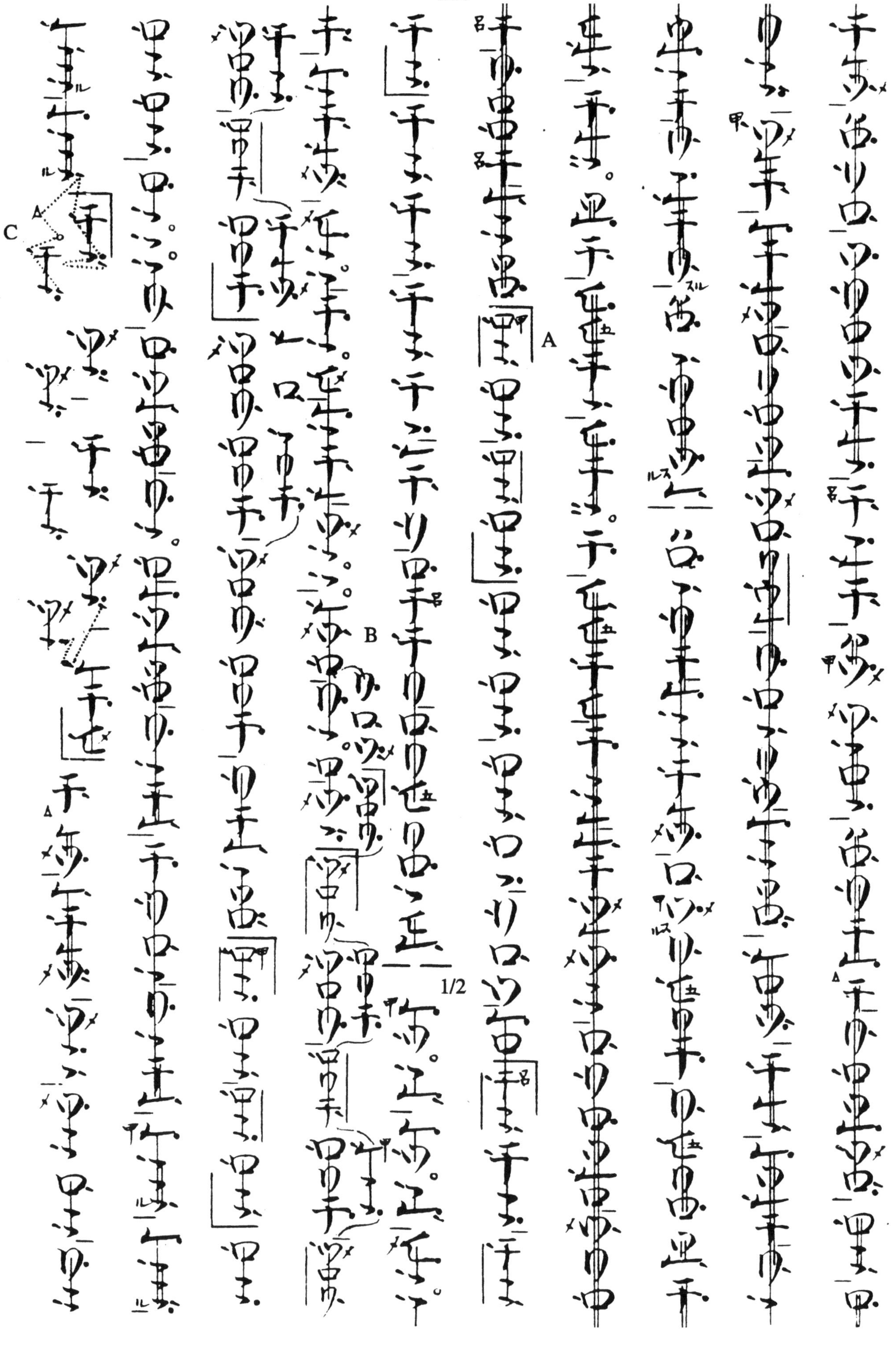

A

B

1/2

C

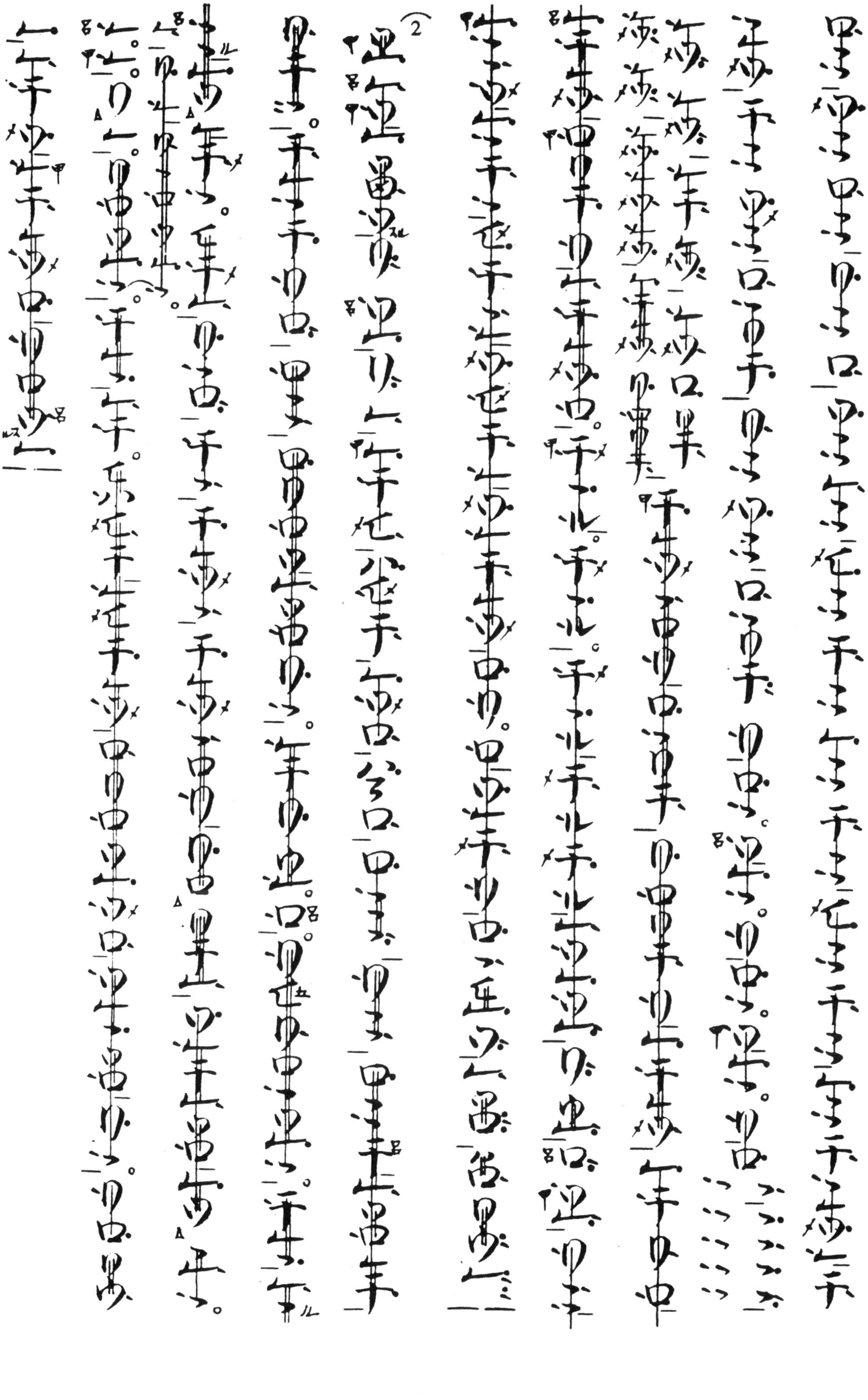

2

**
Londondary Air

****
Santa Lucia

* Amazing Grace

** The Tennessee Waltz

*** Venezuela

****
Rock of Ages

***
Lock Lomand

*
Old Folks At Home

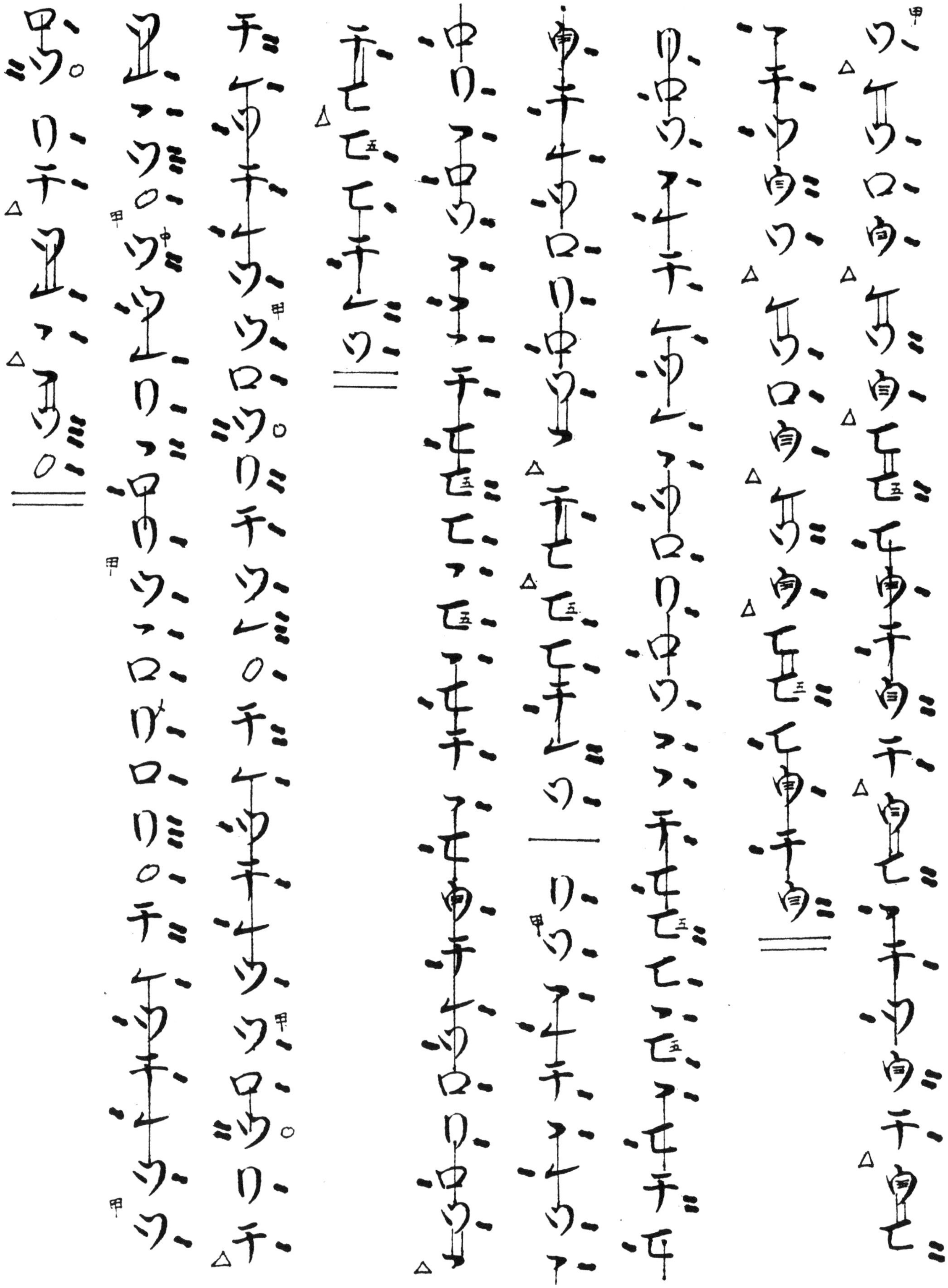

**
Scarborough Fair

ヒ中

HI CHU MERI

**
Shanendoah

***
El Condor Pasa

リ中

RI CHU MERI

This Peruvian tune is traditionally played on the 'Quena', and so is well suited for the Shakuhachi.

****
Swing Low
Sweet Chariot

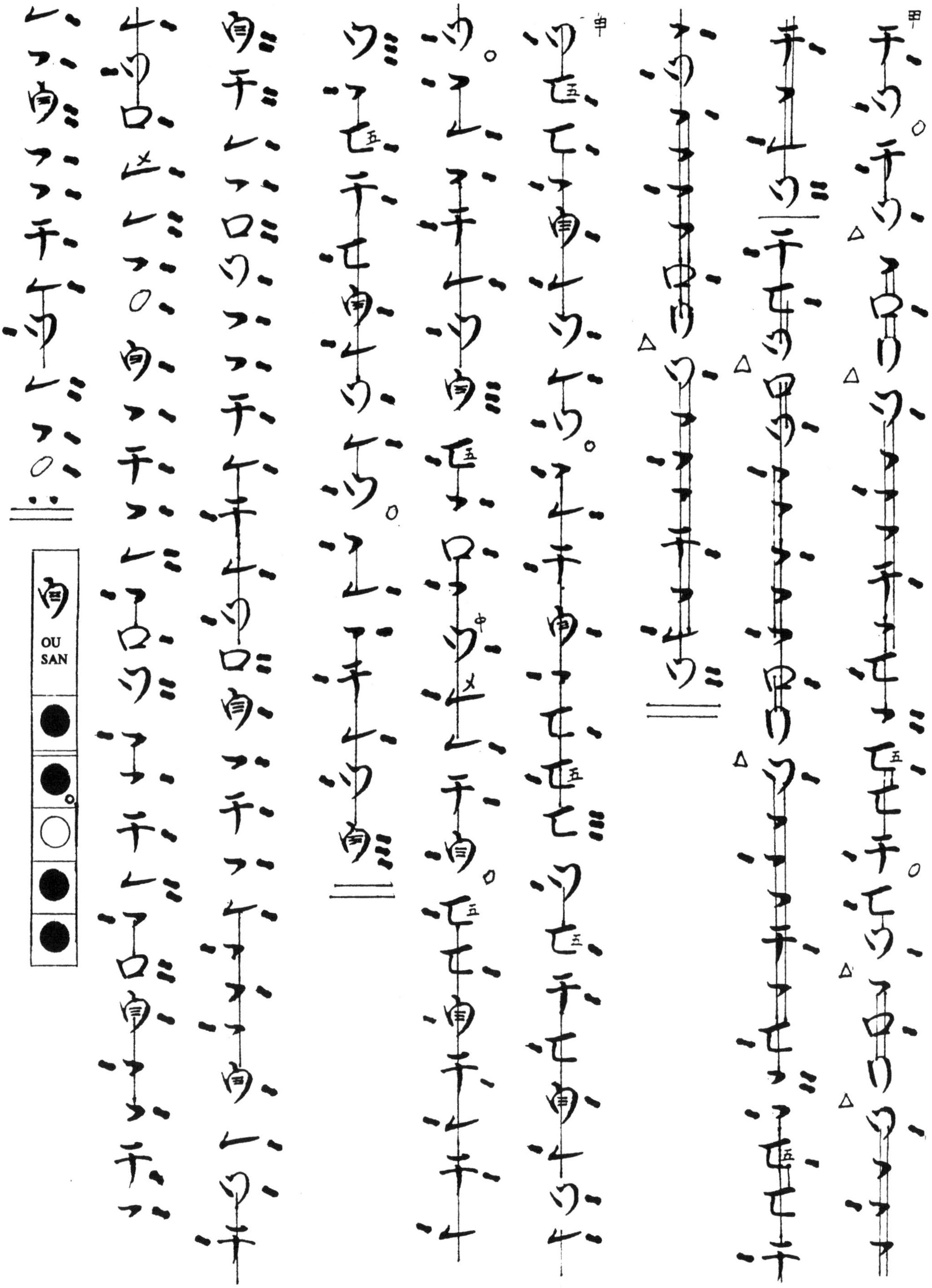

***
It Came Upon a
Midnight Clear

**
Shule Shule

OU
SAN

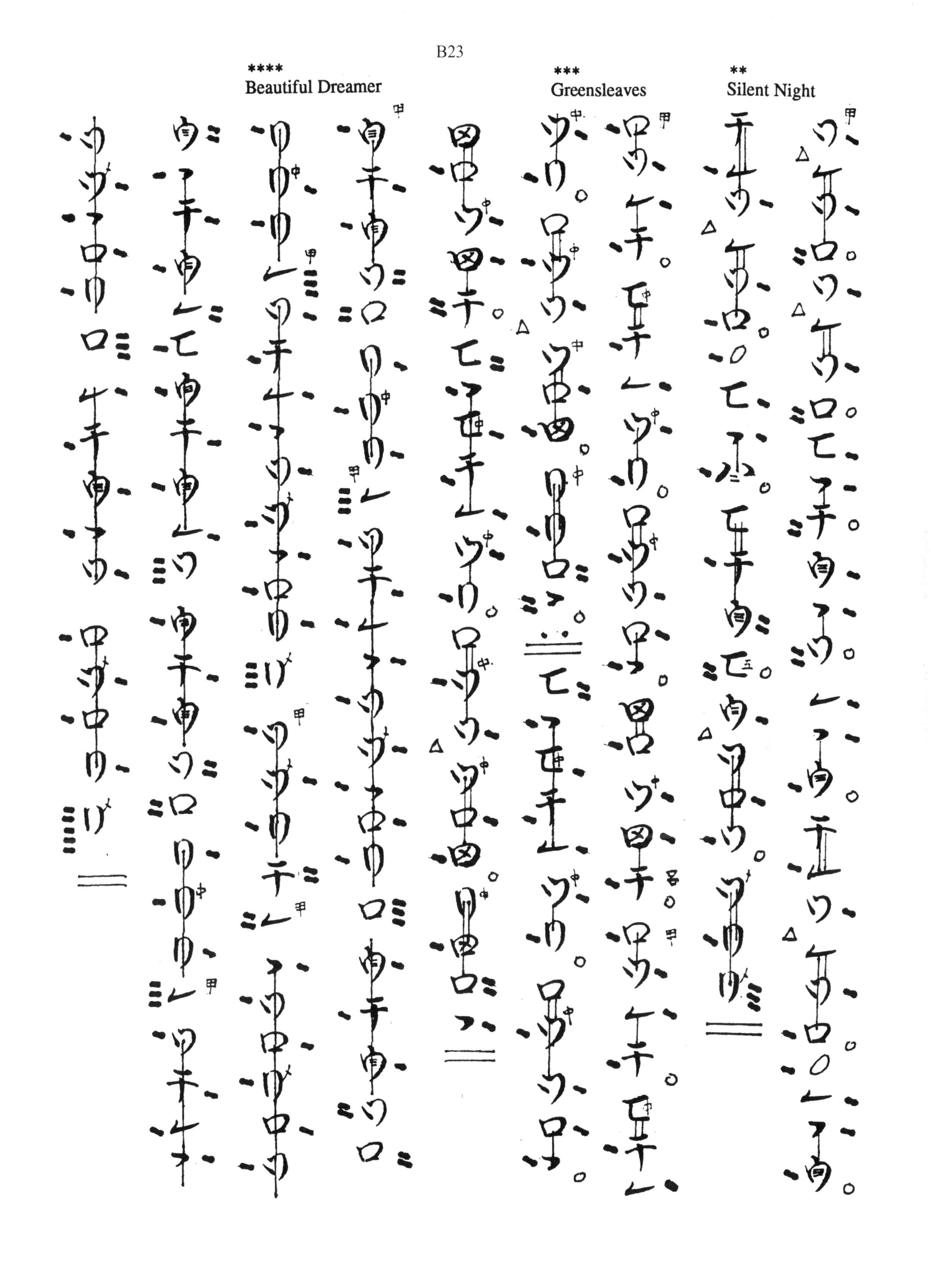

**
Silent Night

***
Greensleaves

****
Beautiful Dreamer

This is the complete notation for "HI FU MI". It takes about 20 minutes to play. It has a few new phrases in it. Study page B25 for hints on these. Improvise when you are unsure of what to do.

一二三鉢返寿調

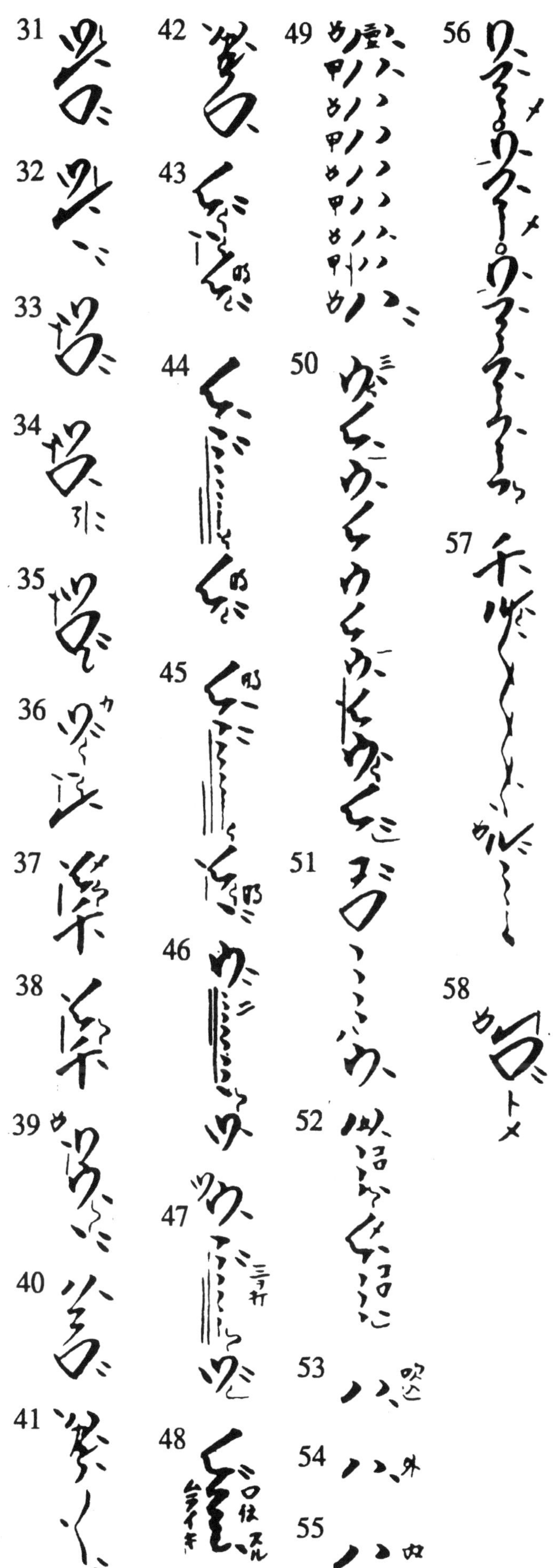

Common Hon Kyoku Phrases

The following, #31 to #58, are common phrases used in Hon Kyoku. See their notation at right. A selection of these is recorded on the last band of the Shakuhachi Lesson Tape. This, and "HI FU MI" (Band 24), should give you enough to go on.

31. Slide gradually from TSU to RE, then slide slightly to RO.

32. Shift abruptly from TSU MERI to TSU and then to RE.

33. Shift from (TSU) MERI to OH MERI, then do an ATARI of RO as you abruptly shift to RO.

34,35. End each RO in RO MERI - two beats for #34 and one beat for #35.

36. TSU is played KARI for the first beat. Then it returns to the usual MERI. It returns to KARI with an articulation on the upbeat. Then it returns to MERI before going to RE.

37. When HI is MERI, CHI is usually KARI.

Squiggly lines that bend left represent MERI shifts. Those that bend right represent KARI shifts. Here it bends both ways - first left into MERI and then right into KARI.

38. When HI is KARI, CHI is usually MERI. CHI is usually MERI in Hon Kyoku even when not indicated. Playing what sounds right works fine.

39. The squiggly line shows that OU bends up to KARI before the ATARI. Play OH KARI by extending your finger off hole #1 and #3, but not off the flute. Also extend the chin out to maximize the KARI. Then shift abruptly back to MERI on the ATARI.

40. The volume of HA diminishes almost to silence just before an abrupt shift to RO.

41. HA goes from MERI to KARI, then after a RU tap on hole #2, goes back to MERI, then back to KARI again.

42. Notice the small KARI symbol placed inside the HA. HA rises abruptly from MERI to KARI just before the right beat mark.

43. Listen to the grace note OU, then HI, then HI MERI, then HI with articulation, then HI MERI again followed by a trill to HI GO.

Ashi no Sirabe (Reed Tune)

芦(アシ)の調

Ban Shiki Cho (Foundation Rhythm)

盤渉調

44. Listen to the volume changes and where the breath is taken.

45. HI GO ATARI's shift to HI ATARI's.

46. Slightly but rapidly shake the flute towards and then away from the lip.

47. Like #46, but shake at the end of OU, as shown by the double line.

48. You can use this, MURA IKI, on most notes. The blast of air and sound occurs on the full KARI of the note. Then it lowers to MERI with a little YURI. (This is played in the next Hon Kyoku, "Ban Shiki Cho", to the left)

49. The first HA goes slightly KARI before it shifts to high octave. Also notice the increase in tempo.

50. This begins with a low octave grace note OU. Notice the increasing tempo.

51. Play this, KO RO, by playing HA, opening and closing holes #1 and #2 alternately, quickly and smoothly. Notice the grace note HA before OU.

52. This is a KO RO of HA GO and HI MERI. Play HA GO and HI MERI as usual, but open and close holes #1 and #2 alternately like #51. Slide off hole #2 when going to HI MERI.

53. Thumb makes RU type articulation on the back hole.

54. Thumb brushes counter clockwise across hole #5

55. Thumb brushes clockwise across hole #5.

56. The first two OSHI YURIs end in MERI. The remainder are never overly MERI, and end in KARI.

57. Each repeat mark means to repeat CHI and RU. Then play a series of RUs in low octave.

58. Most Hon Kyoku end with this. When playing RE, leave hole #1 closed.

NOTE: These points, numbers 31 to 58, are from our "Blowing Zen II Booklet". It wasn't necessary to include numbers 1 to 30 because most of this information is already covered in "Blowing Zen".

Also, be sure to download the MP3 files of the Western melodies and the other Hon Kyoku pieces (pages B24 and B26 - B28) at: Centertao.org/learn-zen

This piece is called "Kumoi Jishi" which means Cloud Lion. Play it at a little faster tempo than "Hi Fu Mi". Always play TSU at KARI pitch and play HI MERI in place of CHI KARI (HI MERI plays closer to the pitch required).

雲井獅子

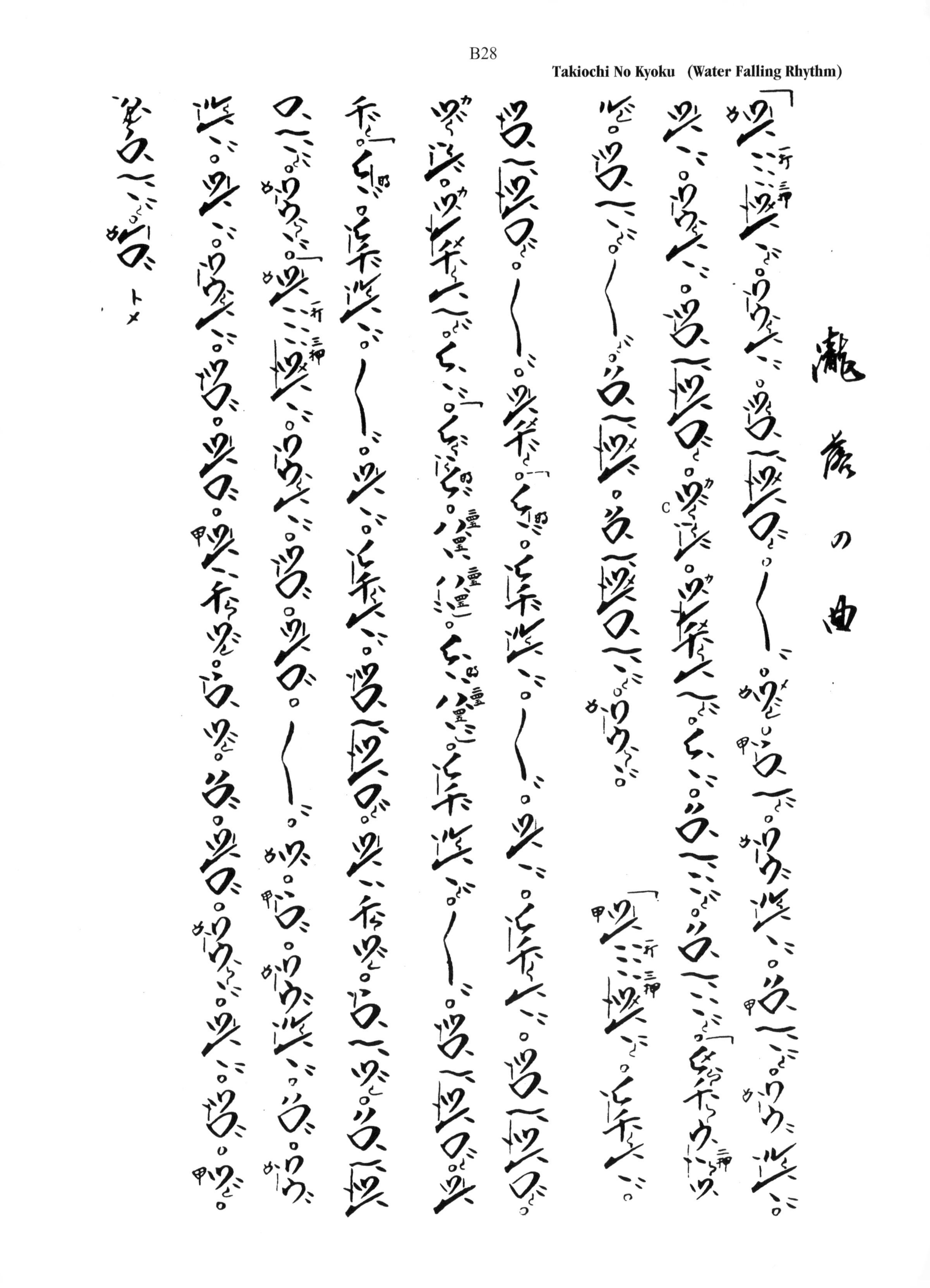

Takiochi No Kyoku (Water Falling Rhythm)

瀧落の曲

THE SHEET MUSIC

One inconvenience you'll find in playing the sheet music is that you must interrupt your playing while you turn to the next page of notation. To solve this problem try the following:

Xerox the sheet music. Then glue the first page of notation to the second, and these in turn to the next and so on which will result in a single sheet of notation 20 plus feet. You now fold this long sheet accordion fashion. This allows you to lay open to any length of notation and read and play continuously.

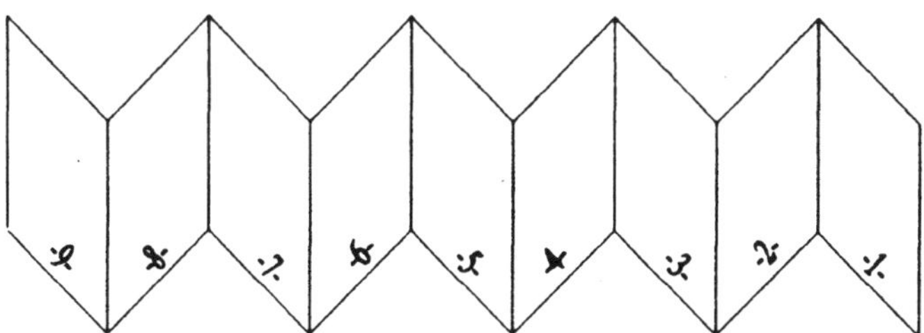

In order to have enough margin to glue on, you must position each page of notation on the copy machine so that you have a wider margin on the left side of each page. Doing a careful job will result in a much better finished product

SAN KYOKU PIECES, Page 1 - 14
It takes a while to find San Kyoku music really pleasurable to play or listen to. After much playing you gradually acquire an aesthetic appreciation for it. For most Westerners it is mostly just noise in the beginning. Even so, it is important to play it awhile because it trains technique and timing. Whether you want to play it long enough to develop a love for it is another matter. Actually the more skilled you become at Hon Kyoku the more you will be able to use the sensitivity learned through it in San Kyoku, which in turn will make it more satisfying to play.

If you have studied "Blowing Zen" conscientiously you should know all you need to for the San Kyoku in this booklet. If you are unsure of some parts, try to improvise. Here and there you will find double columns of notation. Play the right column and if you are playing with someone else, they play the left.

FOLK MUSIC, Page 46 - 54
The folk tunes are nice to play for a change. They have a more recognizable melody which can be more pleasing to western ears. Try playing them at different tempos using side to side sway timing or 1/2 timing.

HON KYOKU PIECES, Page 14 - 23
I have included PITCH GRAPHS for these pieces. The graph for each piece contains only the important sections or phrases of the piece which are new, i.e., the ones you have not encountered yet. Don't take these graphs too literally. They are meant to suggest ways to play: to give you an idea of what is possible. But really there are no hard and fast rules.

HON KYOKU PIECES, Page 24 - 45
After studying the pitch graphs and playing the music for the Hon Kyoku on pages 14 to 23, you should know enough to play these pieces, Once you have a firm understanding of what is involved in Hon Kyoku you can improvise with certainty.

Shika No Tone on page 28 is a duet. If you play alone, play both columns one after the other. Kumoi Jishi on page 29 is a duet for two or three players. The main melody is found on the central column. The right hand column is for the 2nd player, and the left hand column is for a third player who plays a NI SHAKU (60.5 cm. long flute). To obtain the highest benefit and pleasure from Hon Kyoku it is important to keep in mind the Taoist principle of 'actionless action'.

PITCH GRAPHS FOR HON KYOKU

(see top of next page)

(A). Title of the Hon Kyoku piece.

(B). The numbers indicate the column in which the following phrases are located, e.g., **2** would be the second column from the right.

(C). Two measure marks (o's) one below the other show that some notation has been left out between them. Take, for example, the pitch graphs of these 3 unconnected phrases from column 1 of Takiochi No Kyoku.

NOTE: The graph lines don't always coincide with the note graphed. Sometimes these lines are below the note and sometimes above.

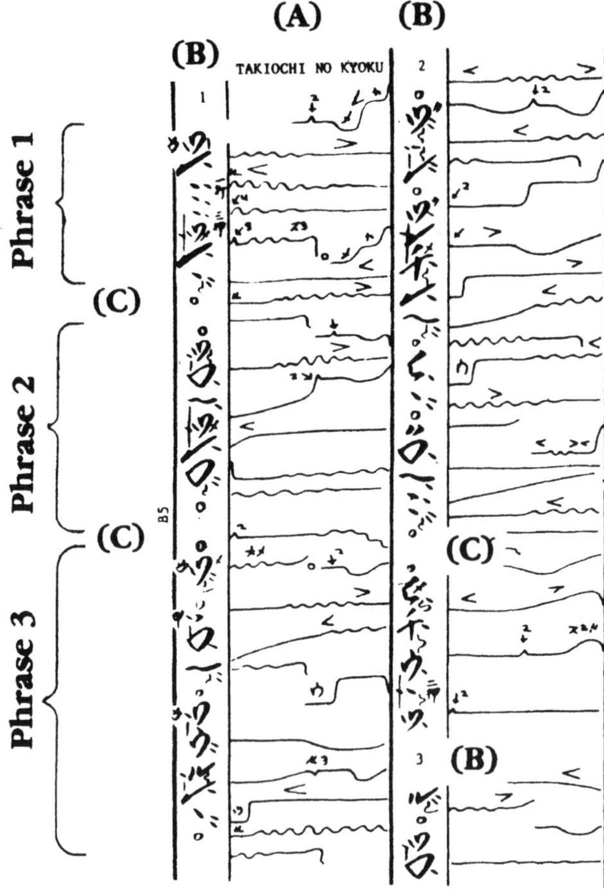

POINTS 1 to 58

Notation, pitch graph symbols and phrases.

NOTATION

1. This HA is played with all the fingers off all the holes, and a slight chin tilt. This is also indicated by a dot inside the HA ( )

2. This indicates that you can repeat the preceding phrase or section, starting at the bracket mark ( ). You need not do this in the beginning years of playing. It is optional.

3. This is similar to a measure mark. It is a good place to breathe if you have not done so earlier.

4. This grace note is called a 'Keshi'. It should be very subtle.

5. The pitch goes to a deep MERI (OH MERI) and then returns to the pitch you were playing.

6. The pitch goes more KARI (sharper) and then it returns, or it slides to the next note.

7. The pitch first goes to a deep MERI, then goes very KARI, and finally slides to the next note.

8. The pitch rises very gradually and slightly towards the end of the note.

9. You make a RU type articulation by striking hole #1 with the ring finger.

10. RU type articulation on hole #2.

11. RU type articulation on hole #3.

12. ATARI type articulation on hole #2.

13. ATARI type articulation on hole #3.

PITCH GRAPH SYMBOLS

14. ATARI (sometimes without ↓) usually with hole number shown.

15. RU (sometimes without ル) usually with hole number shown.

16. MERI

17. OH MERI

18. SURU with hole number usually shown.

19. Quick transition/finer movement.

20. Volume increases.

21. Volume decreases.

22. Tempo increases - play note shorter.

23. Tempo decreases - play note longer.

24. Slight pause for breath.

25. YURI

26. Relative pitch change for the note.

27. KO RO: Play HA but open and close holes #1 and #2 alternately, quickly and smoothly.

28. Slightly but rapidly shake flute toward and then away from lip.

29. Grace note TSU.

30. Grace note OU.

COMMON HON KYOKU PHRASES

The following, #31 to #58, are common phrases used in Hon Kyoku. See their notation on the next page (B4). A selection of these is recorded on the last track of the Blowing Zen CD.

31. Slide gradually from TSU to RE, then slide slightly to RO.

32. Shift abruptly from TSU MERI to TSU and then to RE.

33. Shift from (TSU) MERI to OH MERI, then do an ATARI of RO as you abruptly shift to RO.

34,35. End each RO in RO MERI - two beats for #34 and one beat for #35.

36. TSU is played KARI for the first beat. Then it returns to the usual MERI. It returns to KARI with an articulation on the upbeat. Then it returns to MERI before going to RE.

37. When HI is MERI, CHI is usually KARI.

Squiggly lines that bend left represent MERI shifts. Those that bend right represent KARI shifts. Here it bends both ways - first left into MERI and then right into KARI.

38. When HI is KARI, CHI is usually MERI. CHI is usually MERI in Hon Kyoku even when not indicated. Playing what sounds right works fine.

39. The squiggly line shows that OU bends up to KARI before the ATARI. Play OH KARI by extending your finger off holes #1 and #3, but not off the flute. Also extend the chin out to maximize the KARI. Then shift abruptly back to MERI on the ATARI.

40. The volume of HA diminishes almost to silence just before an abrupt shift to RO.

41. HA goes from MERI to KARI, then after a RU tap on hole #2, goes back to MERI, then back to KARI again.

42. Notice the small KARI symbol placed inside the HA. HA rises abruptly from MERI to KARI just before the right beat mark.

43. Listen to the grace note OU, then HI, then HI MERI, then HI with articulation, then HI MERI again followed by a trill to HI GO.

44. Listen to the volume changes and where the breath is taken.

45. HI GO ATARI's shift to HI ATARI's.

46. Slightly but rapidly shake the flute towards and then away from the lip.

47. Like #46, but shake at the end of OU, as shown by the double line.

48. You can use this, MURA IKI, on most notes. The blast of air and sound occurs on the full KARI of the note. Then it lowers to MERI with a little YURI.

49. The first HA goes slightly KARI before it shifts to high octave. Also notice the increase in tempo.

50. This begins with a low octave grace note OU. Notice the increasing tempo.

51. Play this, KO RO, by playing HA, opening and closing holes #1 and #2 alternately, quickly and smoothly. Notice the grace note HA before OU.

52. This is a KO RO of HA GO and HI MERI. Play HA GO and HI MERI as usual, but open and close holes #1 and #2 alternately like #51. Slide off hole #2 when going to HI MERI.

53. Thumb makes RU type articulation on the back hole.

54. Thumb brushes counter clockwise across hole #5

55. Thumb brushes clockwise across hole #5.

56. The first two OSHI YURIs end in MERI. The remainder are never overly MERI, and end in KARI.

57. Each repeat mark means to repeat CHI and RU. Then play a series of RUs in low octave.

58. Most Hon Kyoku end with this. When playing RE, leave hole #1 closed.

Hon Kyoku symbols and notation.

ロ	RO
ツ	TSU
レ	RE
ウ	OU
チ	CHI
リ	RI
ハ	HA
(1)	HA (open holes)
ヒ	HI
	HI GO
	RYO
甲	KAN
	ATARI + 2 beat marks
	NAYASHI
ル	RU
	YURI
カ	KARI
メ	MERI
(2)	REPEAT PRECEDING PHRASE (optional)
(3)	MEASURE 'marks'

(4) (5) (6) (7) (8) (9) (10) (11) (12) (13)

Pitch graph symbols.

(14) (15) (16) (17) (18) (19) (20) < (21) > (22) (23) (24) (25) (26) (27) (28) (29) (30)

Examples of some common phrases used in Hon Kyoku which are recorded on Track 27.

(31) (32) (33) (34) (35) (36) (37) (38) (39) (40) (41) (42) (43) (44) (45) (46) (47) (48) (49) (50) (51) (52) (53) (54) (55) (56) (57) (58)

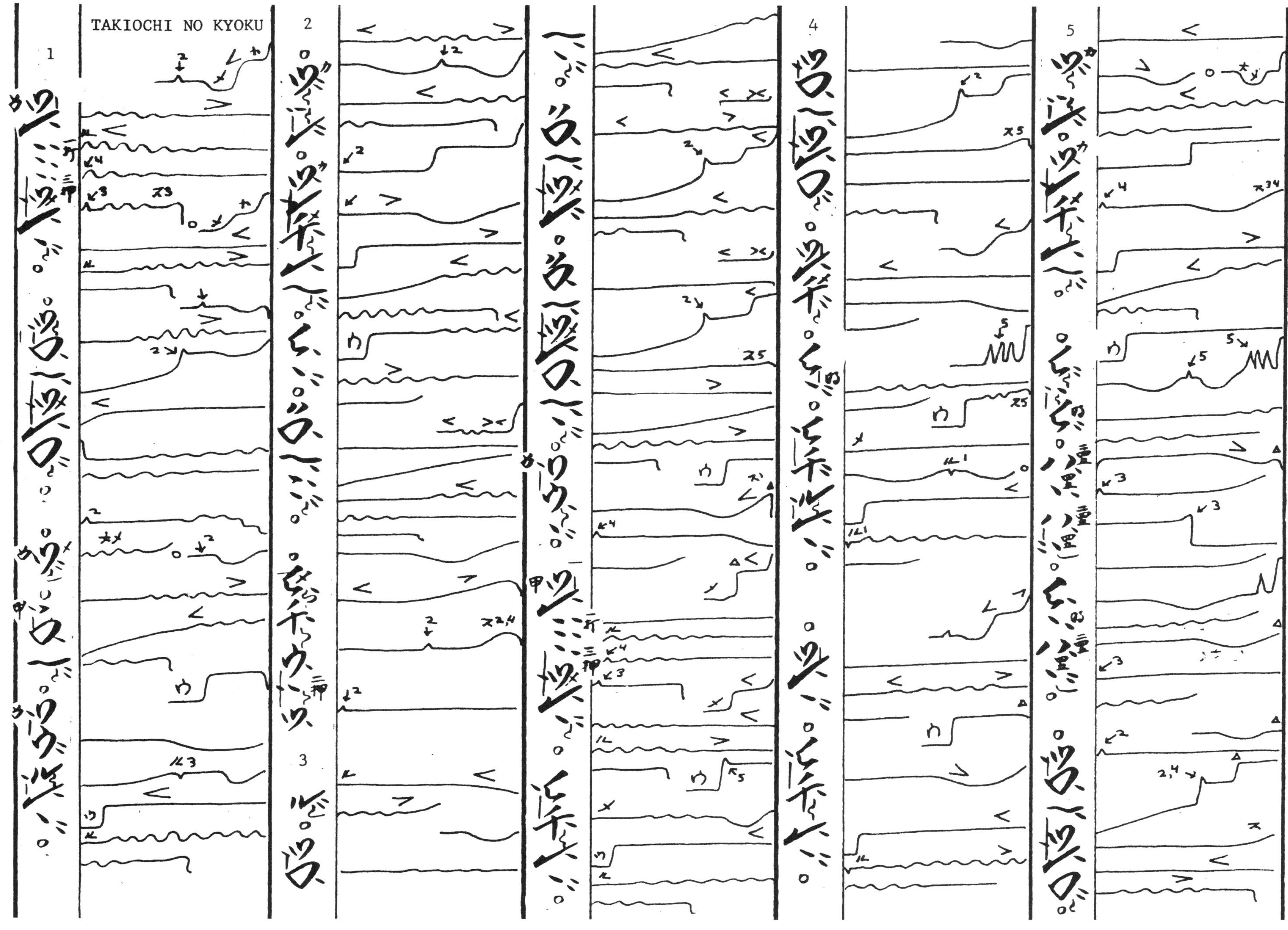
TAKIOCHI NO KYOKU
1
2
3
4
5

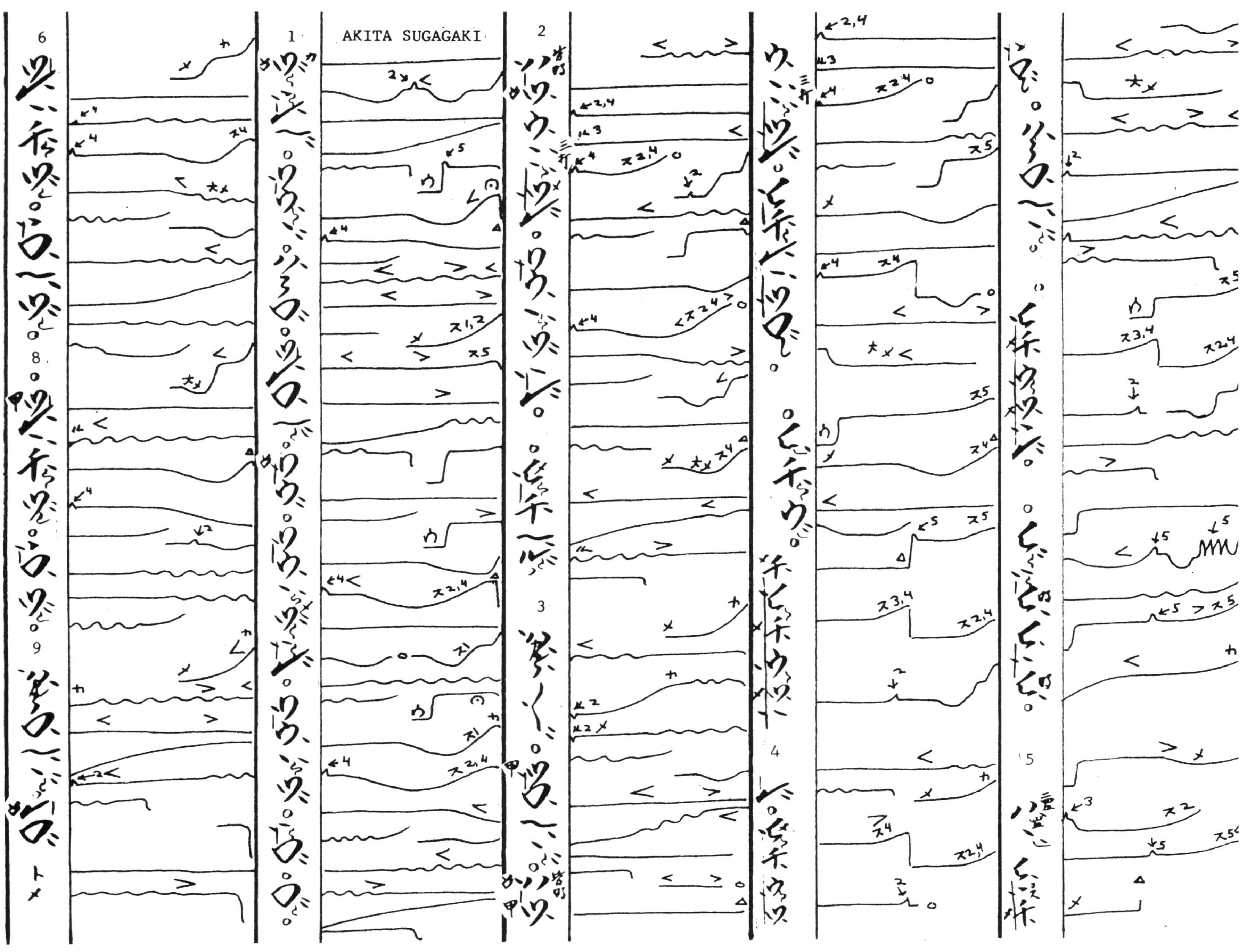
AKITA SUGAGAKI

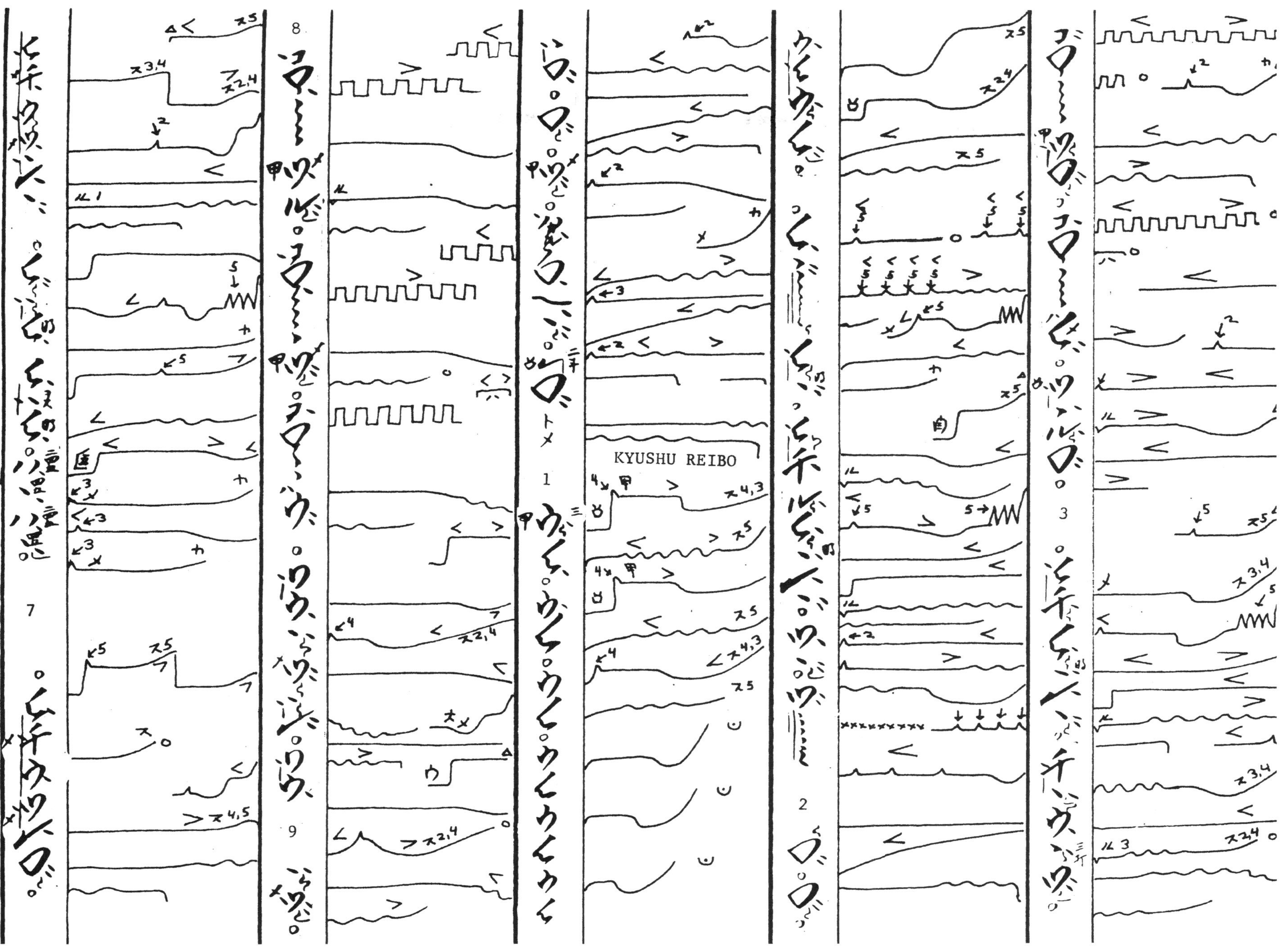
KYUSHU REIBO

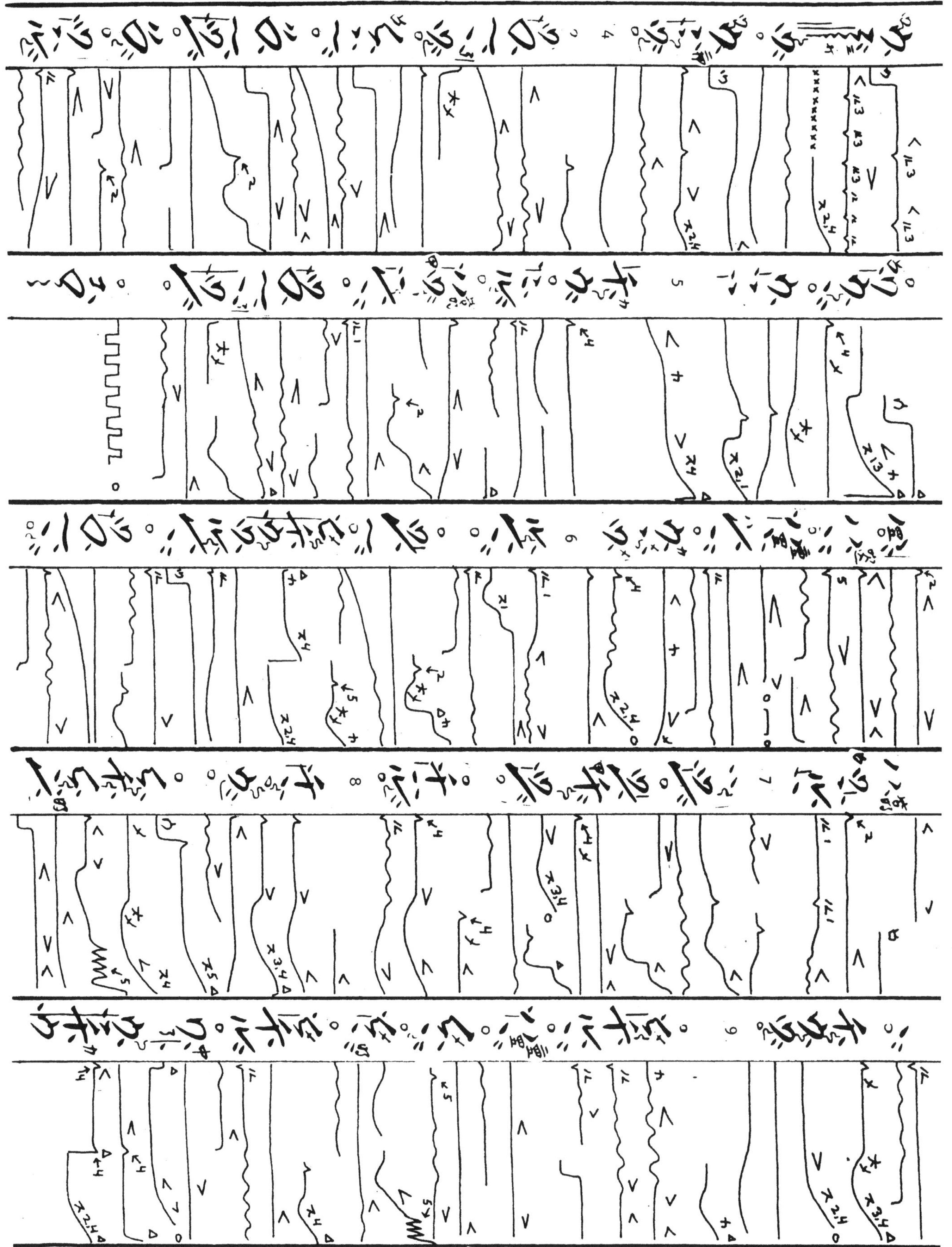

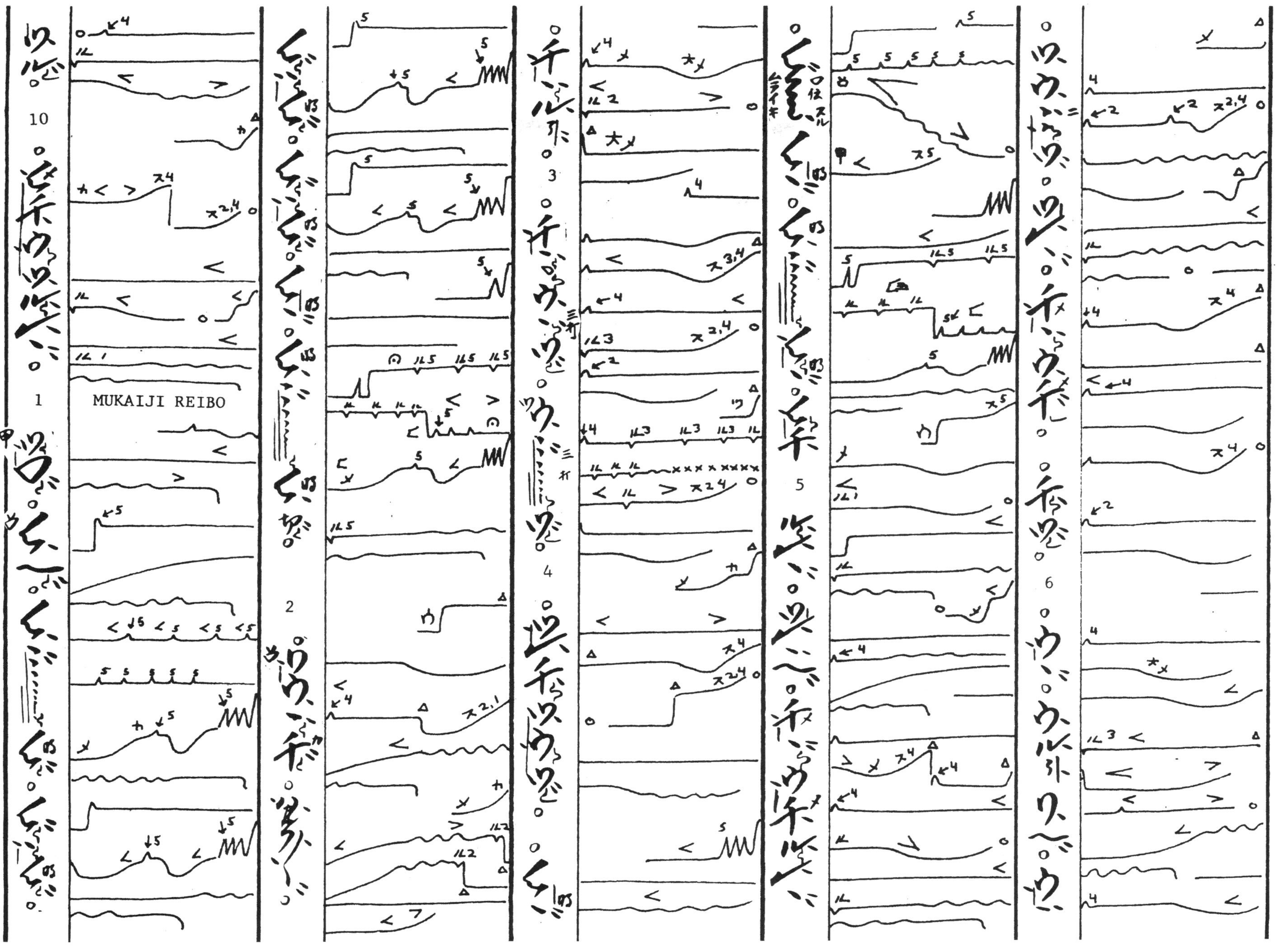
MUKAIJI REIBO

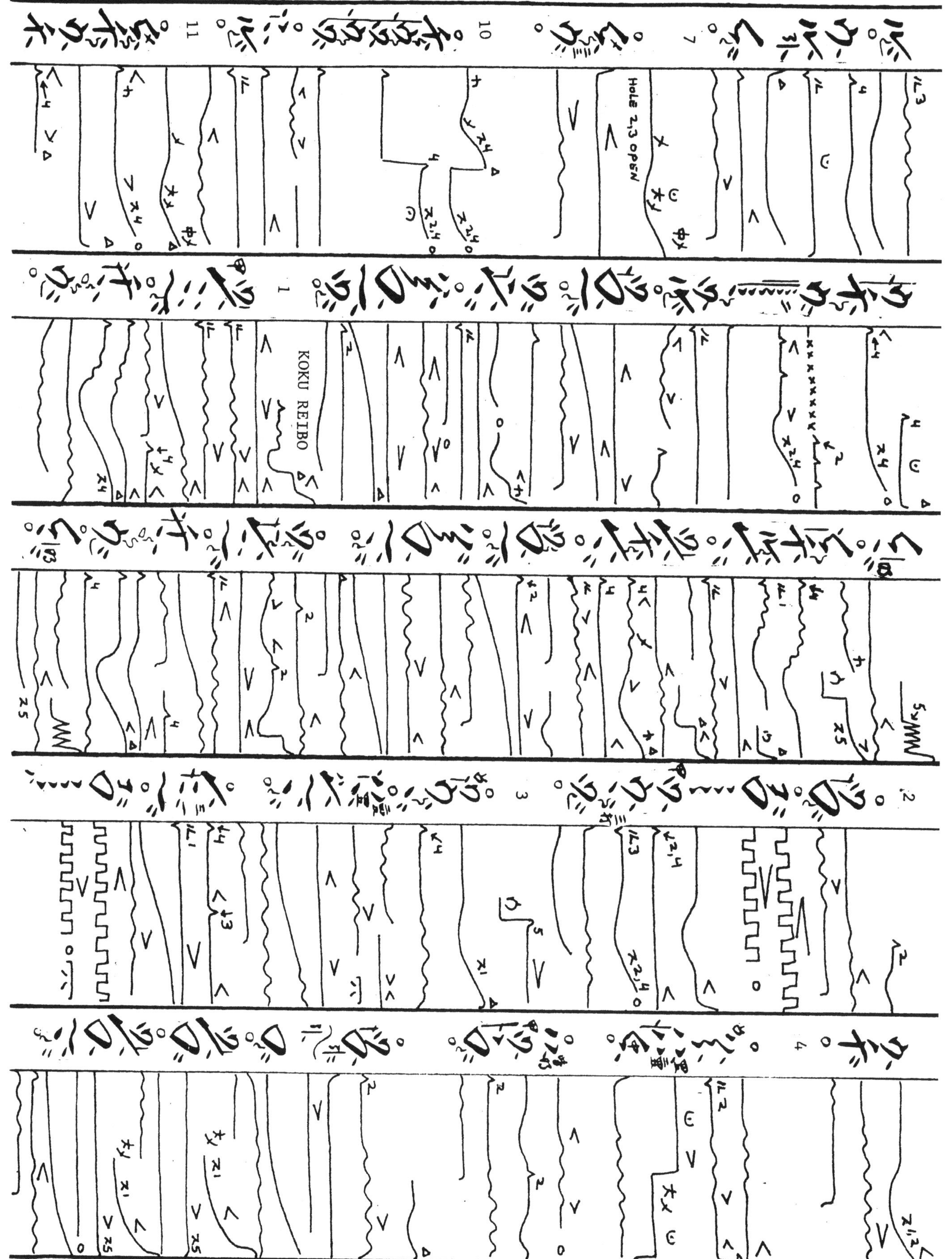

B11

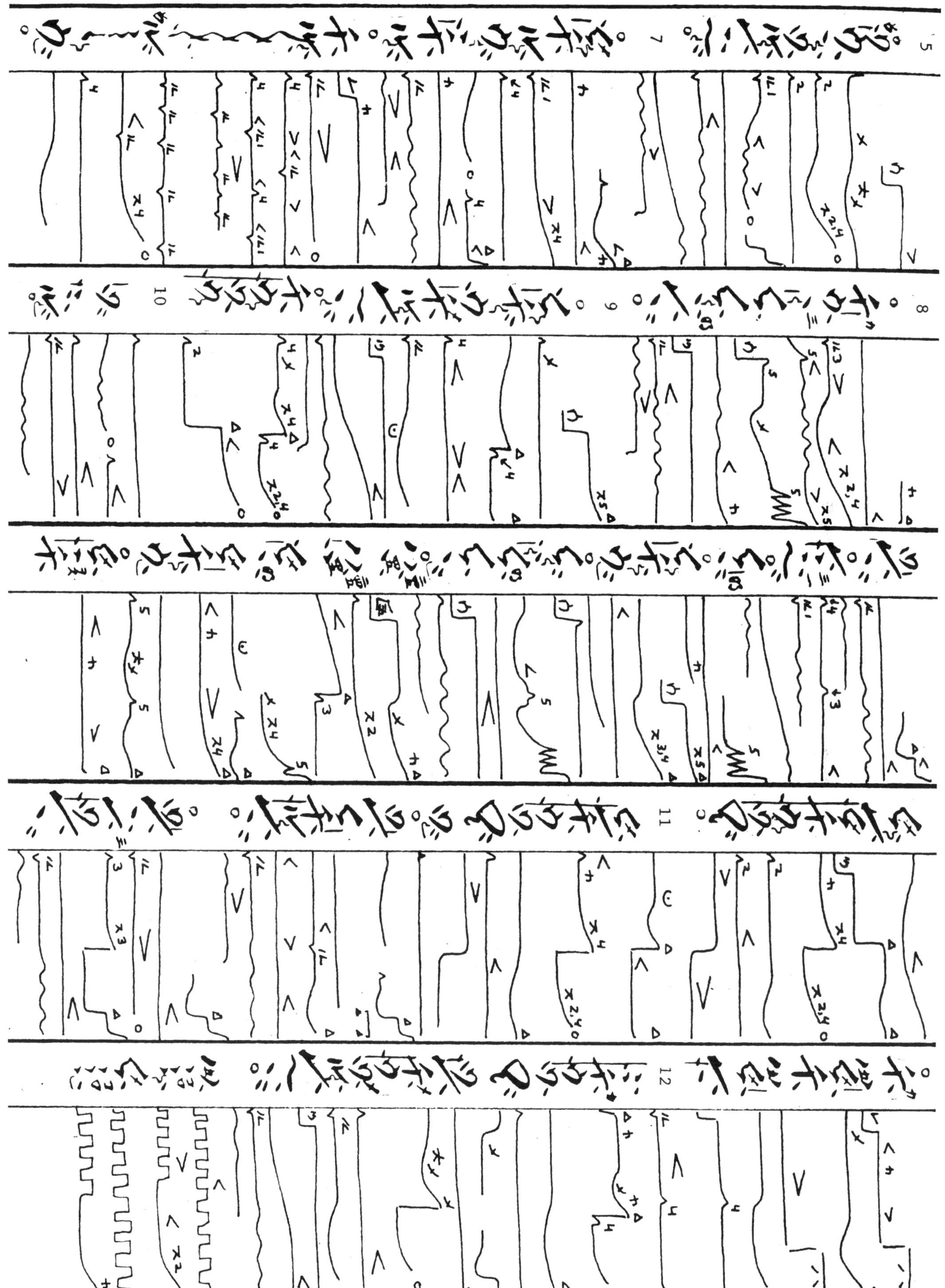

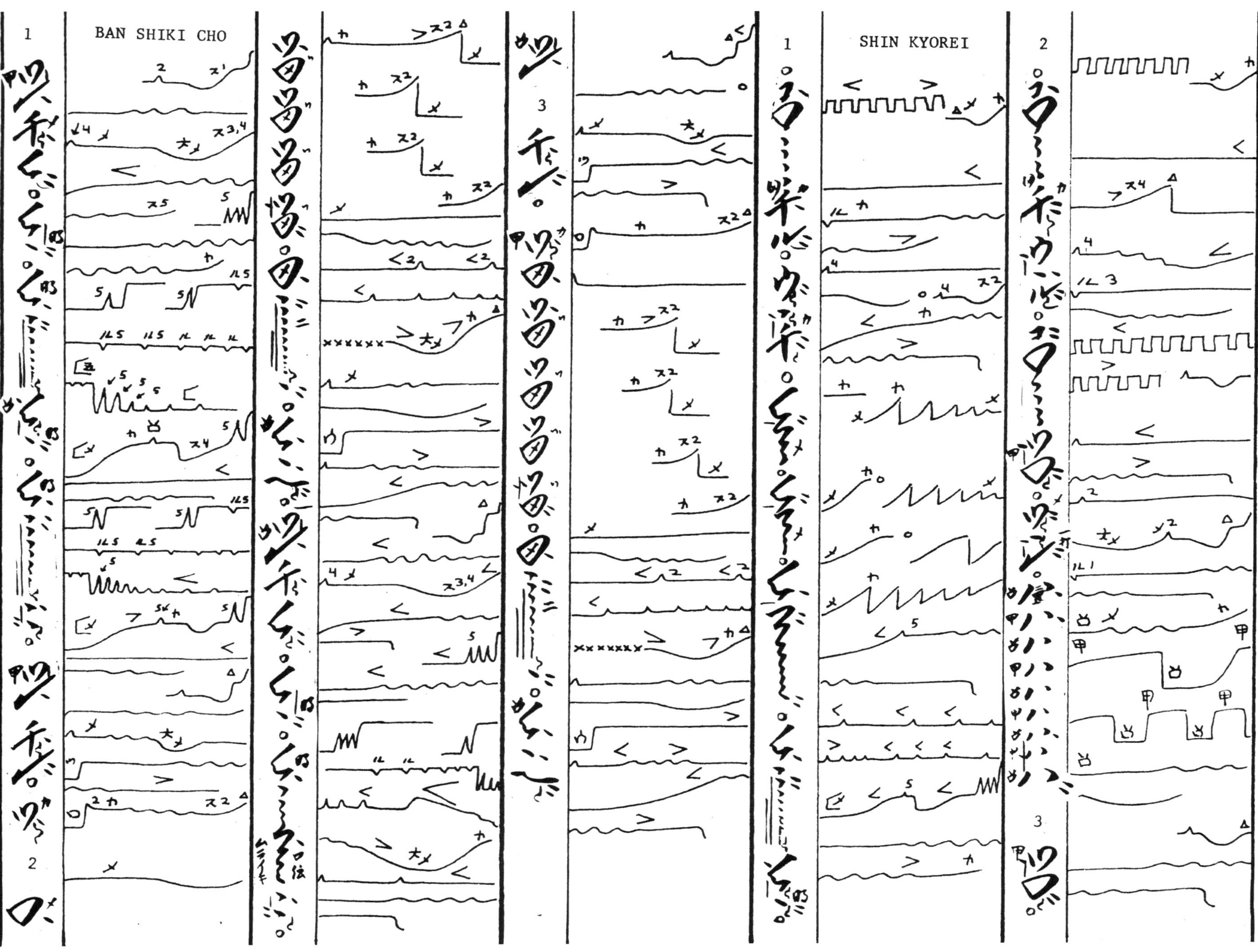
BAN SHIKI CHO
SHIN KYOREI

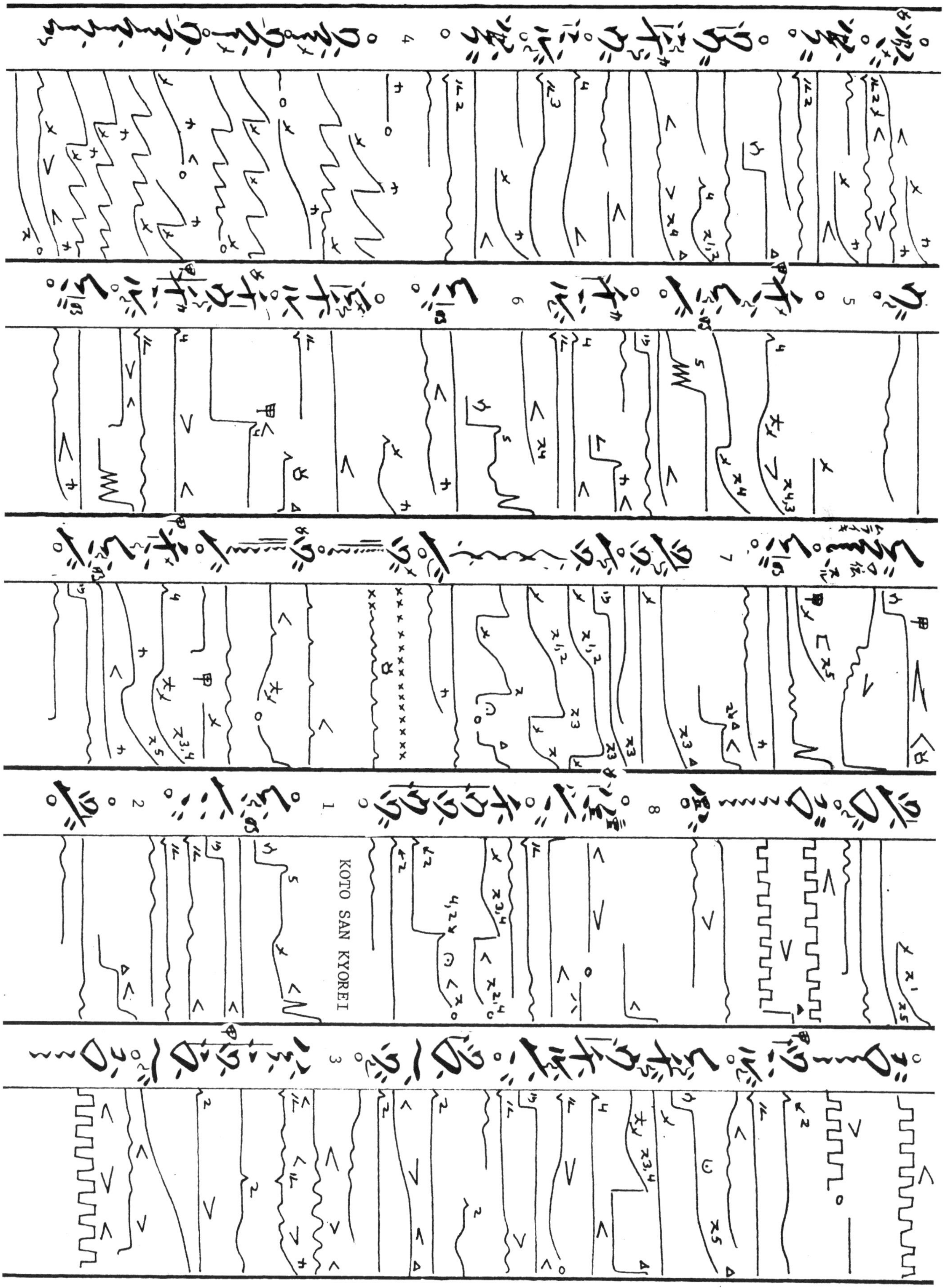

KOTO SAN KYOREI

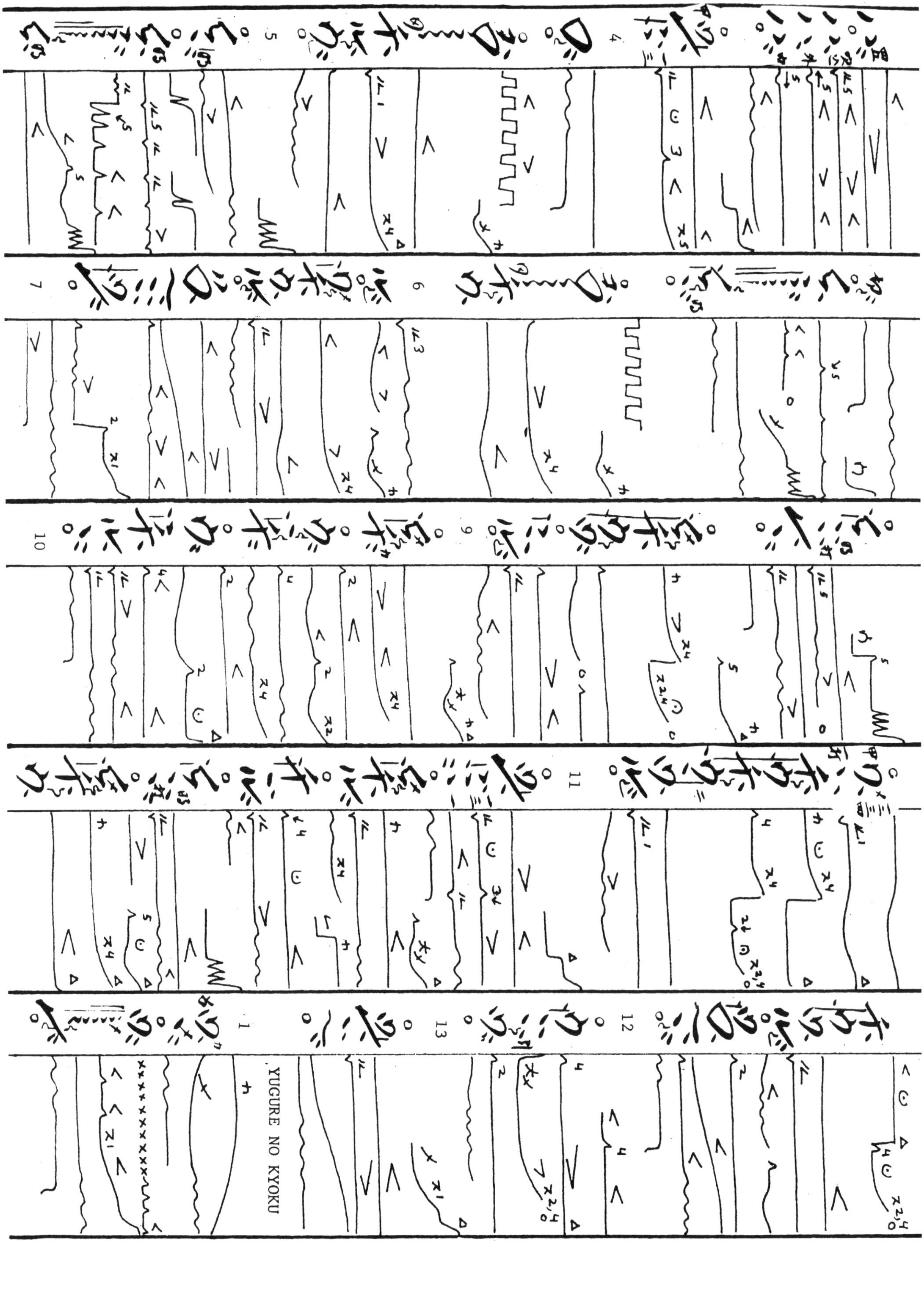

YUGURE NO KYOKU

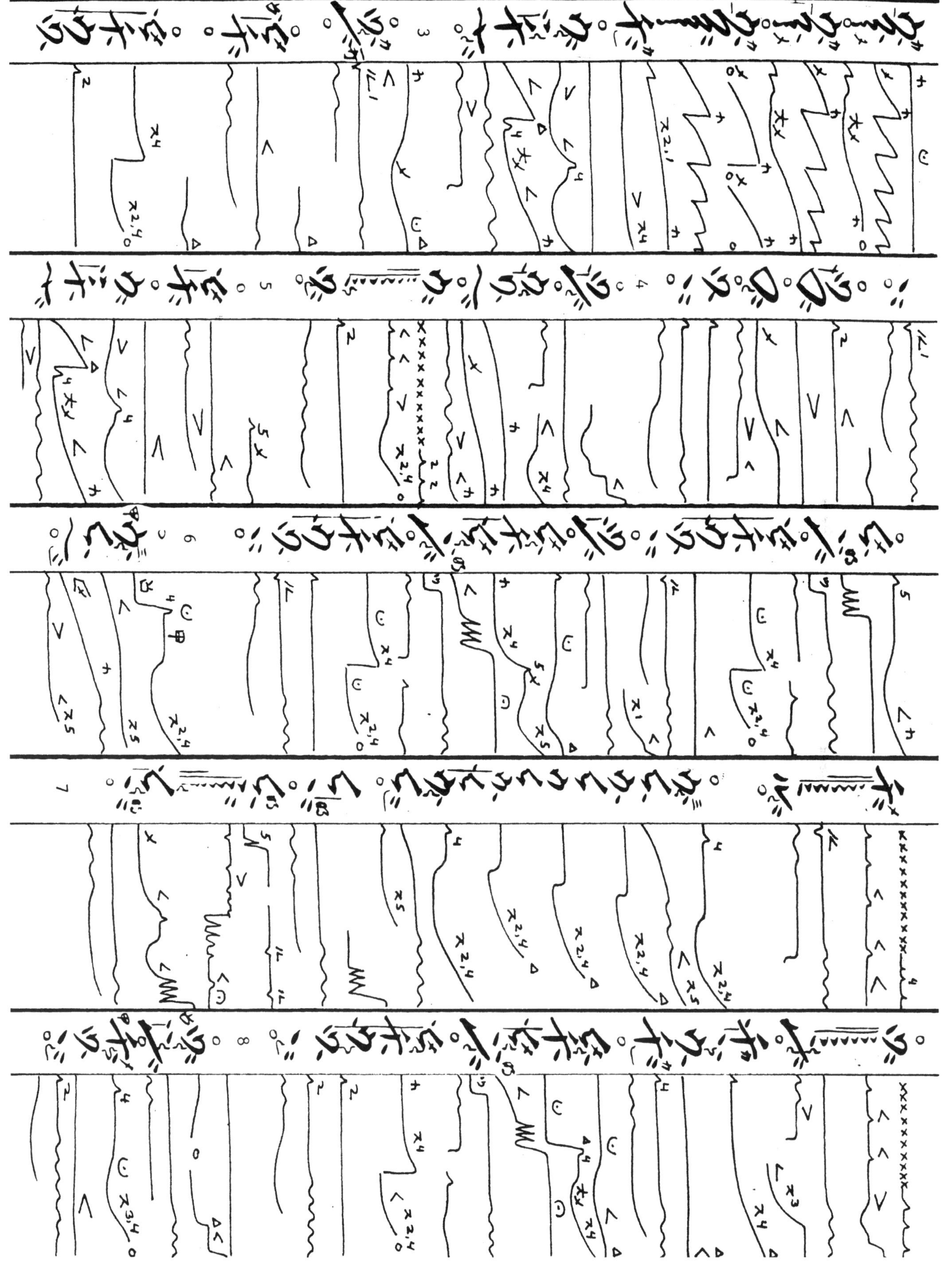

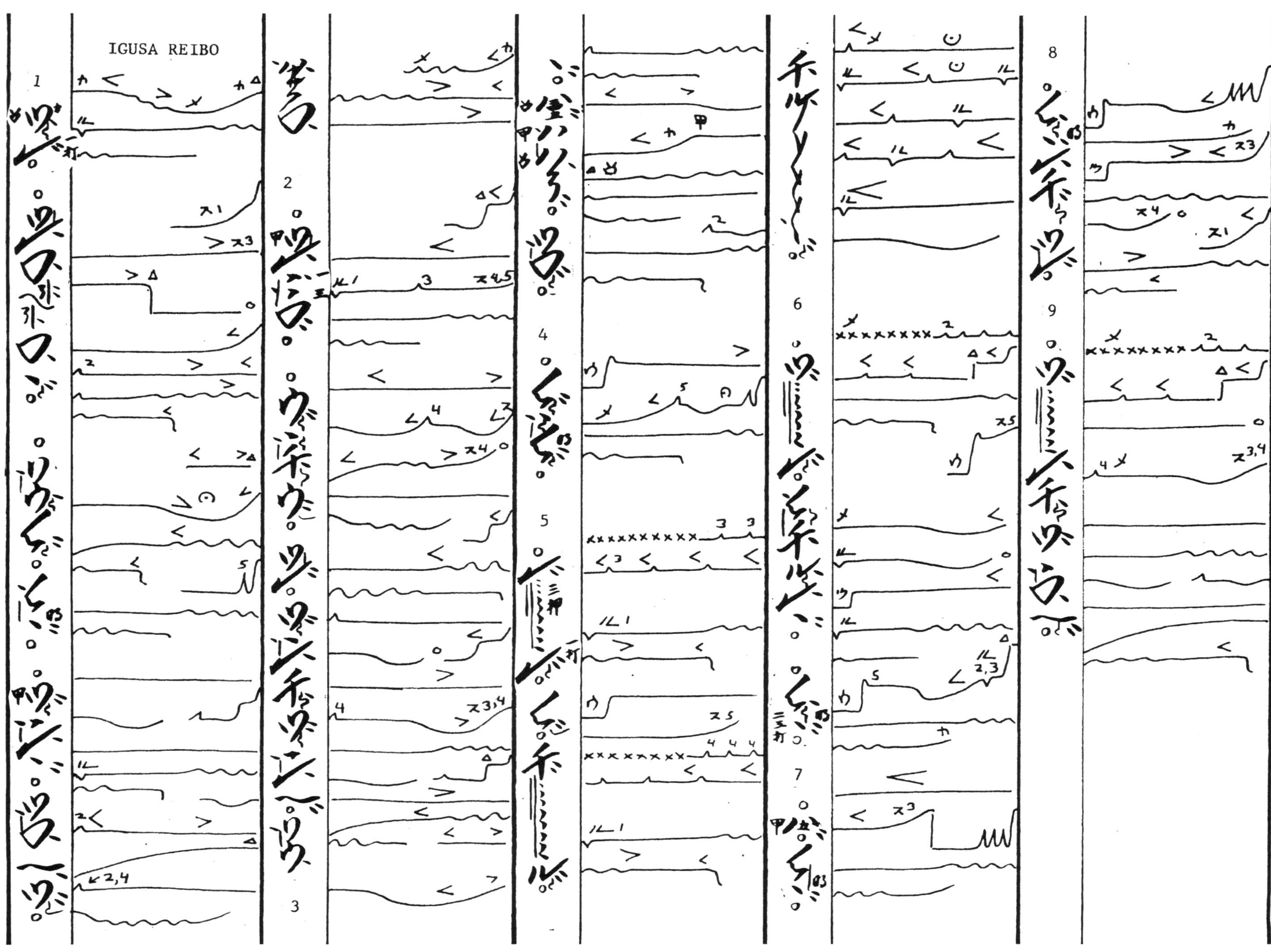
IGUSA REIBO

BLOWING ZEN II

This section carries on where "Blowing Zen" left off. It contains musical scores for additional Hon Kyoku, San Kyoku and Japanese folk music.

Go on line!

Downloads MP3 sound files of many of the Hon Kyoku in this book, bonus materials, and other information at: Centertao.org/blowingzen Also, be sure to revisit the site once in awhile as we will continue to place additional resources there.

Problems?

If you have problems with any of this material, and conscientious attempts to solve them fail, please email me a Centertao.org or write. *Enclose a self-addressed stamped envelope* and send to: Center For Taoist Thought And Fellowship, 406 Lincoln St., Santa Cruz, CA. 95060

Copy the sheet music

Copy the music so you can read it while referring to the instructions. You can glue the edges of these copies into one long sheet, moving from right to left, and then fold it in an accordian fashion. This will allow you to play the long pieces without having to turn pages.

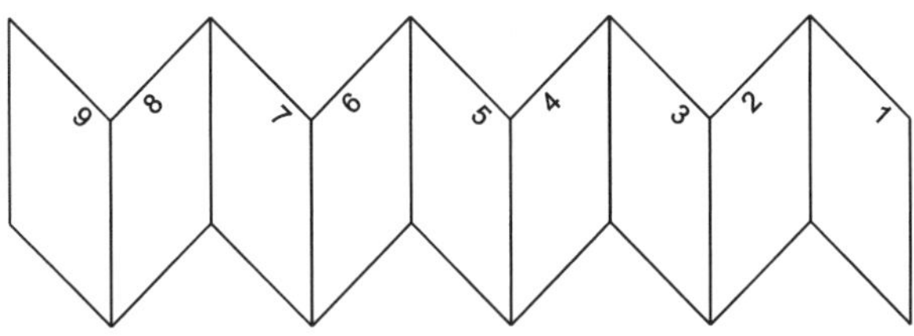

First Published as "Advanced Music Booklet" 1980
Second Revised Edition 1993
Third Edition 2005
Fourth Edition (inclusion into Blowing Zen) 2010, 2012

TABLE OF CONTENTS (Blowing Zen II)

SAN KYOKU MUSIC

Shin Taku Saku — New Long Life, 10 min. .... page 1
Tsu Mikusa — Harvesting Roadside Flowers, 15 min. .... page 3
Hachidan — Eight Steps, 11 min. .... page 7
Cha No Yu — Tea Ceremony, 12 min. .... page 9
Midare — Mixed Up Conversation, 12 min. .... page 11

HON KYOKU MUSIC

Takiochi No Kyoku — Water Falling Tune, 15 min. .... page 14
Akita Sugagaki — Akita Instrumental, 12 min. .... page 15
Kyushu Reibo — Kyushu Island, Bell Yearning, 24 min. .... page 16
Mukaiji Reibo — Foggy Sea, Bell Yearning, 26 min. .... page 17
Koku Reibo — Empty Sky, Bell Yearning, 28 min. .... page 18
Ban Shiki Cho — Foundation Melody, 5 min. .... page 19
Shin Kyorei — True Empty Spirit, 17 min. .... page 20
Koto San Kyorei — Koto Three Empty Spirit, 25 min. .... page 21
Yugure No Kyoku — Evening Twilight Tune, 16 min. .... page 22
Igusa Reibo — Field Of Rushes, Bell Yearning, 19 min. .... page 23
Sokaku Reibo — The Cranes Nest, Bell Yearning, 22 min. .... page 24
Sagariha No Kyoku — Hanging Leaves Tune, 8 min. .... page 27
Shika No Tone — Distant Mating Sound of Deer, 19 min. .... page 28
Kumoi Jishi — Cloud Well Lion, 7 min. (for 2 Shakuhachi + 1 Nishaku) .... page 29
(Note: Nishaku is a 65.5 cm. long flute - and plays the smaller thinner notation)
Kumoi Jishi (for 1 Shakuhachi) .... page 32
Sayama Sugagaki — Rebel Mountain Instrumental, 15 min. .... page 33
Tsuki No Kyoku — Moon's Tune, 13 min. .... page 34
Meguro Jishi — Meguro (eye black) Lions, 24 min. .... page 34
Ginryu Koku — Dragon Cry, Empty Sky, 40 min. .... page 36
Shimotsuke Kyoku — Retreating From the World Tune, 11 min. .... page 38
Koto Ji No Kyoku — Koto Upright Tune, 5 min. .... page 38
Ashi No Shirabe — Reed's Melody, 5 min. .... page 39
San Ya Sugagaki — Three Bitter Emotions Instrumental, 11 min. .... page 39
Hoshosu — Phoenix Fledgling, 29 min. .... page 40
Akebono Cho — Daybreak Melody 10 min. .... page 41
(Note: You can use a 1.3 to play this in a duet with Hi Fu Mi played with a 1.8)
Akebono Sugagaki — Daybreak Instrumental, 28 min. .... page 42
Namima Reibo — Within the Wave, Bell Yearning, 36 min. .... page 44

FOLK MUSIC

A selection of several different styles of Japanese folk music. .... page 46

INSTRUCTIONS

Symbols, techniques and pitch graphs for Hon Kyoku pieces on page 14 -23 .... pages B1-B16

Note: There are two sets of "**B**" pages, one for each section of this Extended Edition. **B1** through **B28** go with the front section of this book. **B1** through **B16** go with this Blowing Zen II section.

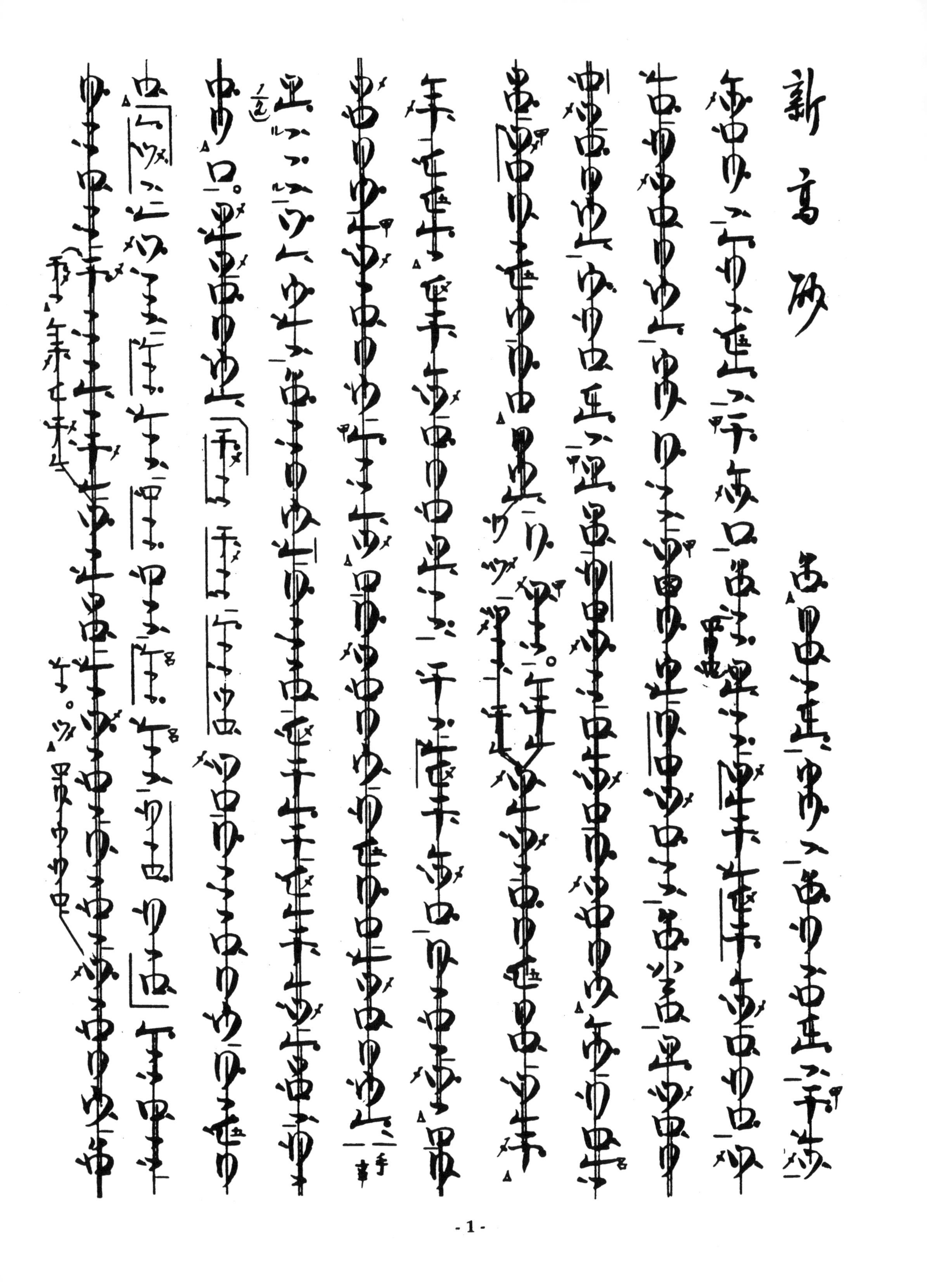

新高砂

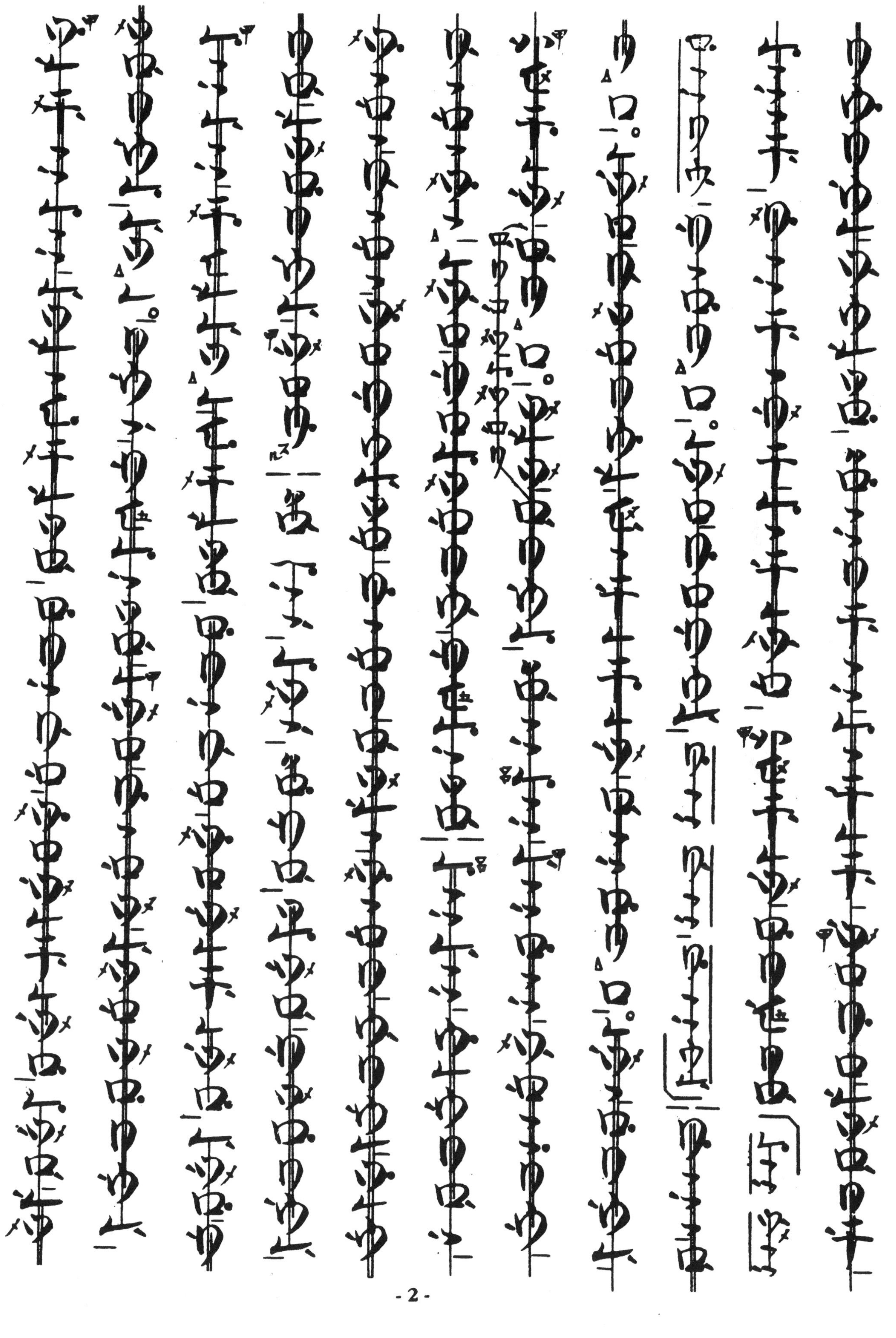

摘草

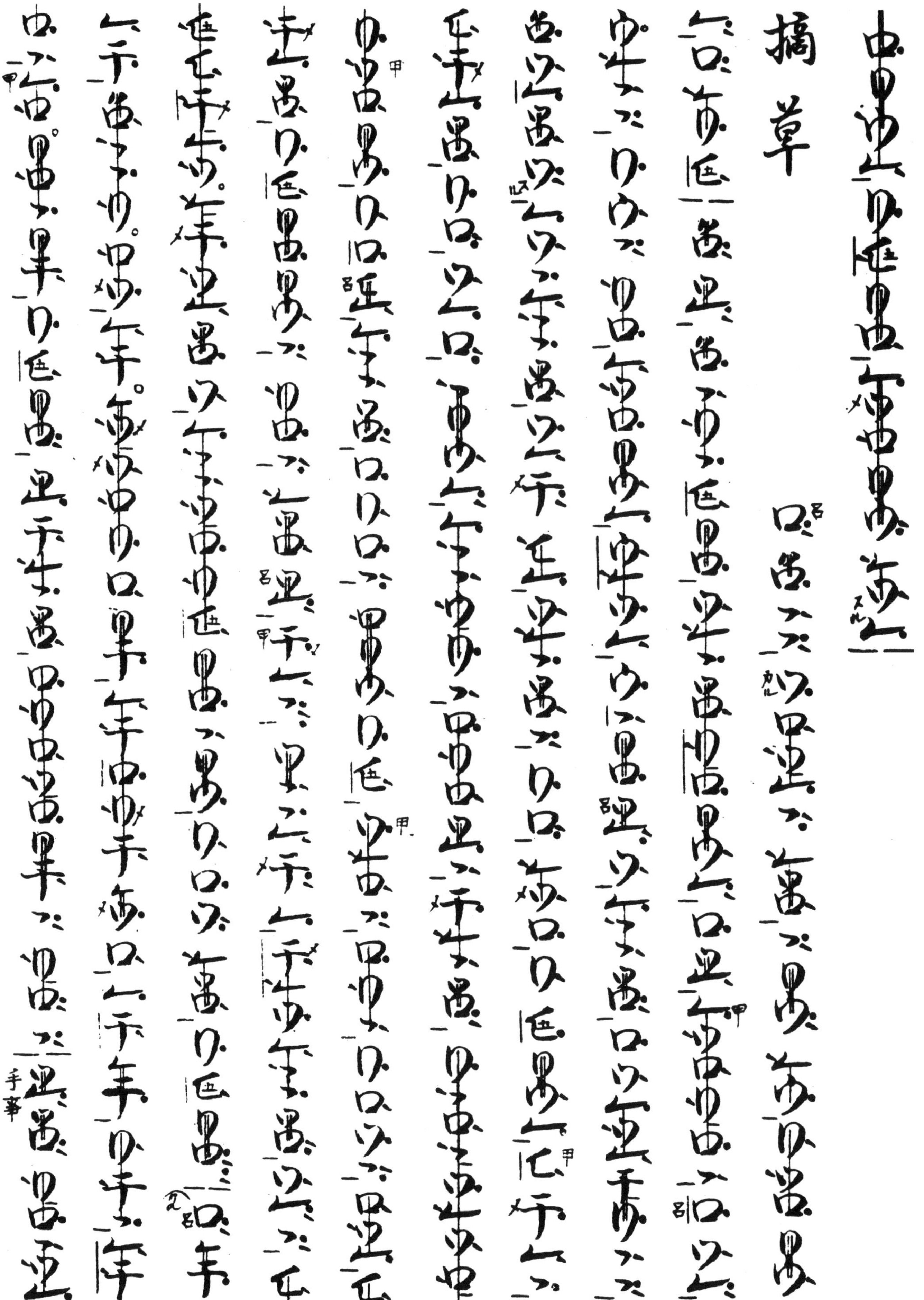

呂

甲

呂

甲

呂

甲

呂

甲

手事

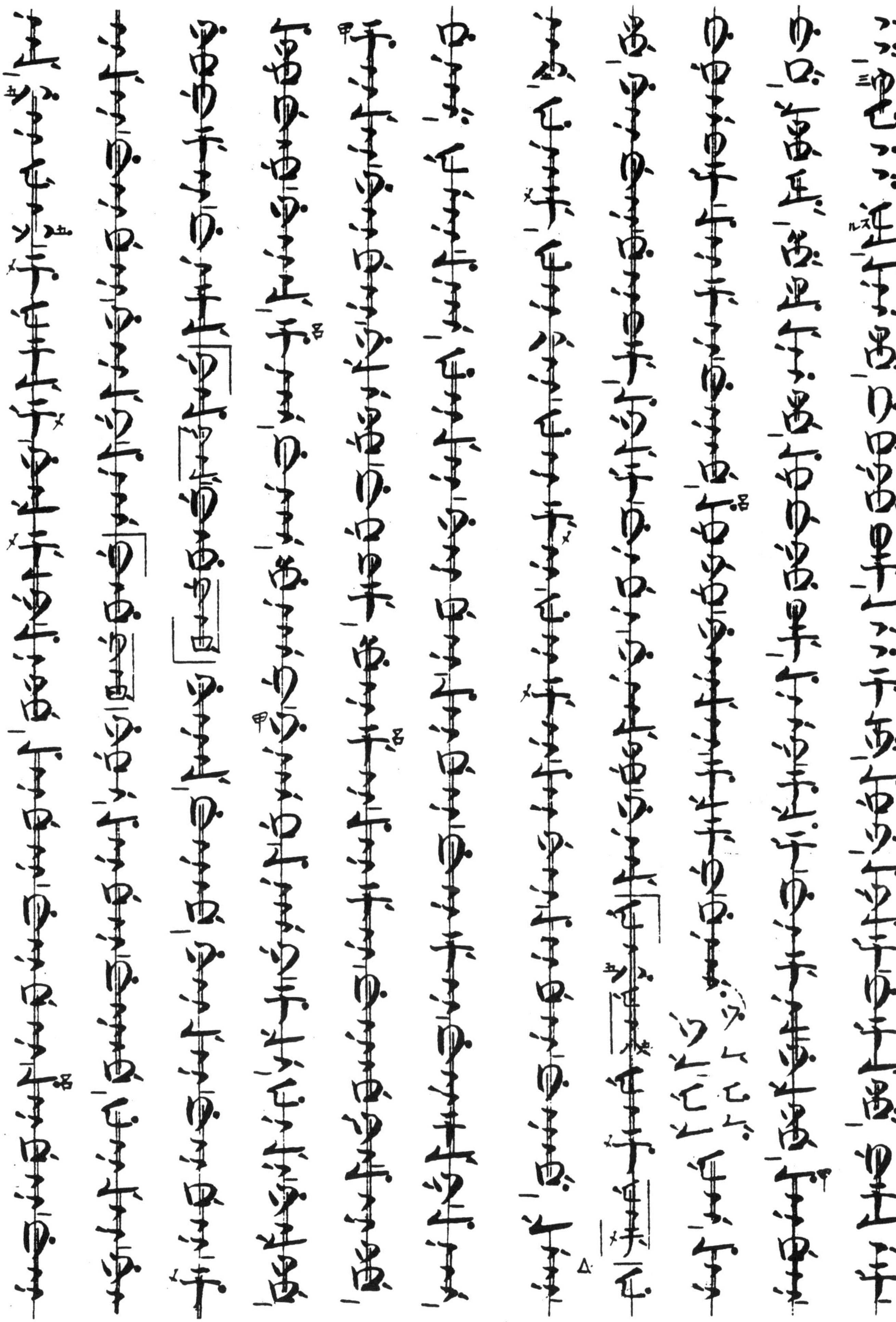

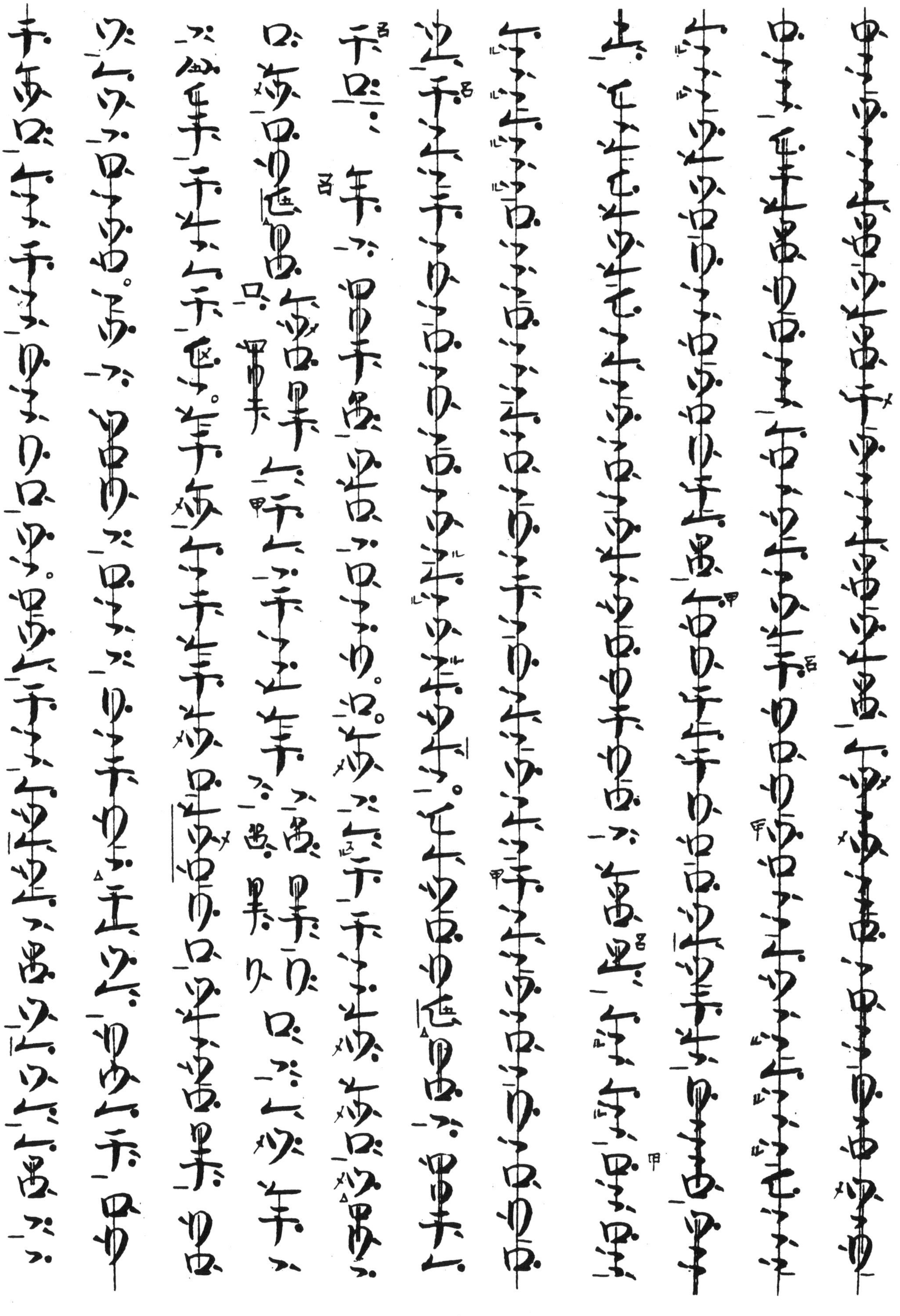

八段之調

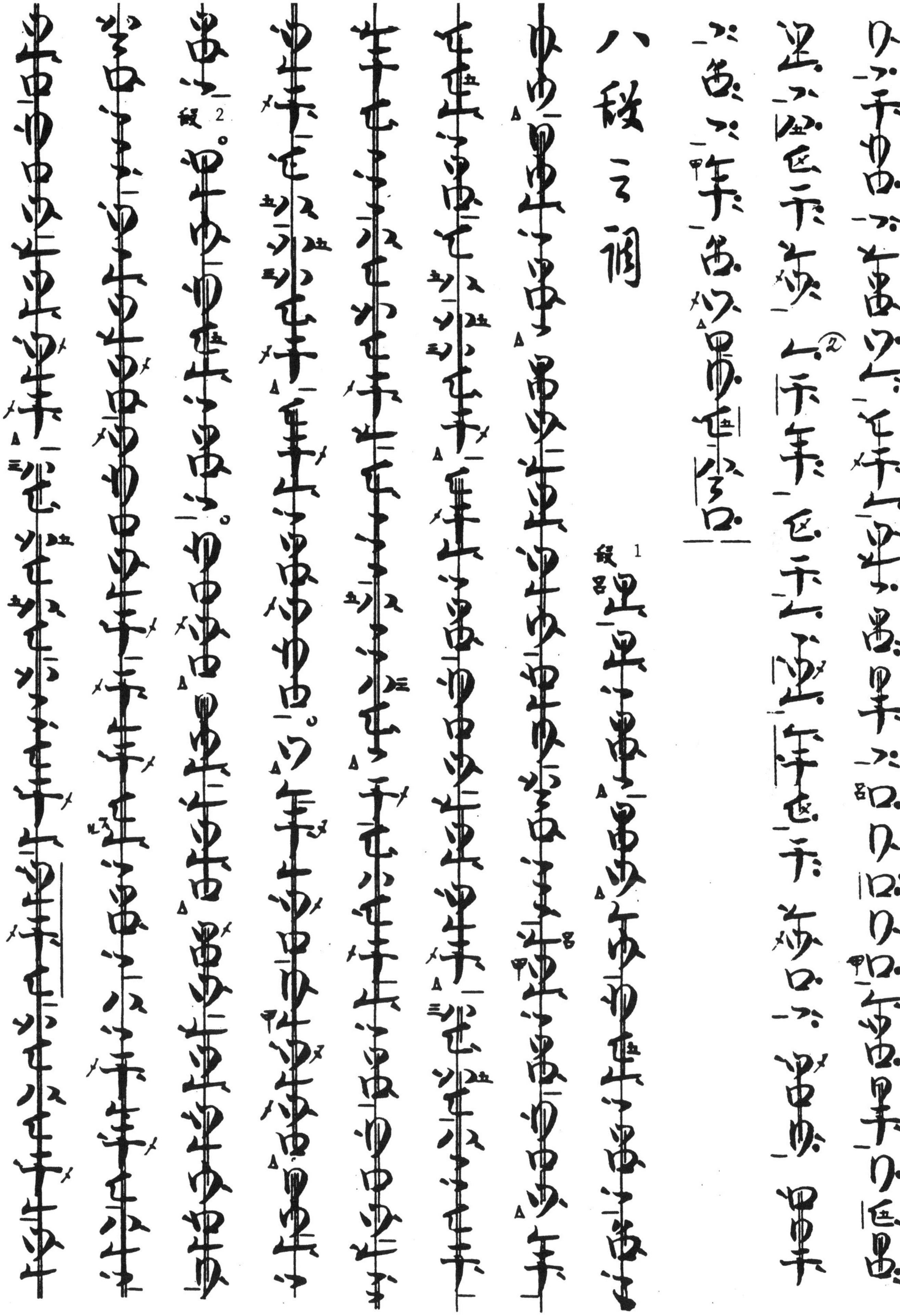

段 1

段 2

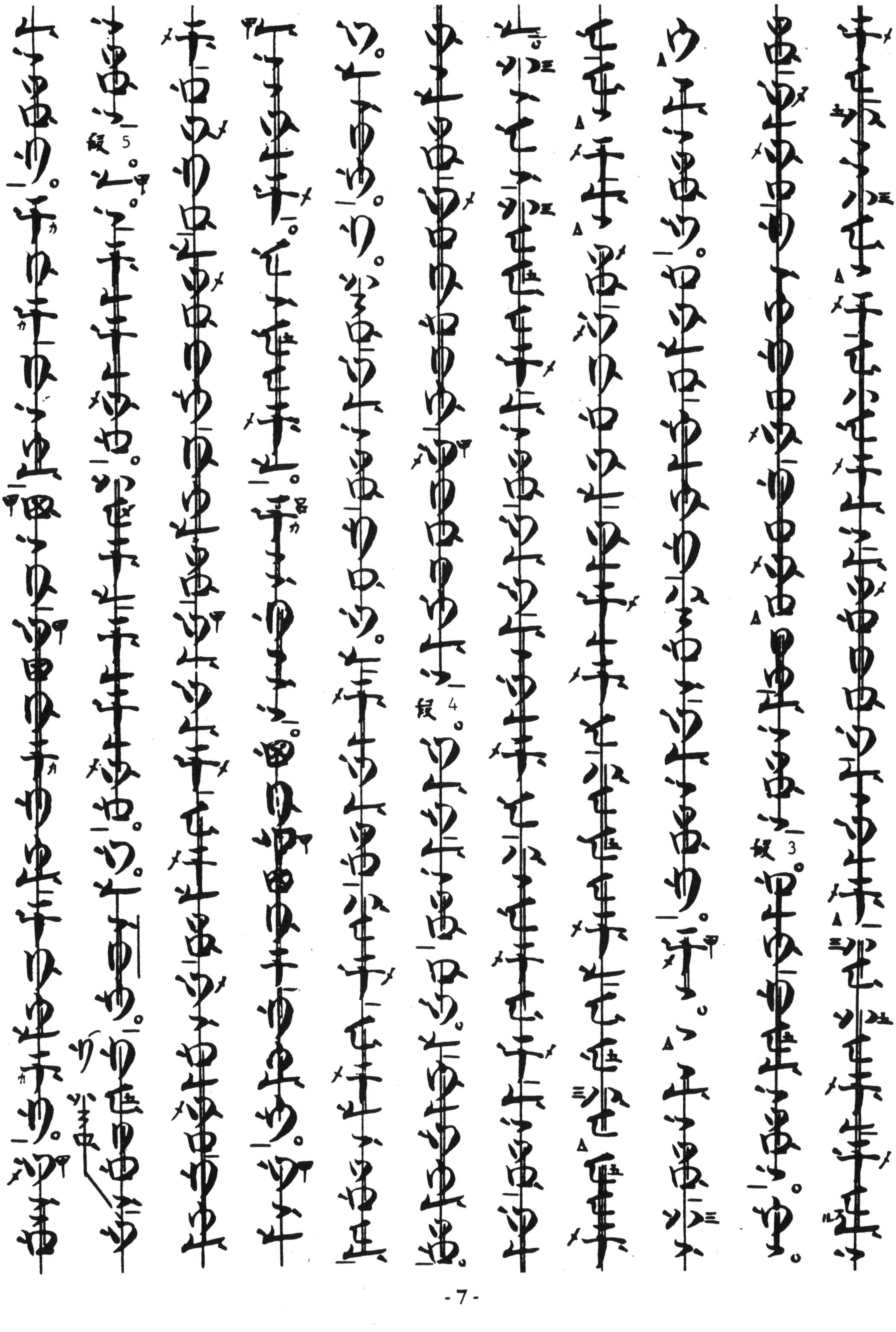

段 3

段 4

段 5

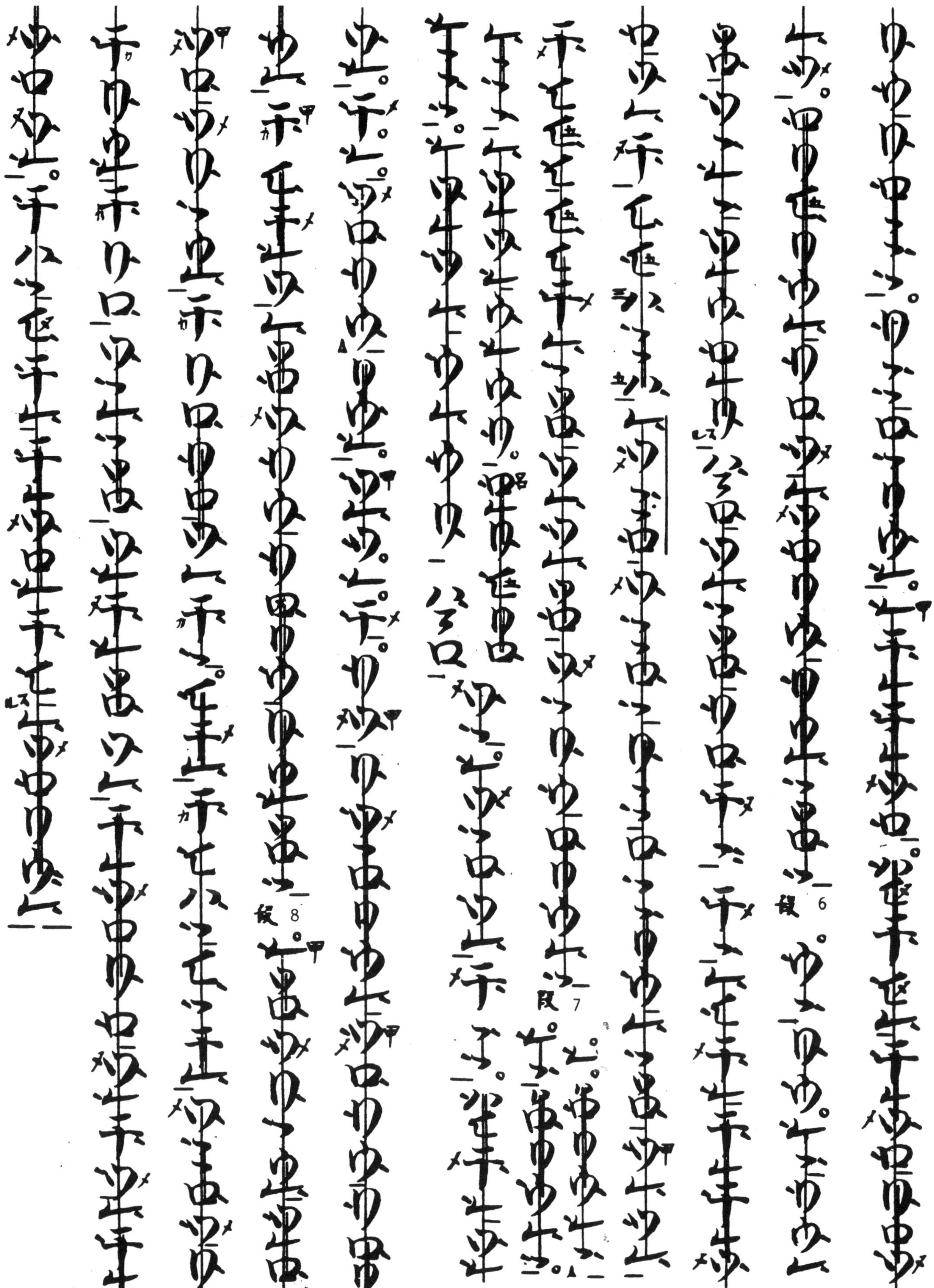

段 6

段 7

段 8

茶湯書院

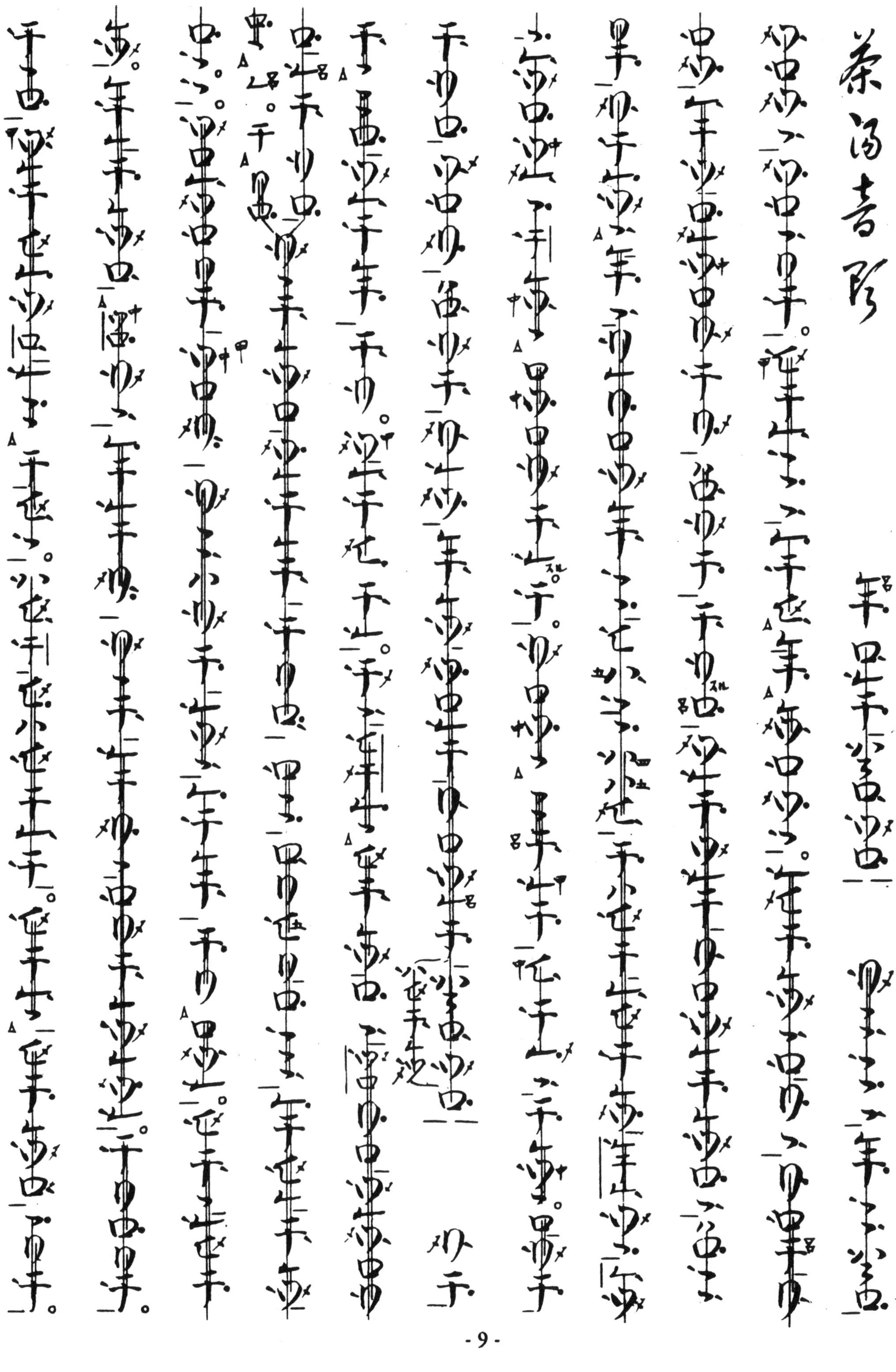

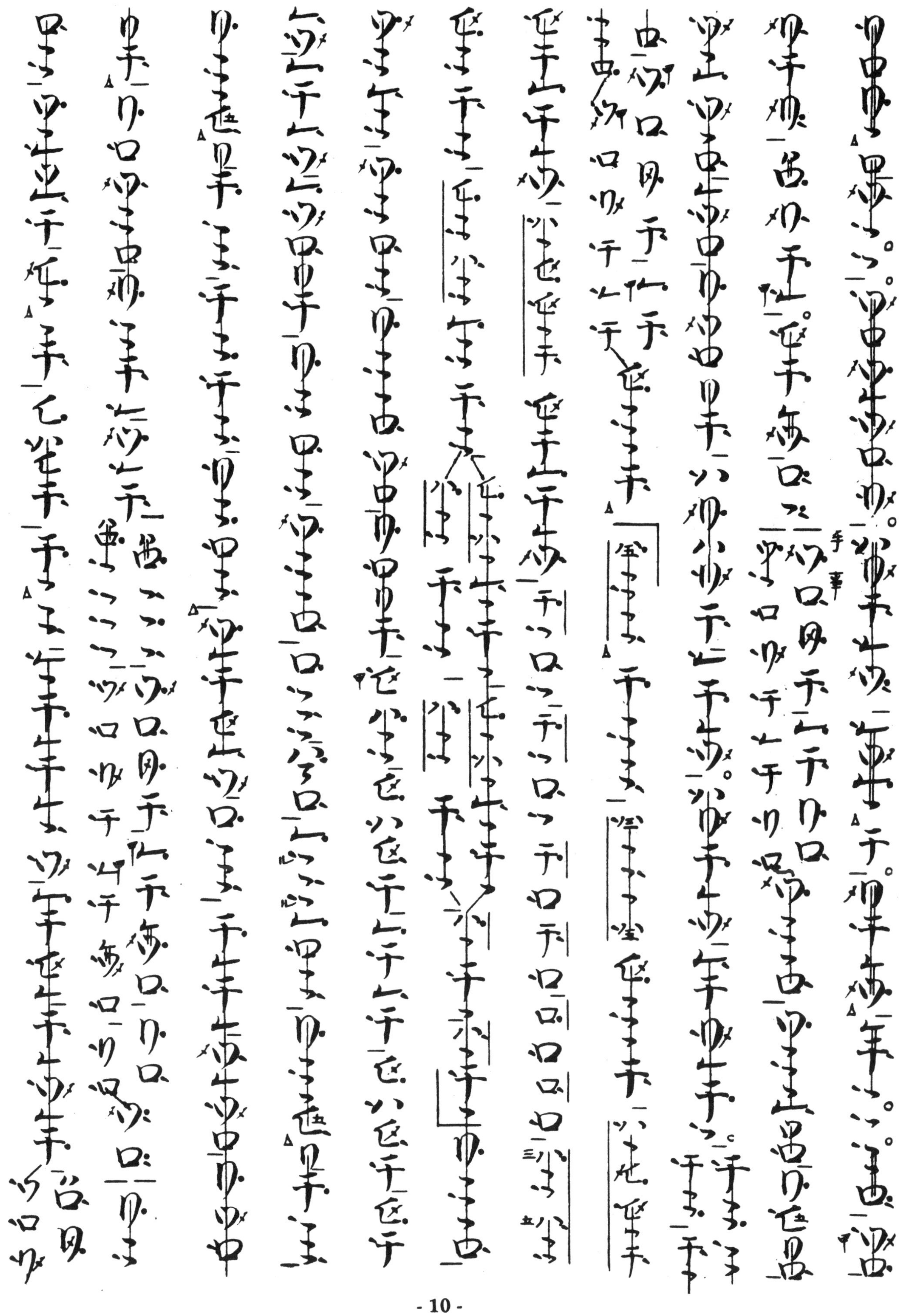

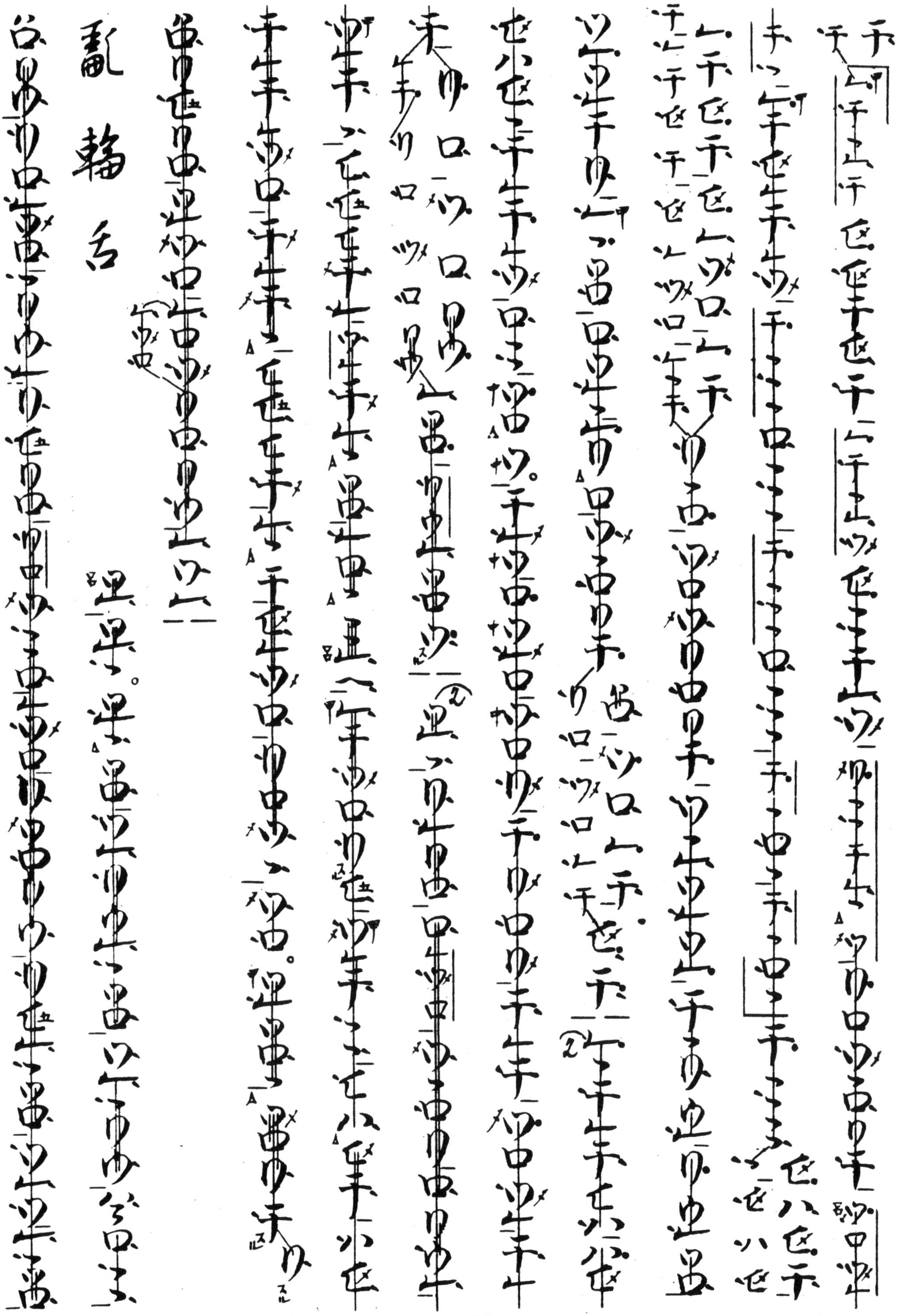

亂輪舌

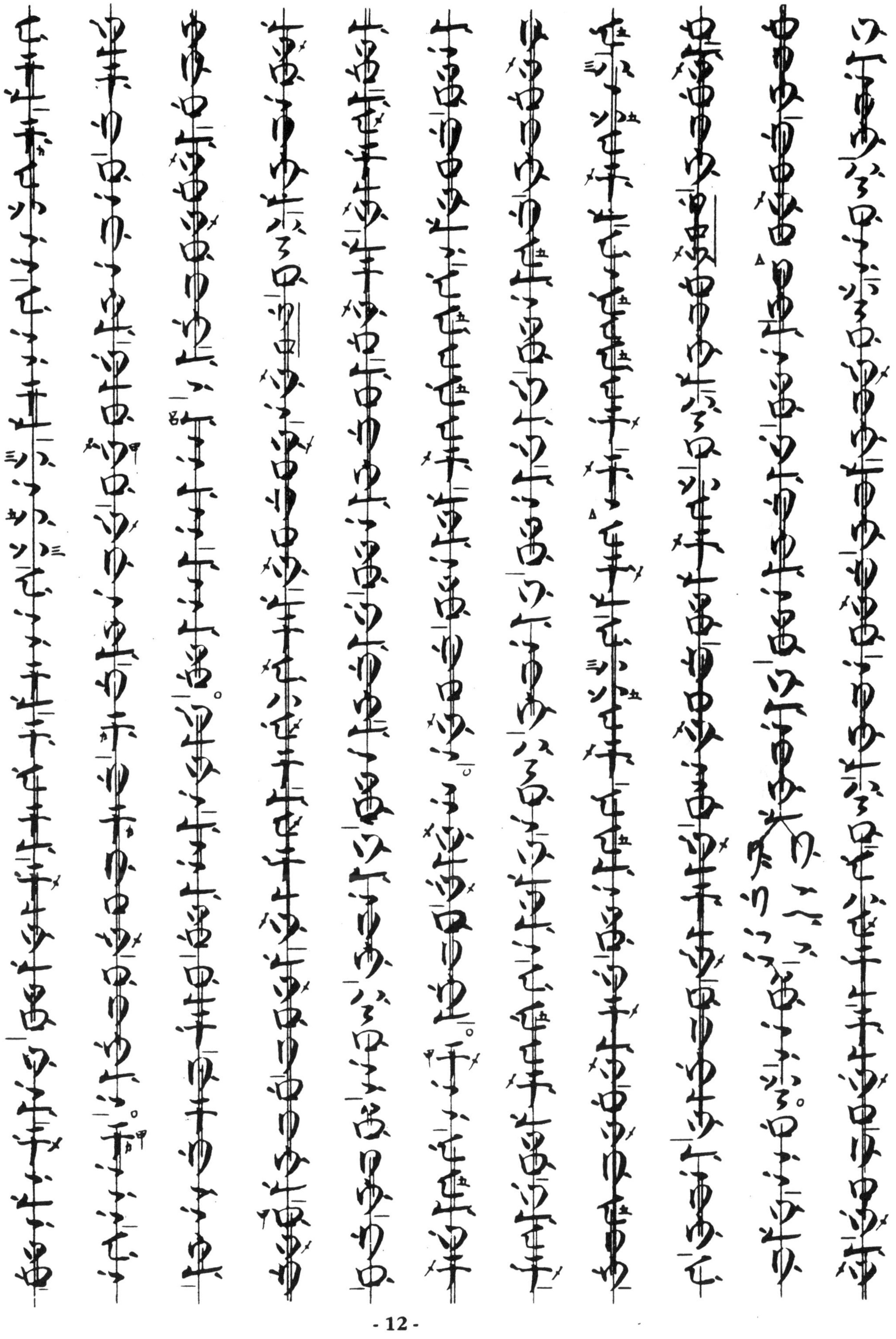

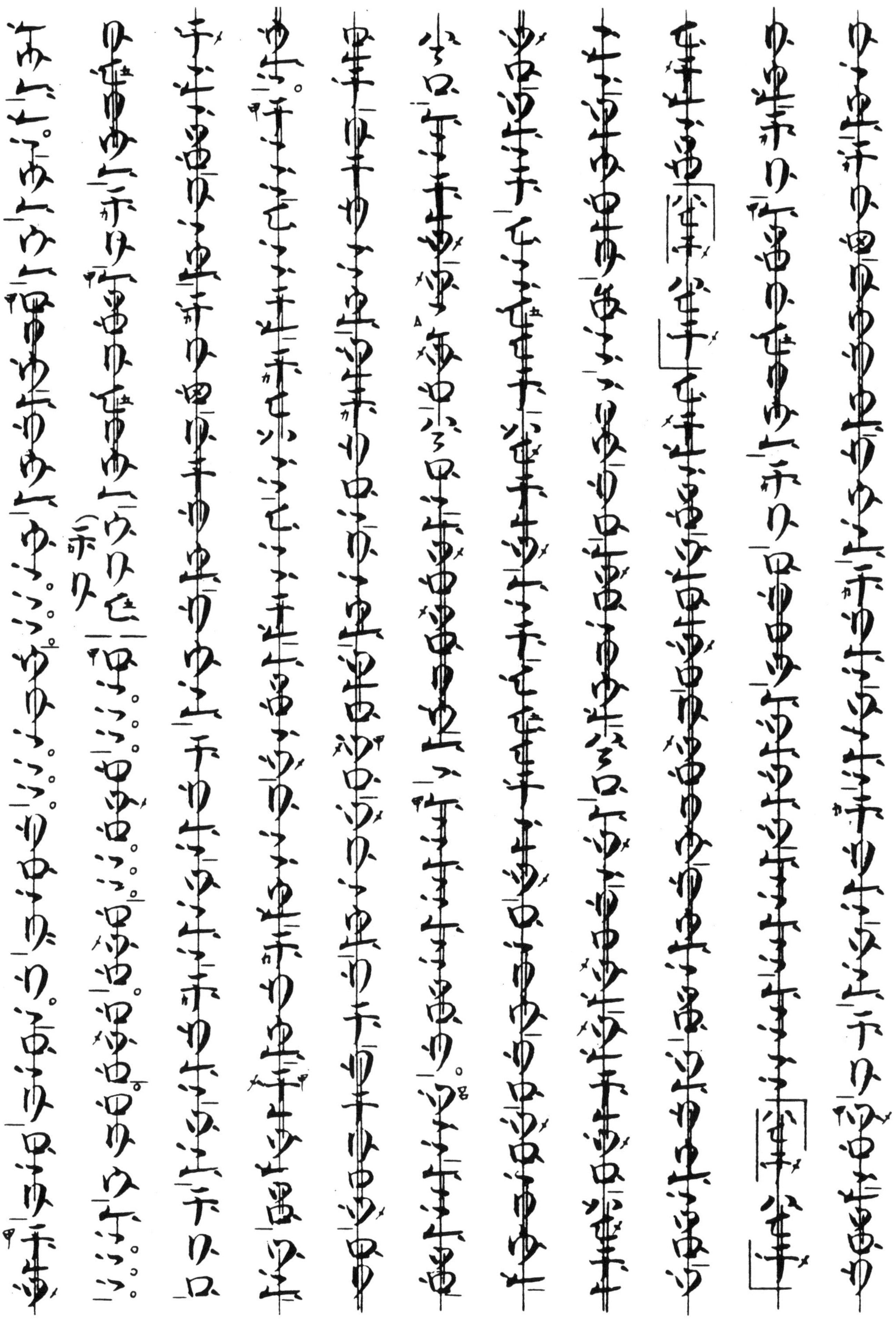

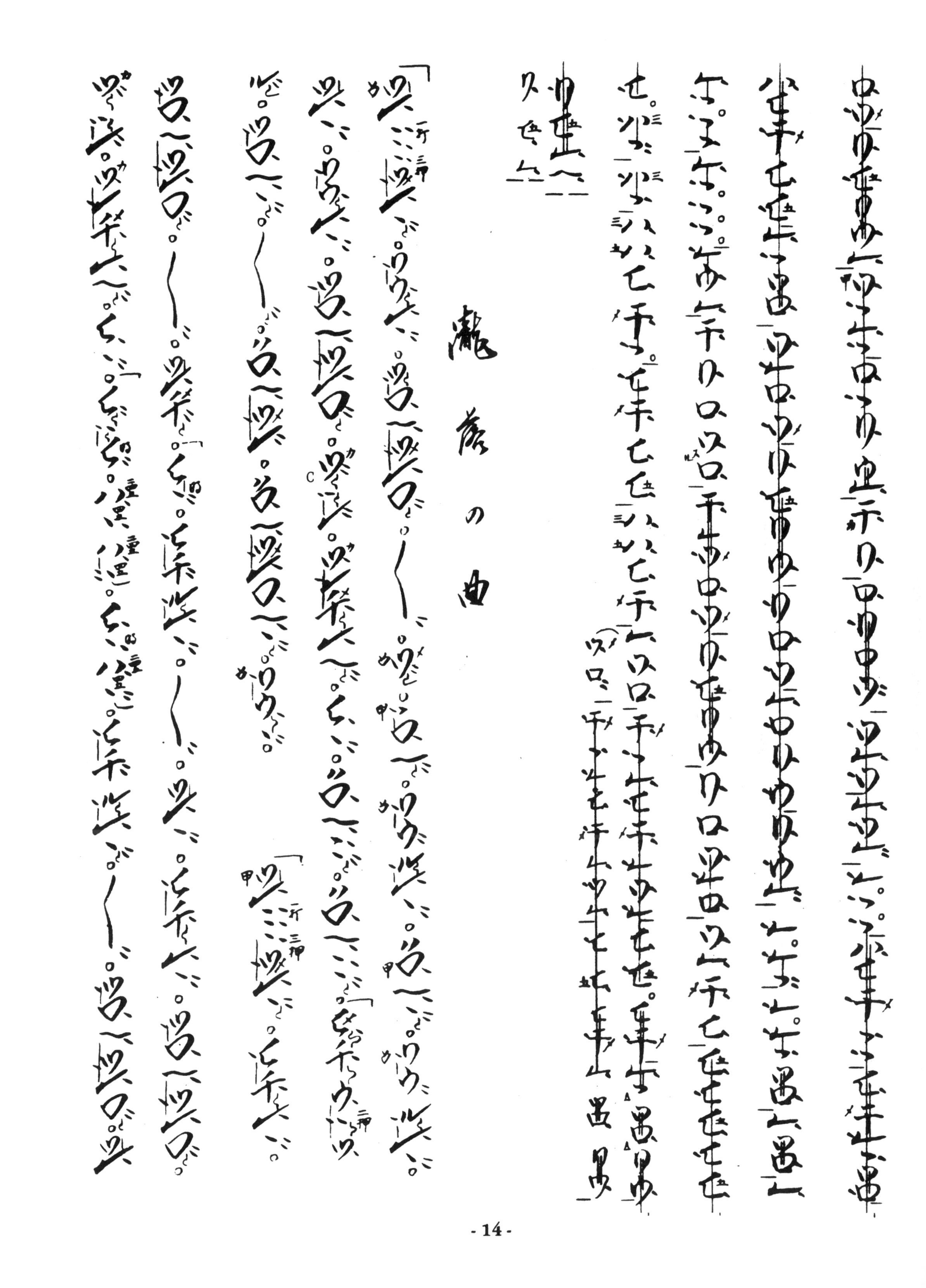

瀧落の曲

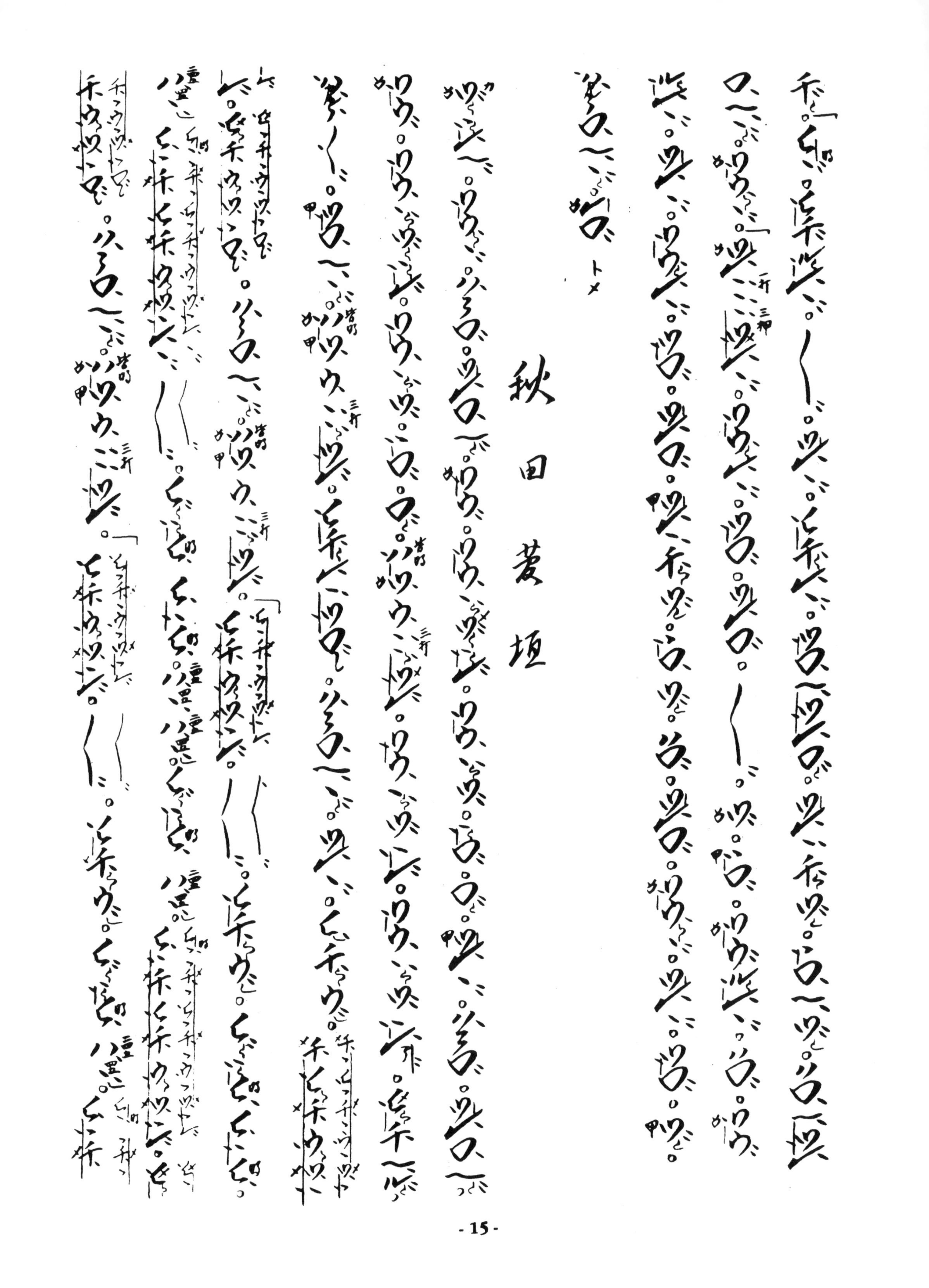

トメ

秋田菅垣

九州鈴慕

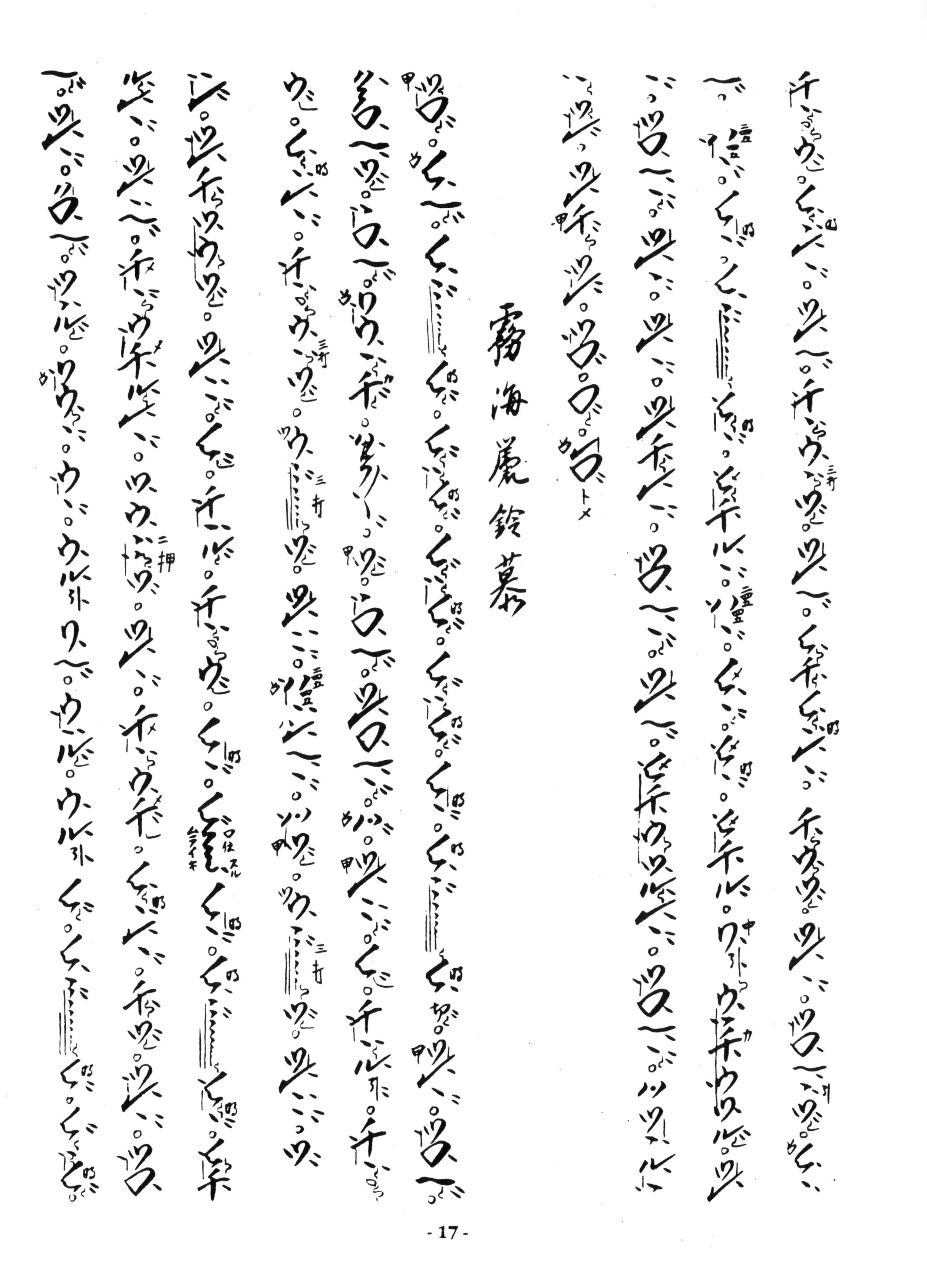

霧海麗鈴慕

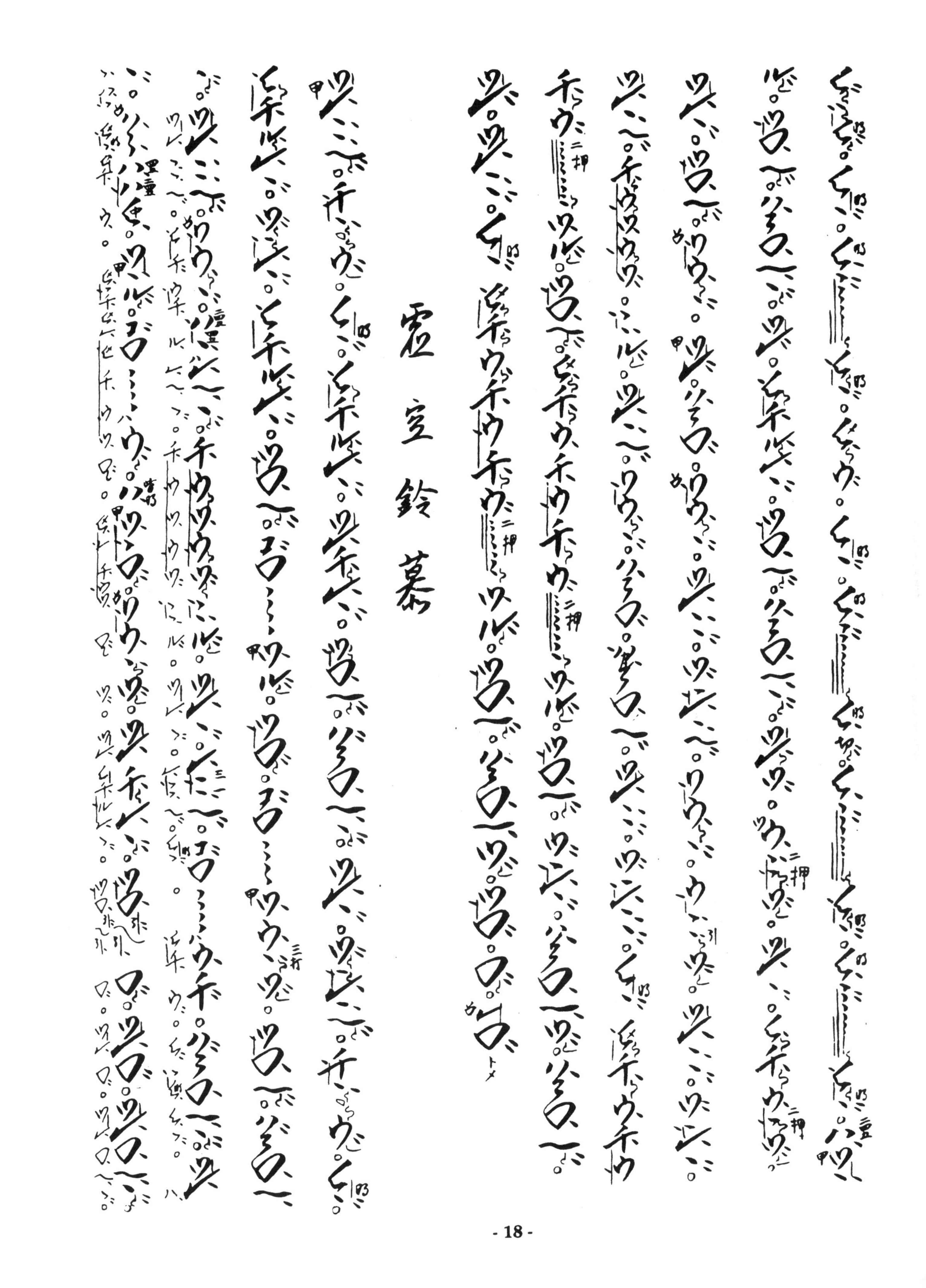

霞空鈴慕

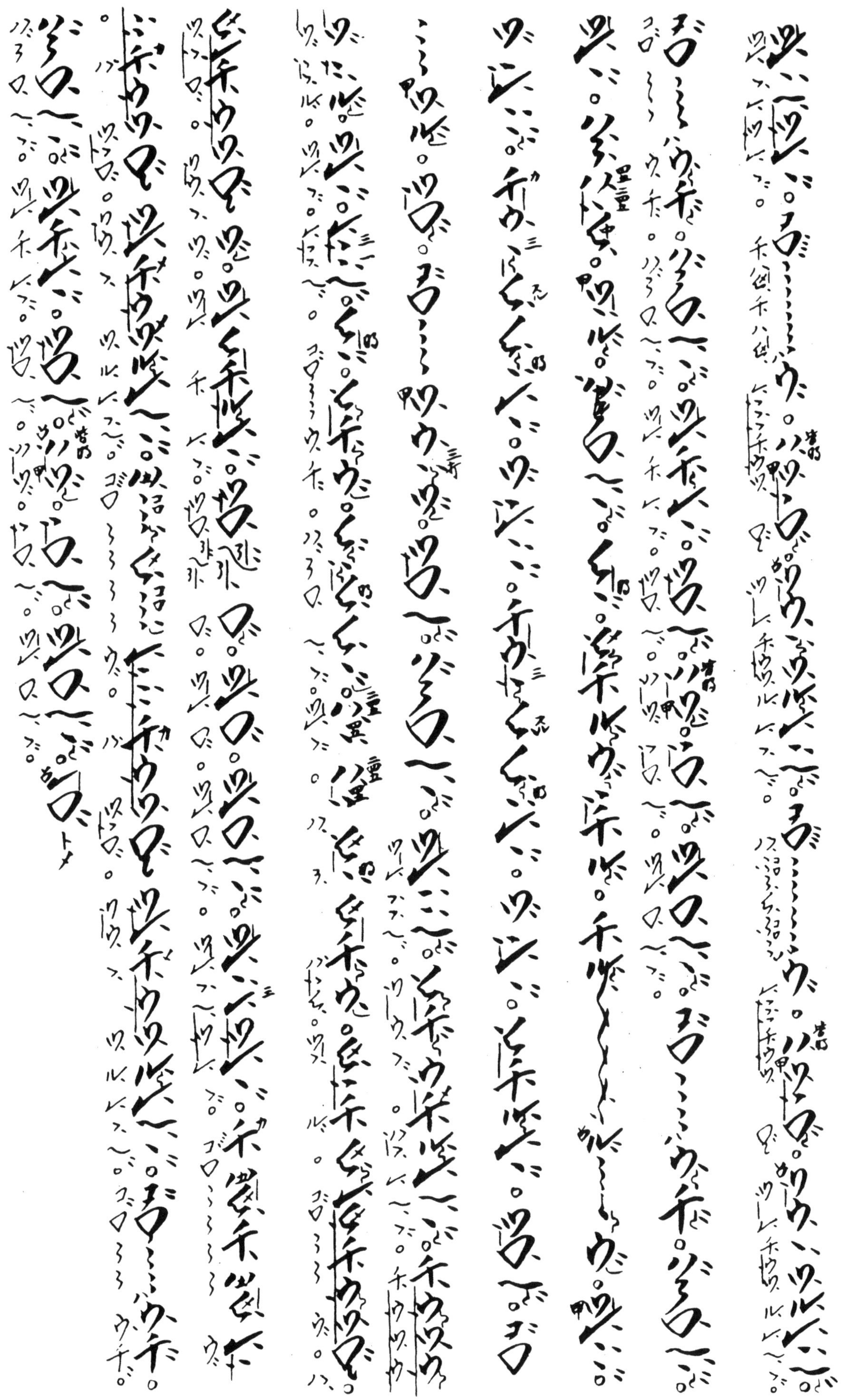

盤渉調

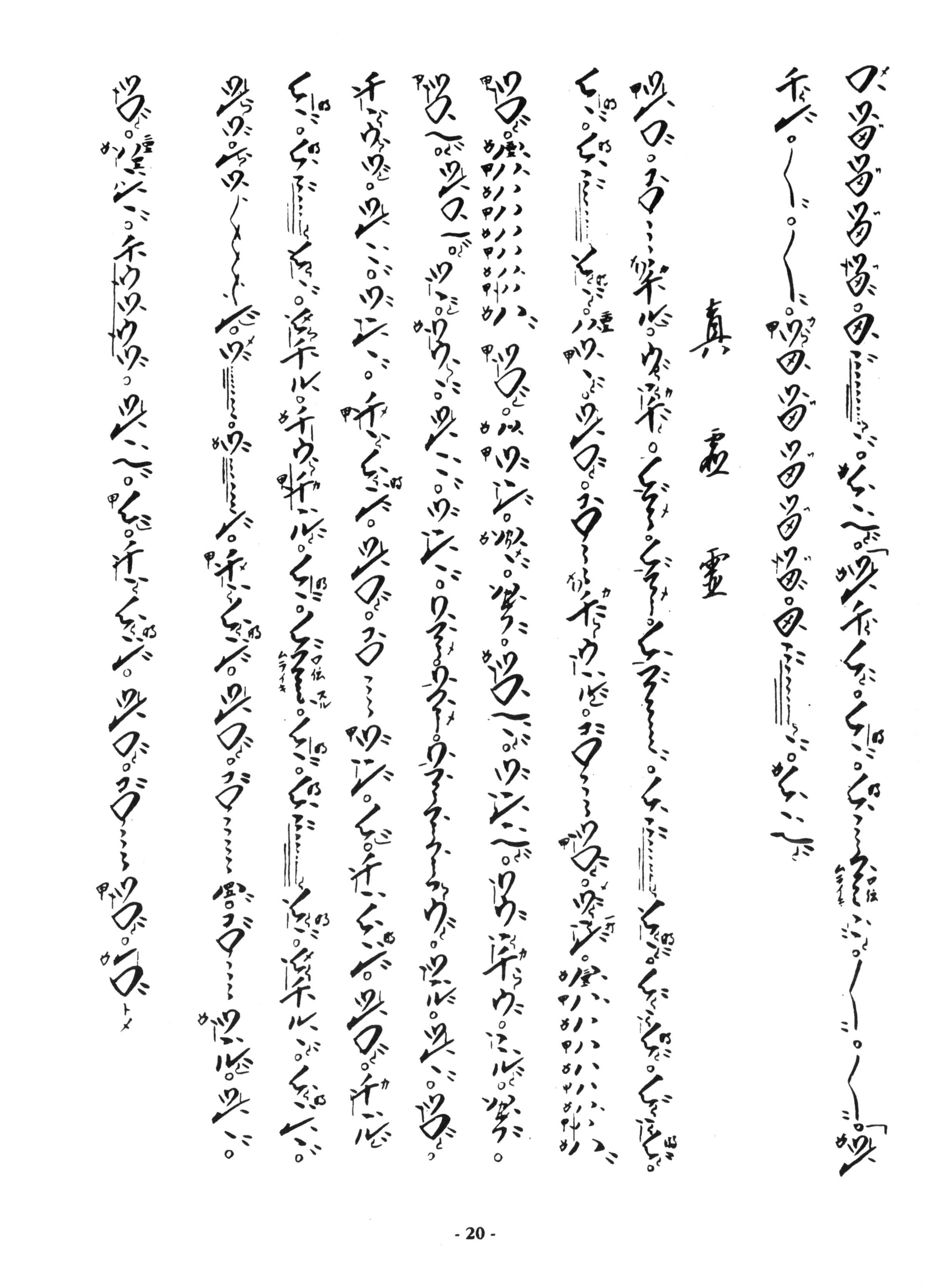

真虚霊

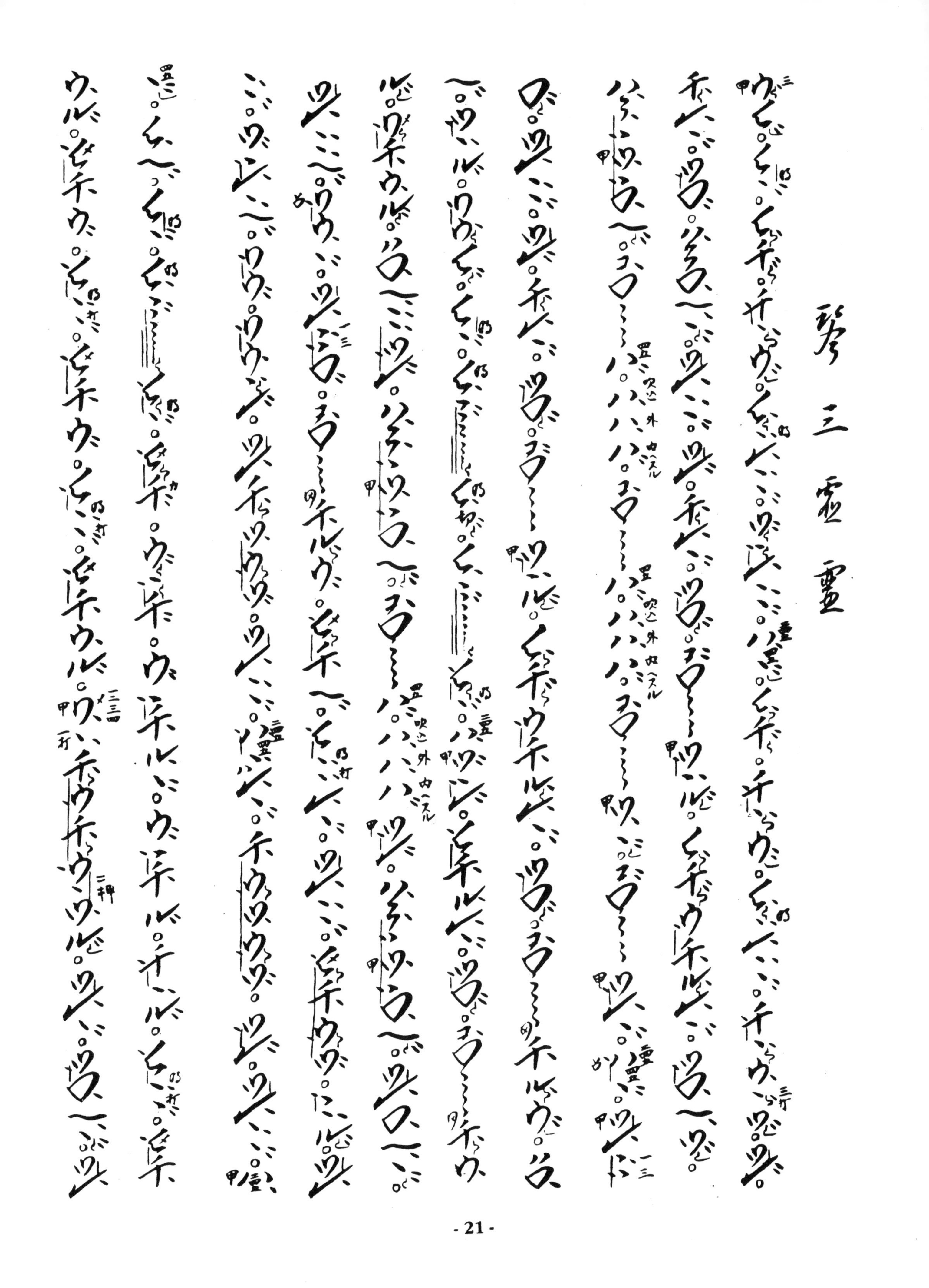

琴三霊

夕暮の曲

葦草鈴慕

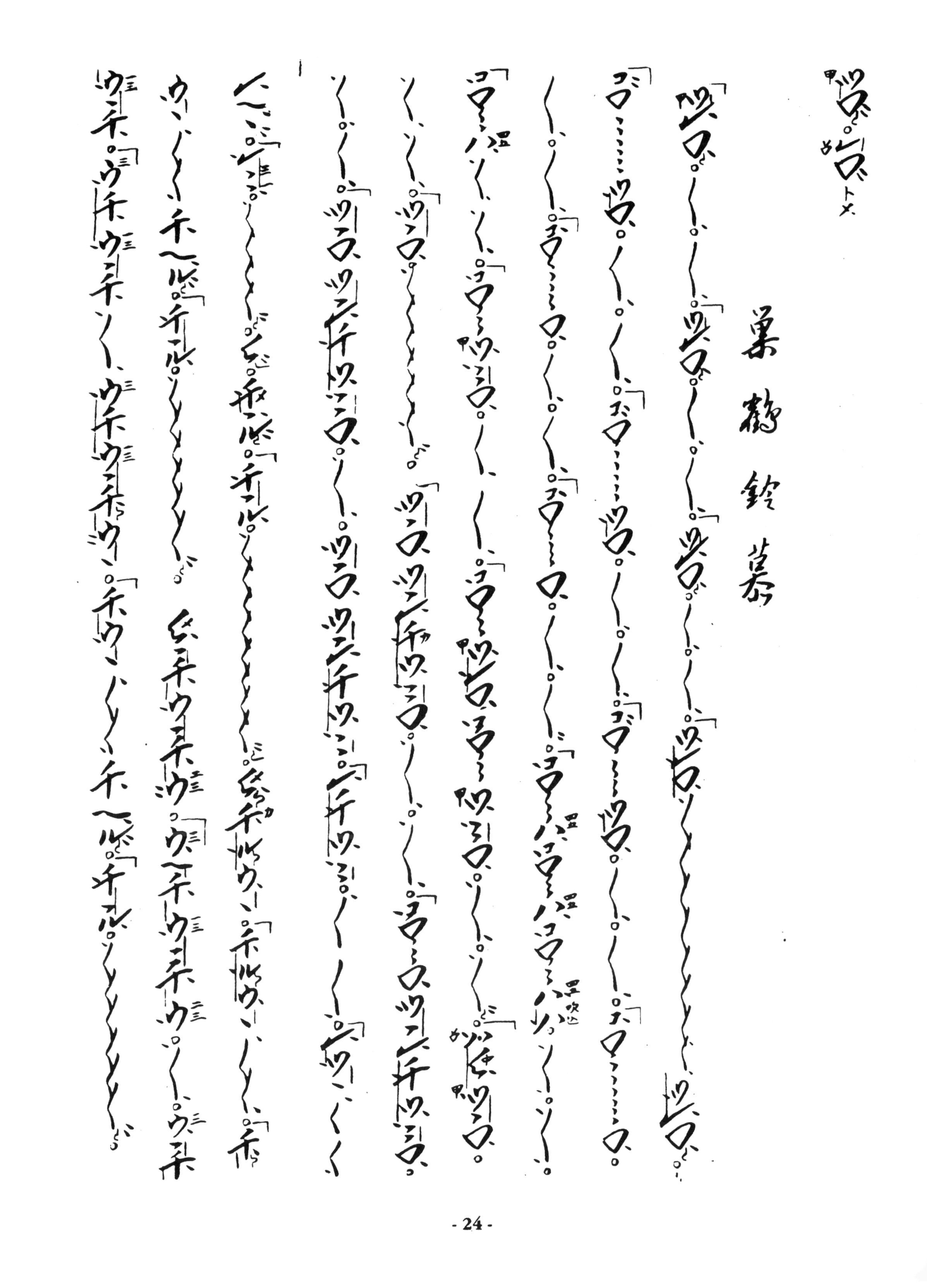

巣鶴鈴慕

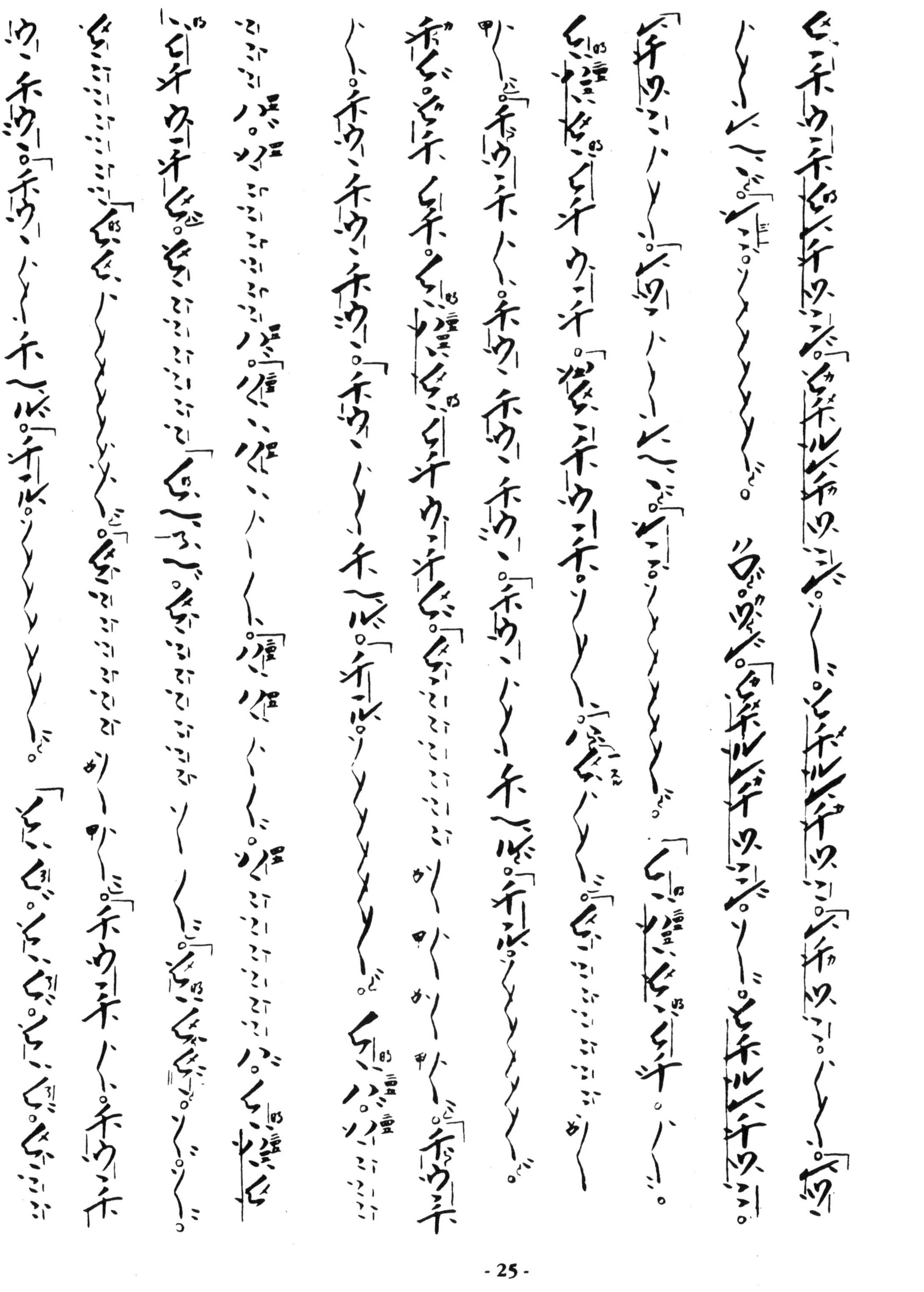

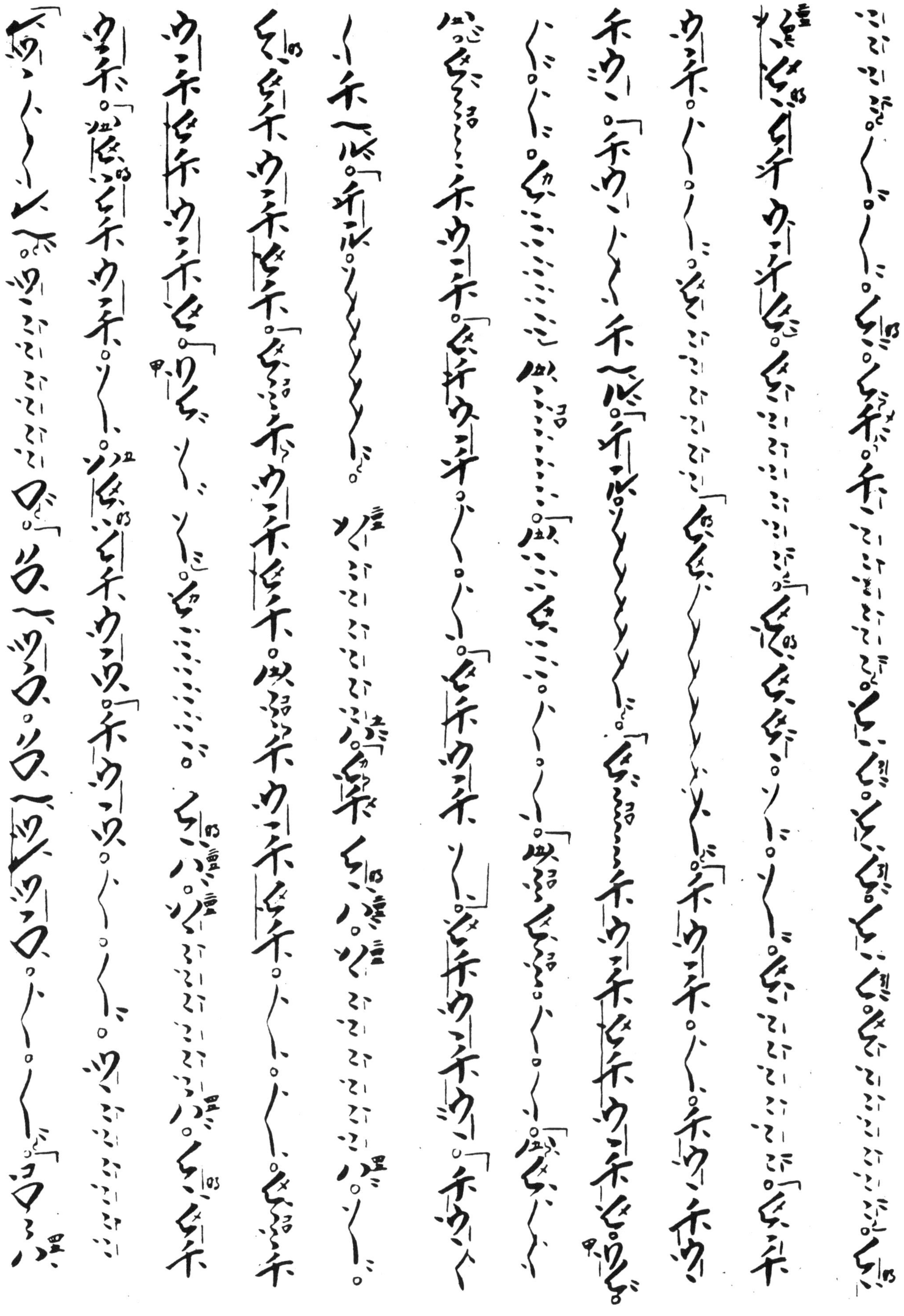

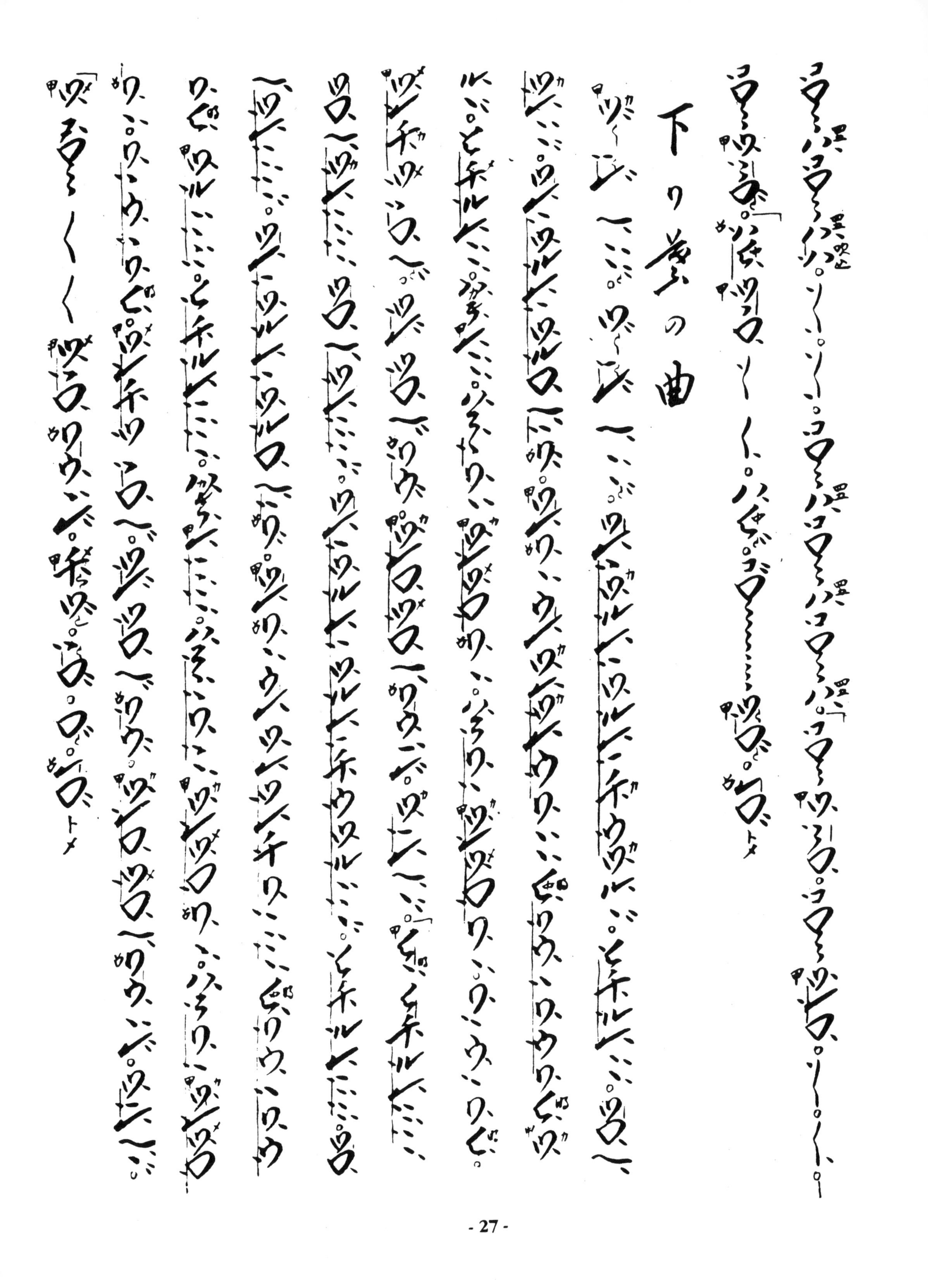

下り葉の曲

鹿の遠音

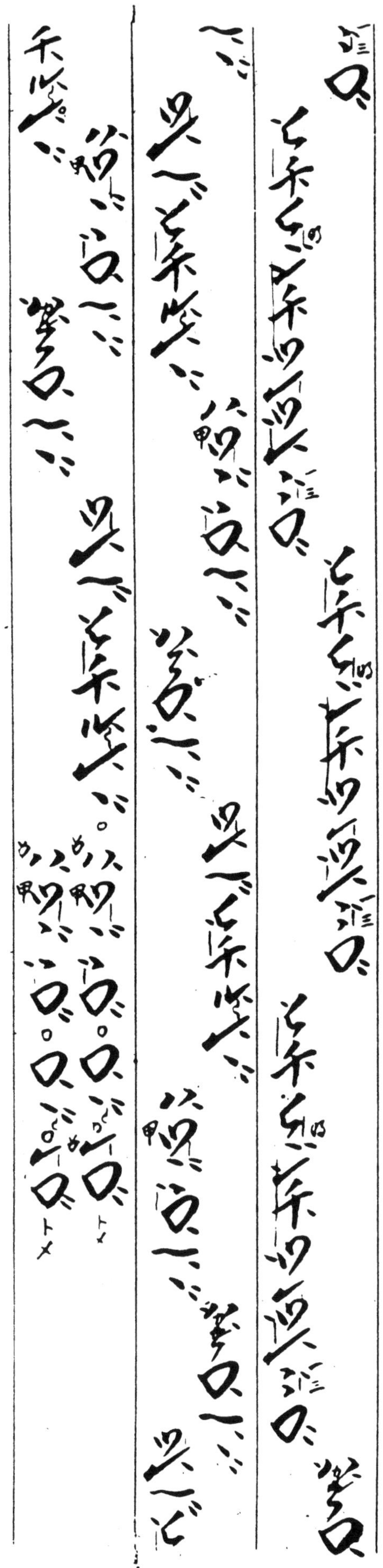

雲井獅子

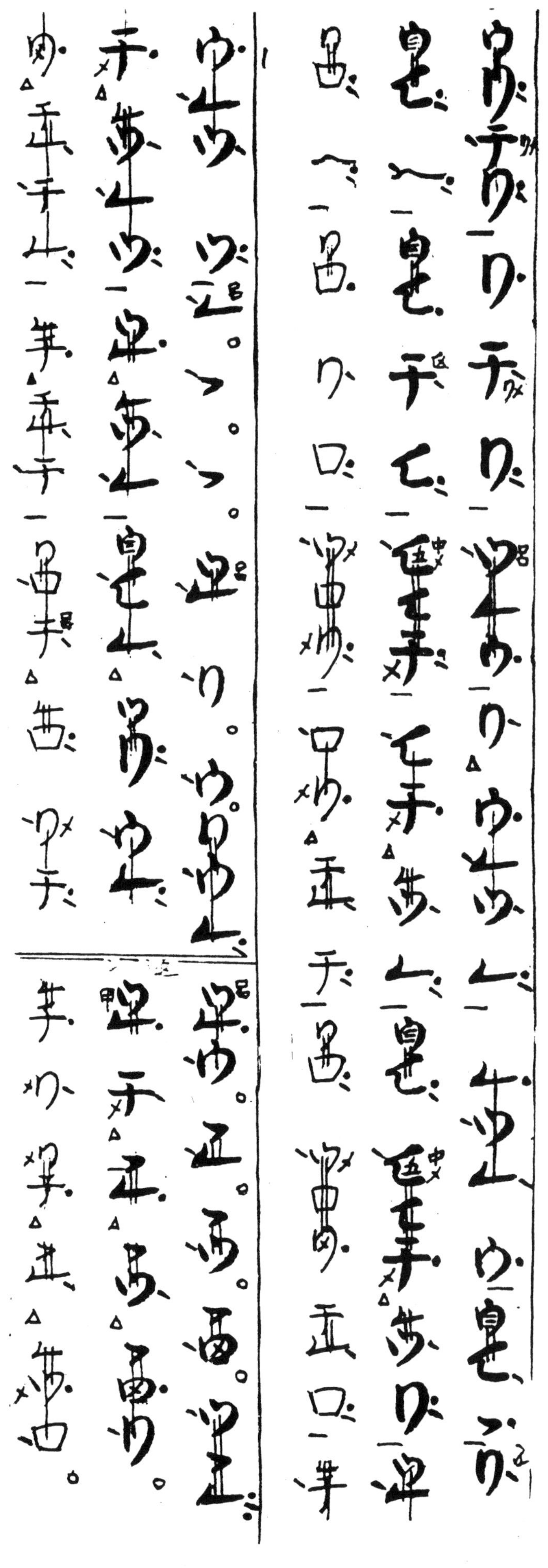

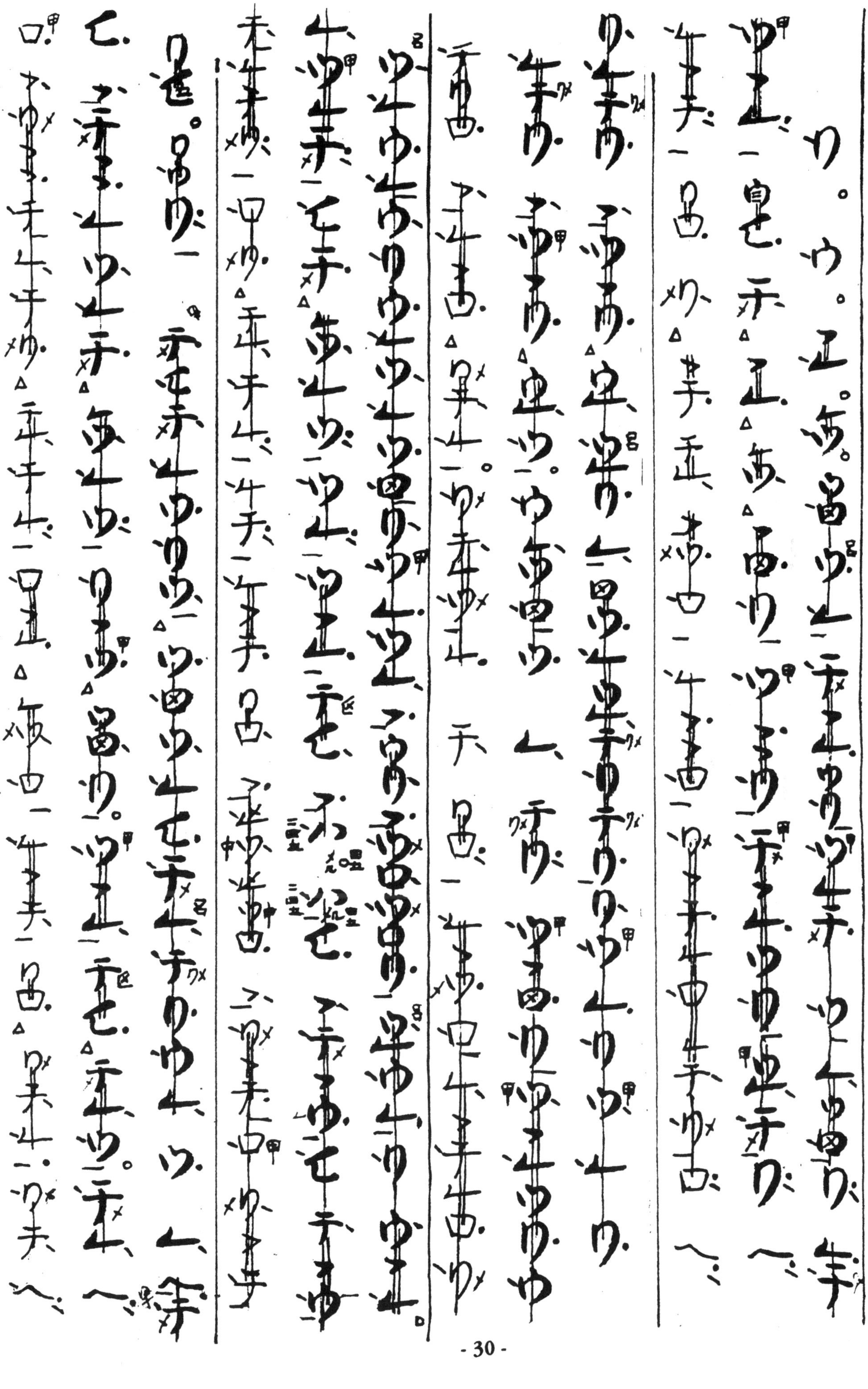

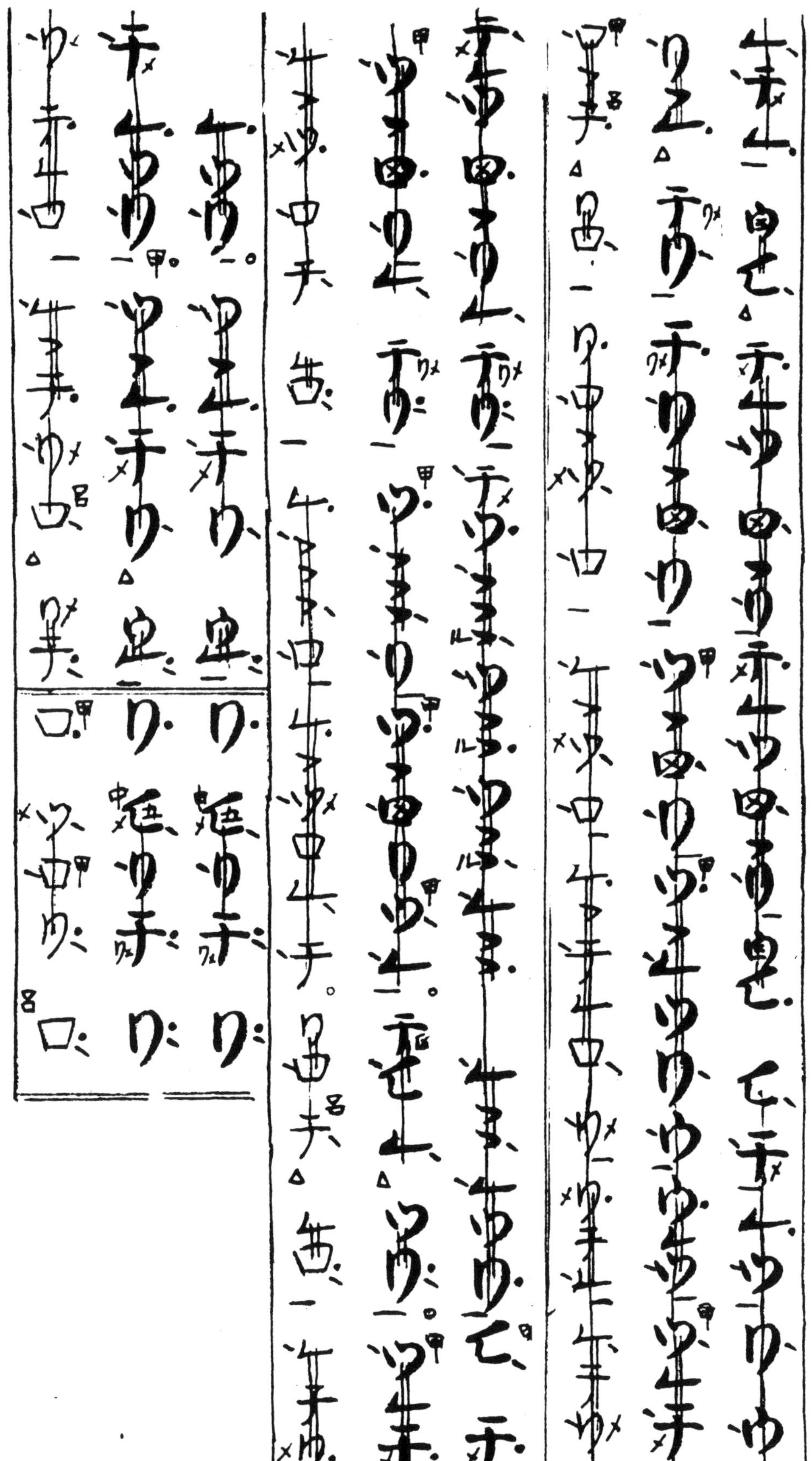

雲井獅子

佐山菅垣

月の曲

同寓獅子

是より△状印へ戻り同様に
都合二へん吹て下へ移る

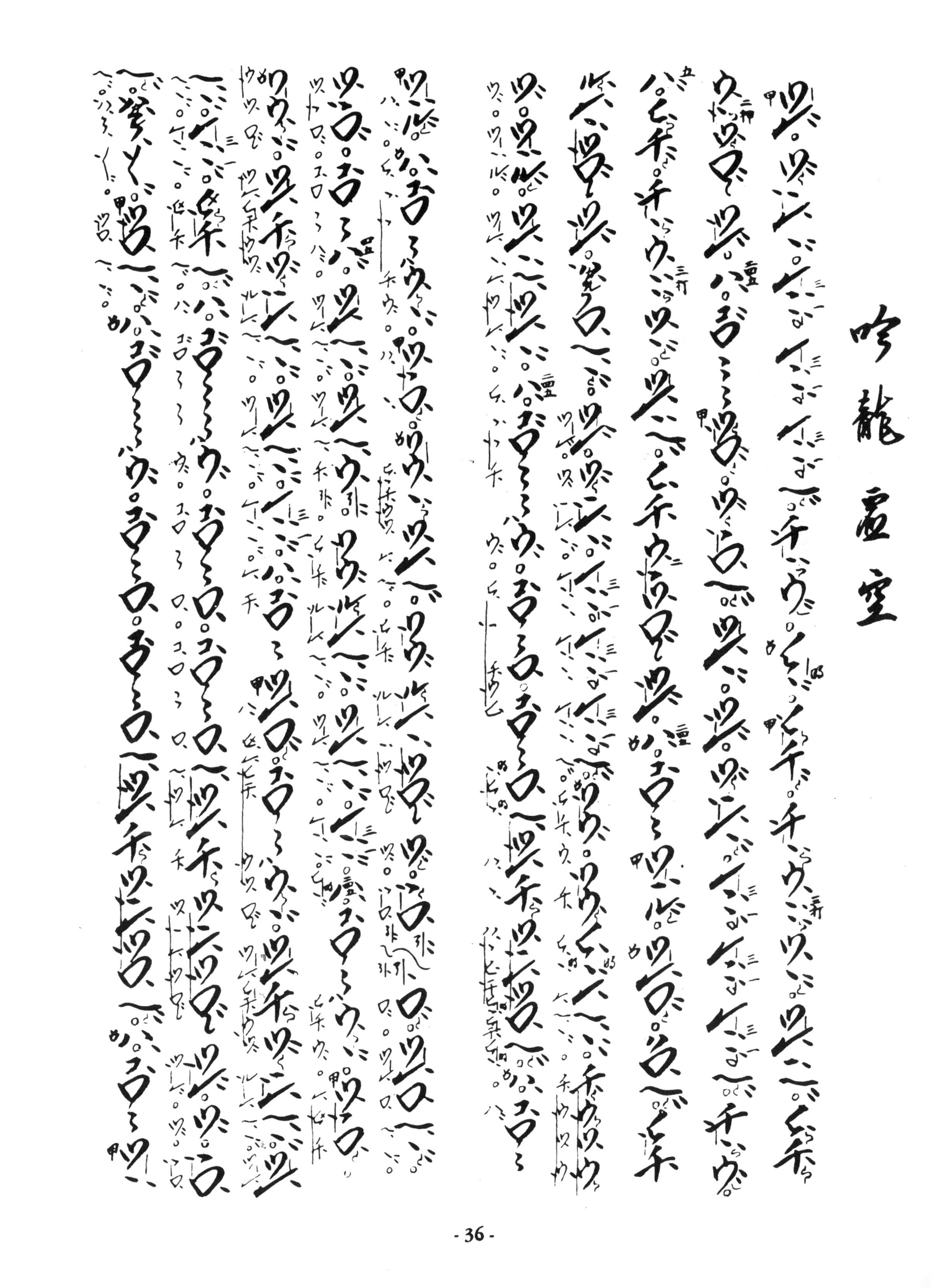

吟龍虚空

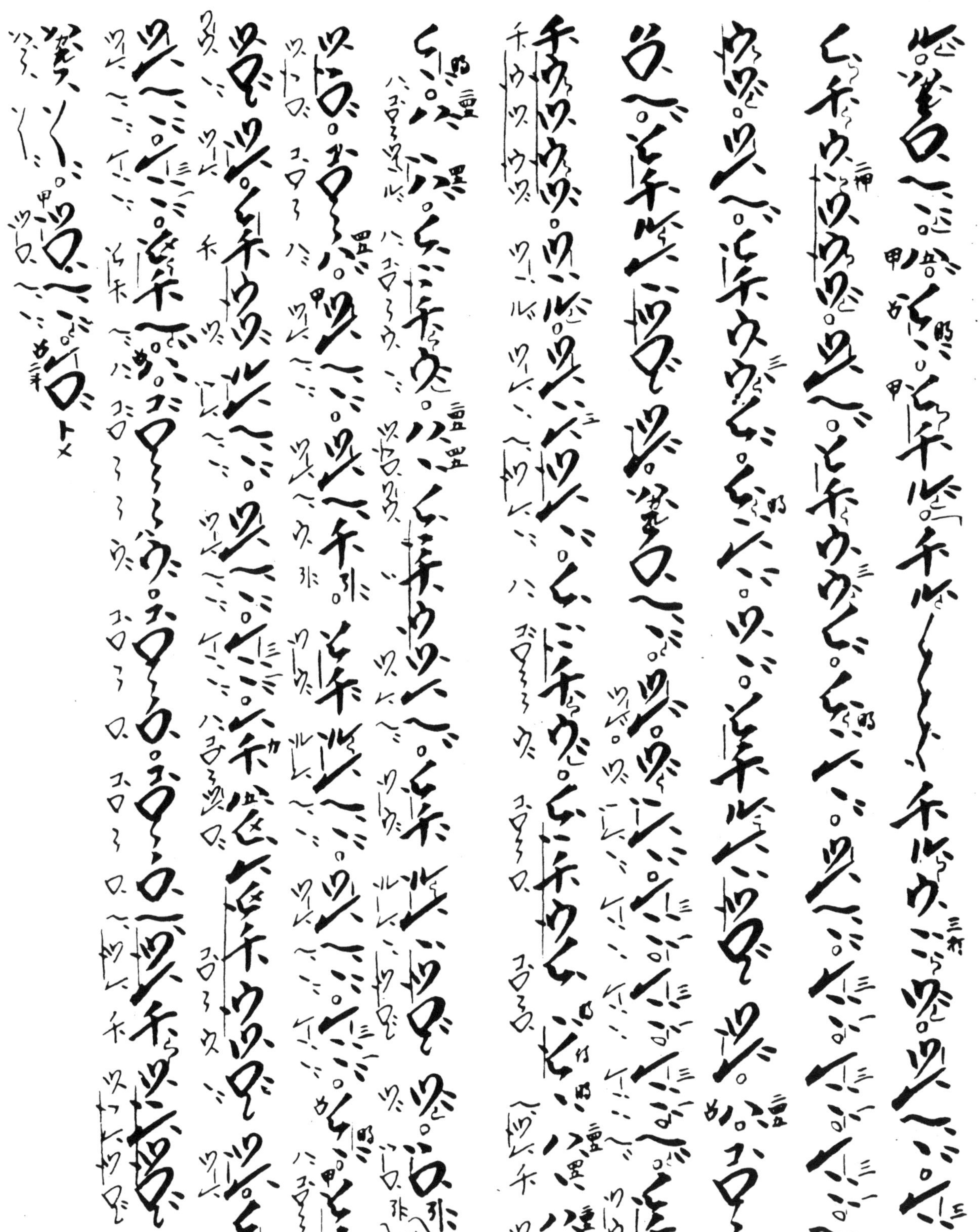

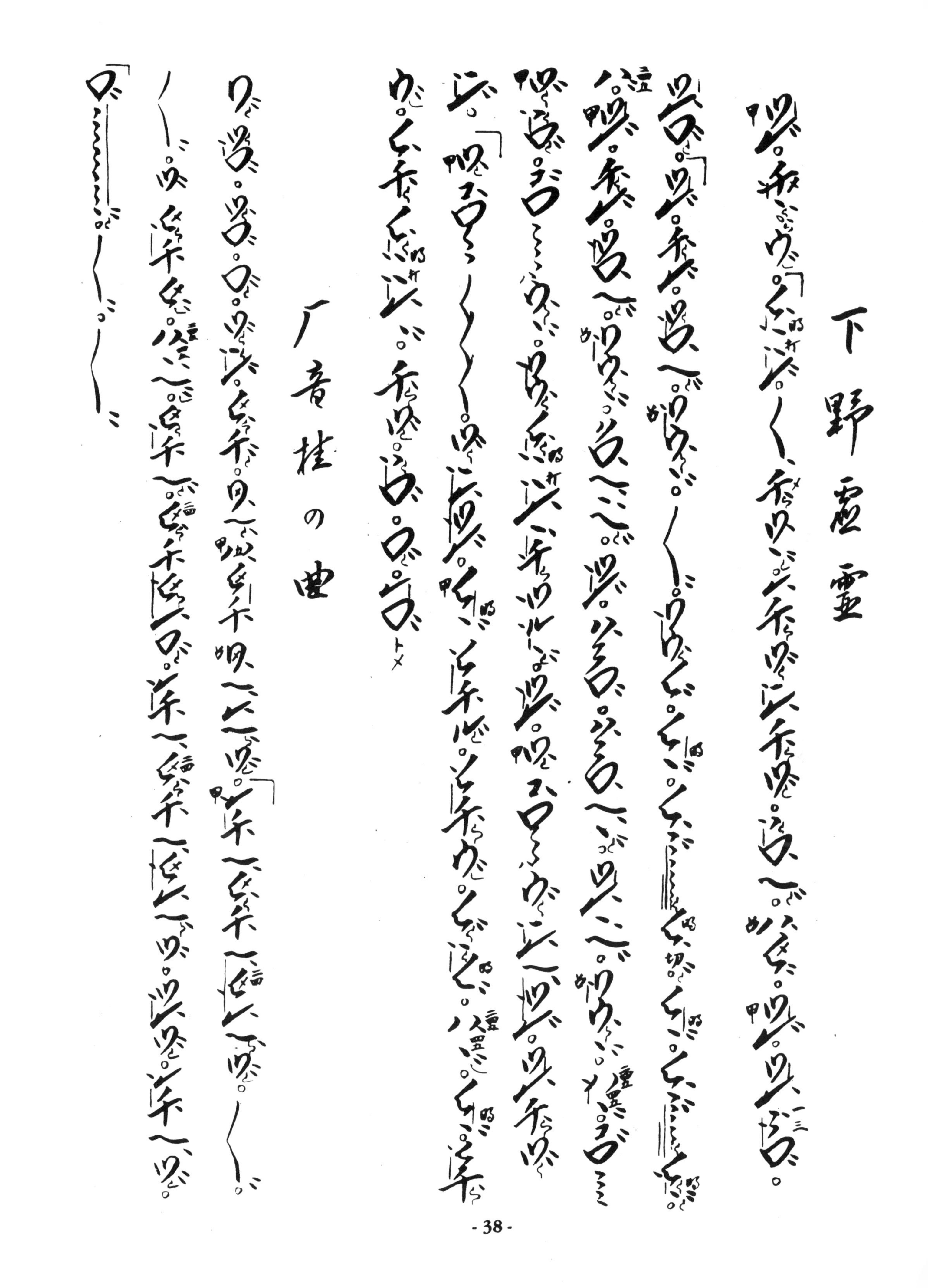

下野虚霊

厂音桂の曲

芦の調

三谷菅垣

鳳将雛

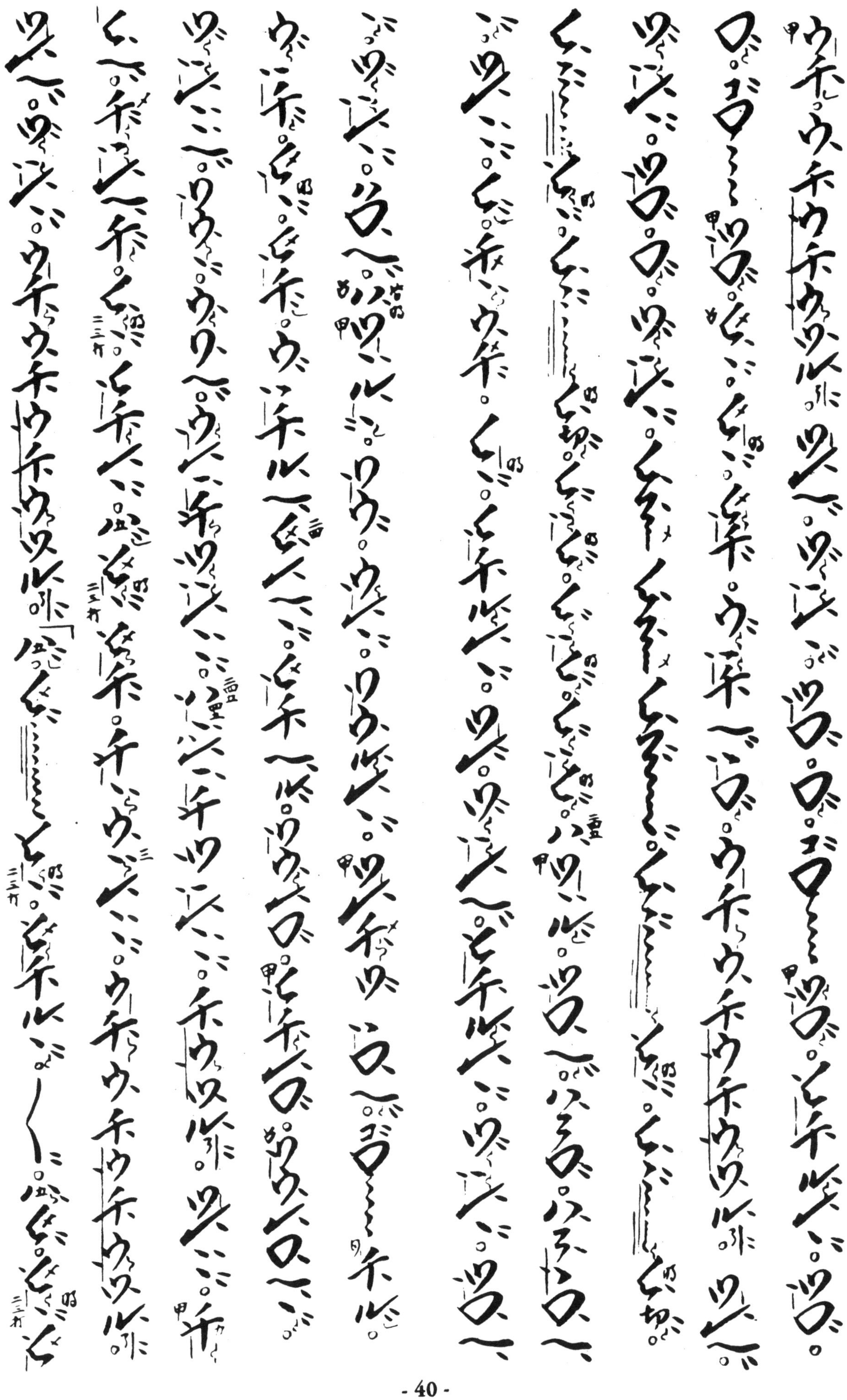

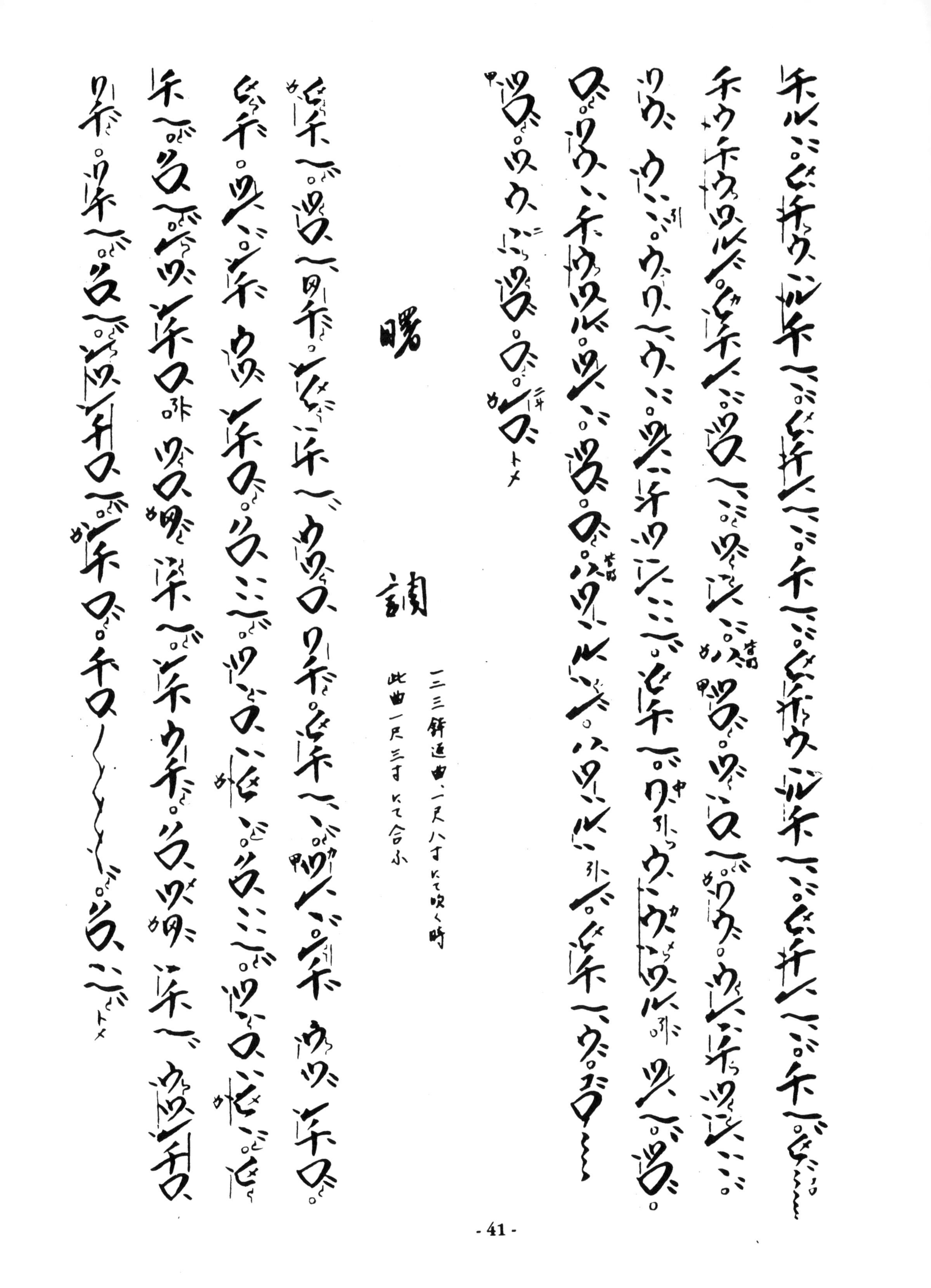

曙調

一三三鉢返曲、一尺八寸にて吹く時
此曲一尺三寸にて合ふ

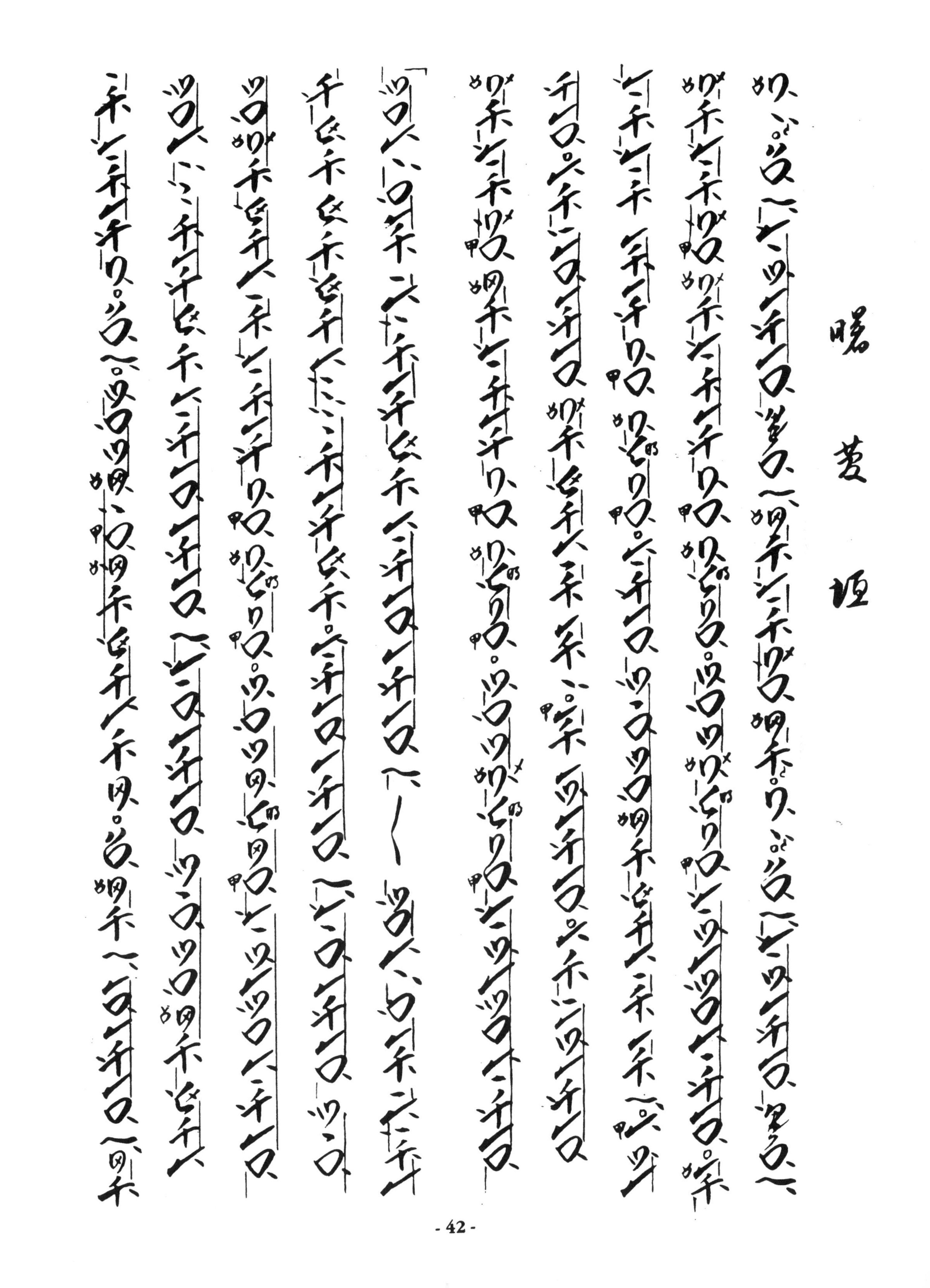

曙菅垣

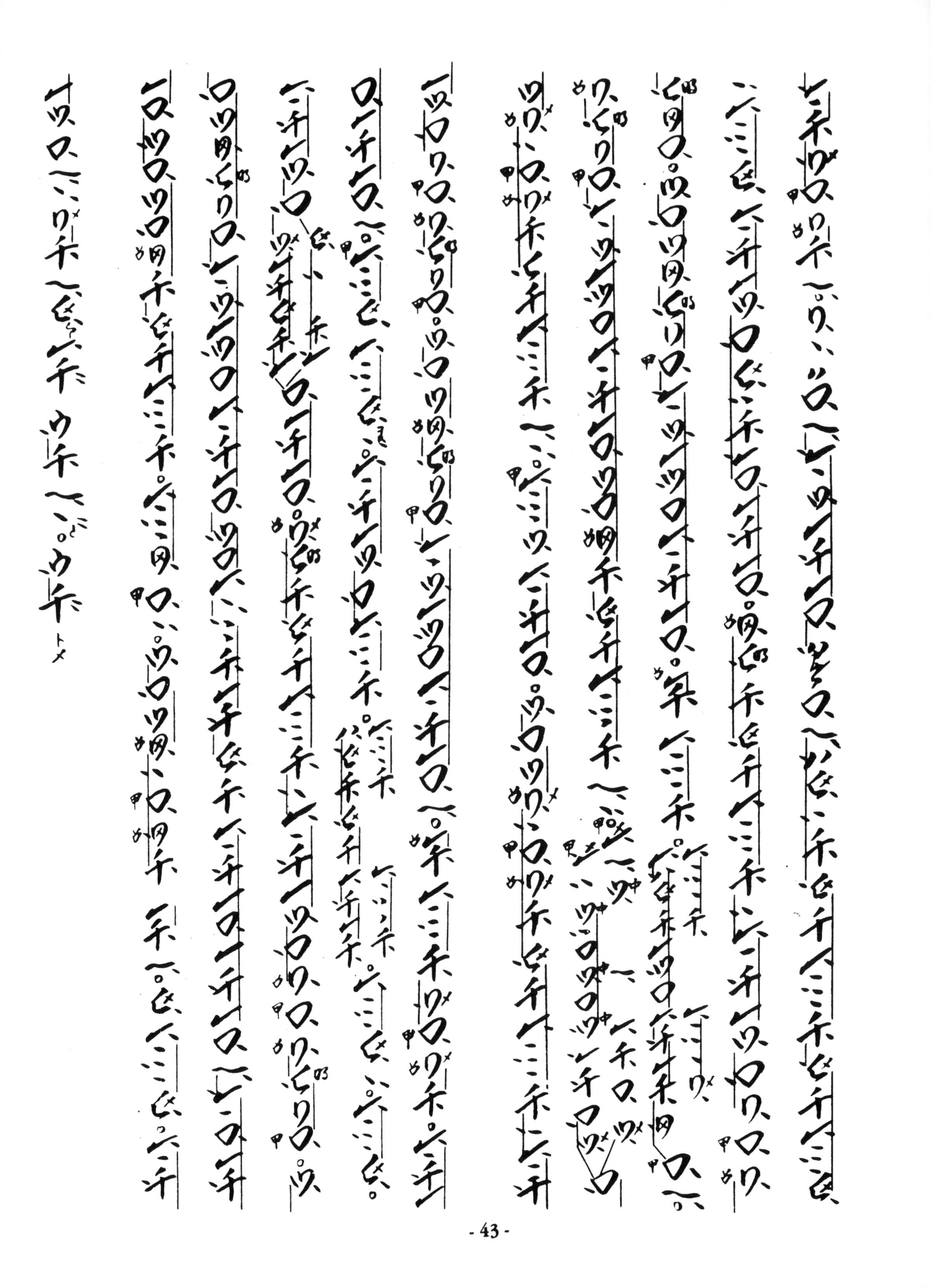

波間鈴慕

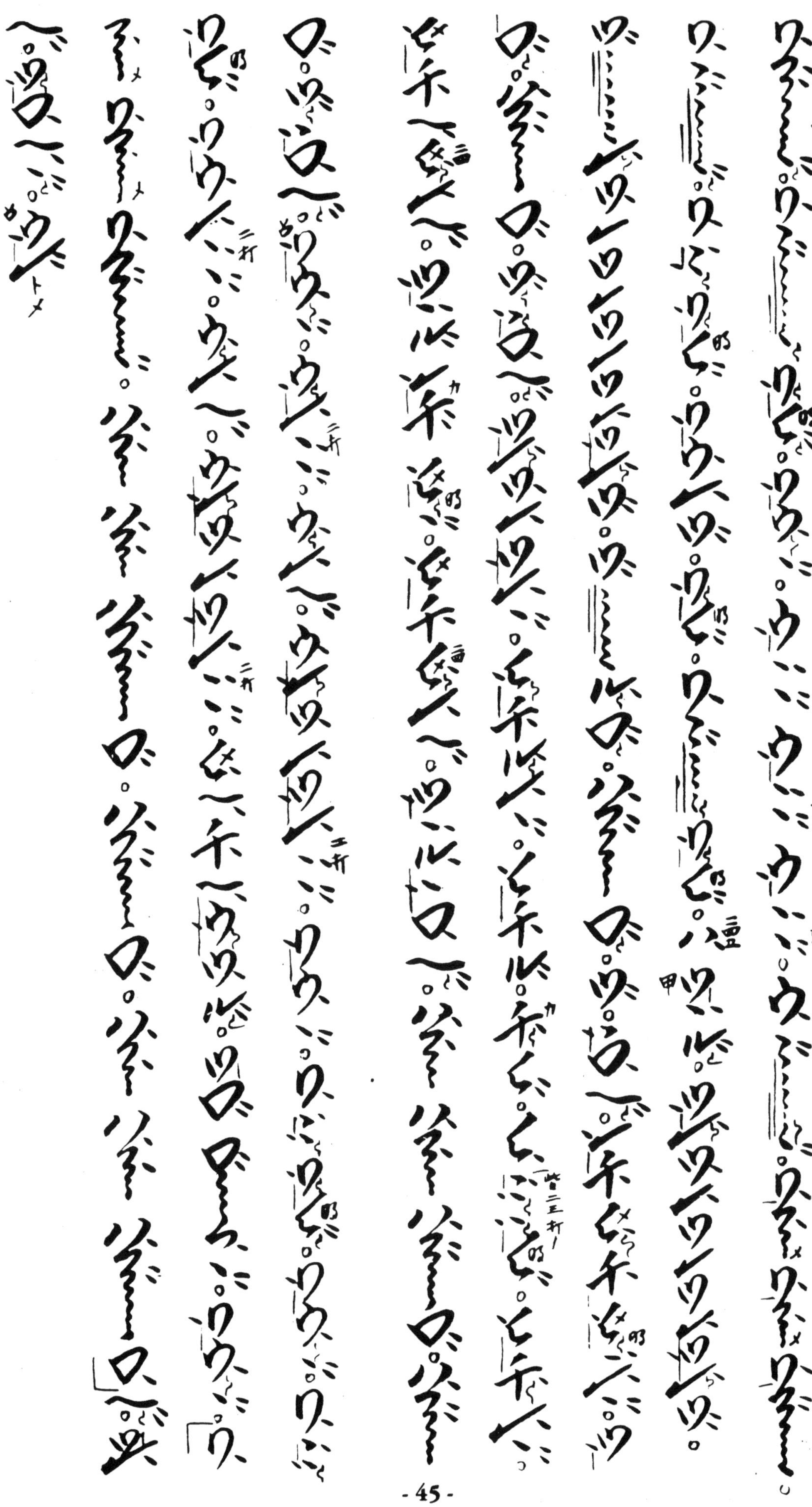

毬と殿様

紅屋の娘

花嫁人形

(rest)

雨降りお月さん

NOTE: The MERI of a note is often indicated by a slash through the note instead of a symbol next to the note. (乙) is the low octave symbol used in this notation.

出船

お江戸日本橋

黒田節

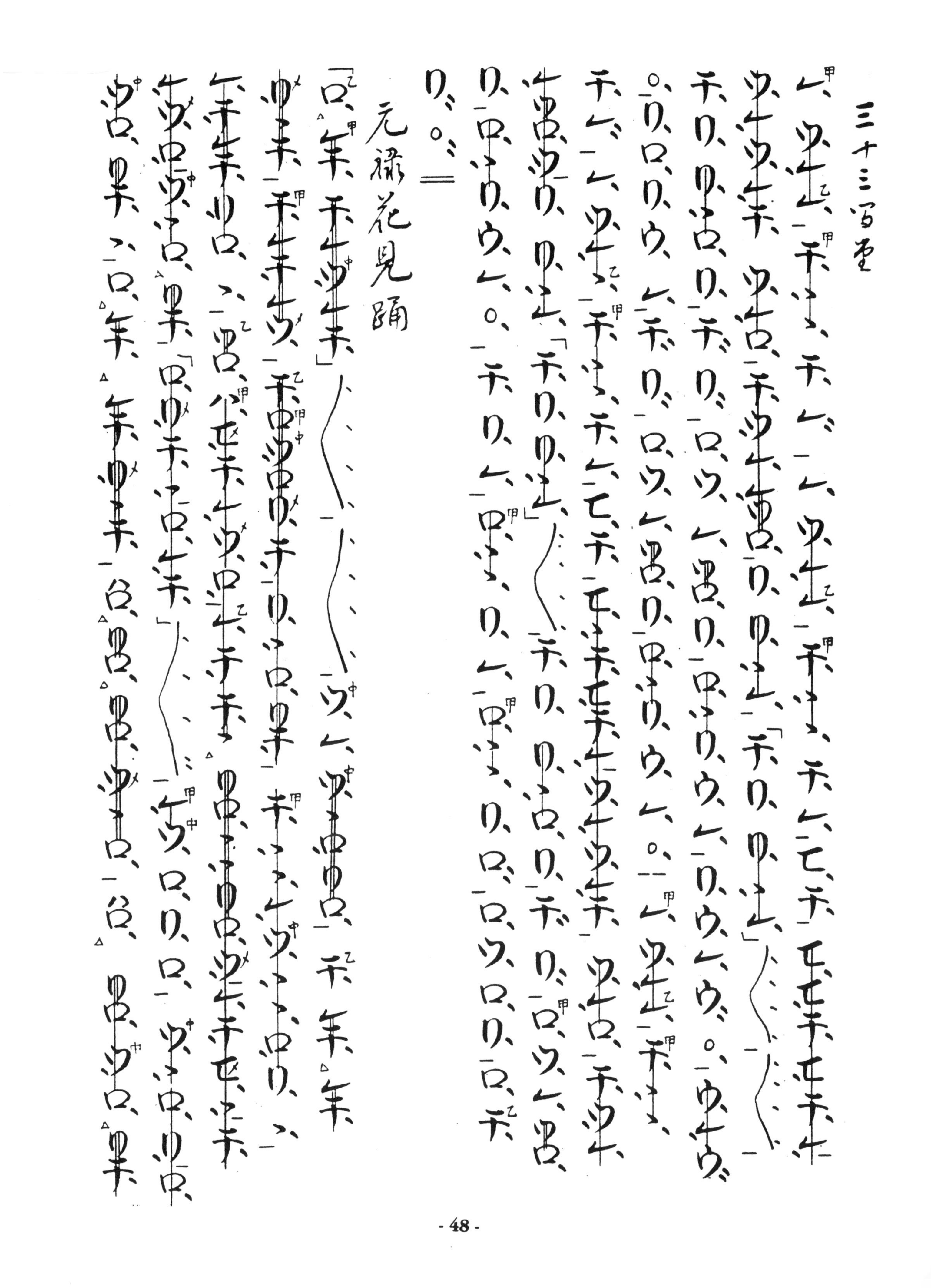

三十三間堂

元禄花見踊

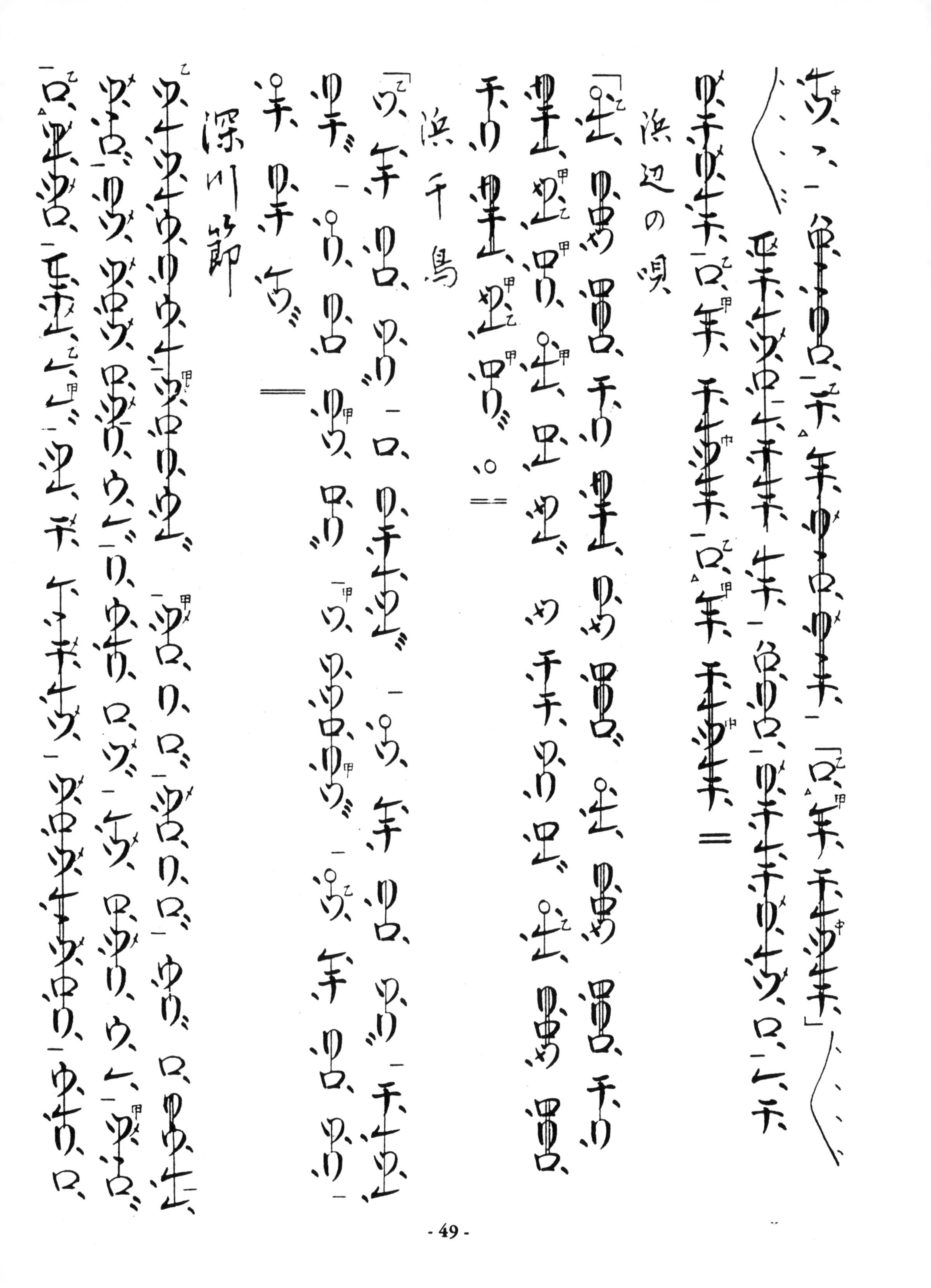

浜辺の唄

浜千鳥

深川節

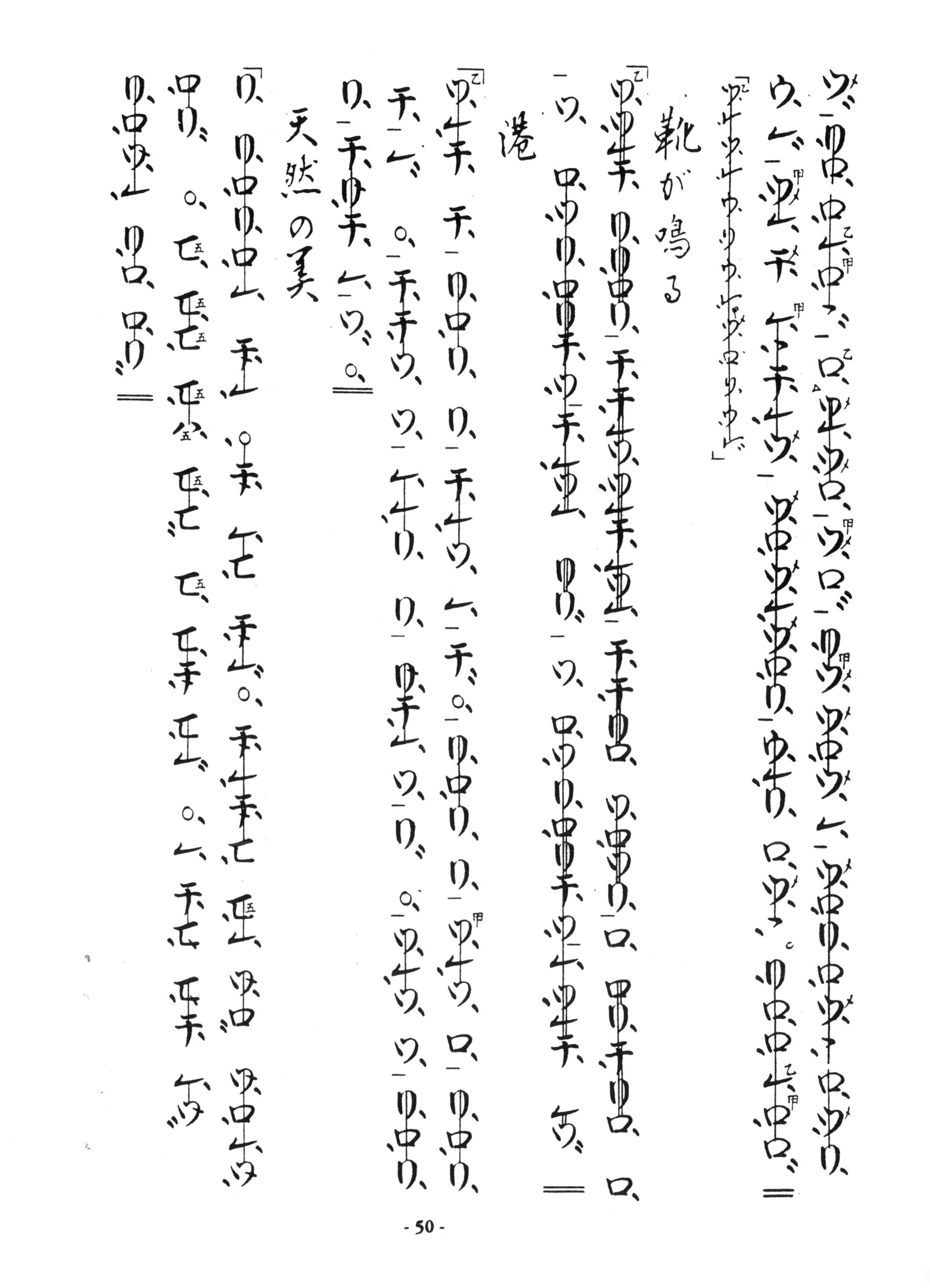

靴が鳴る

港

天然の美

茶摘み

かっぽれ

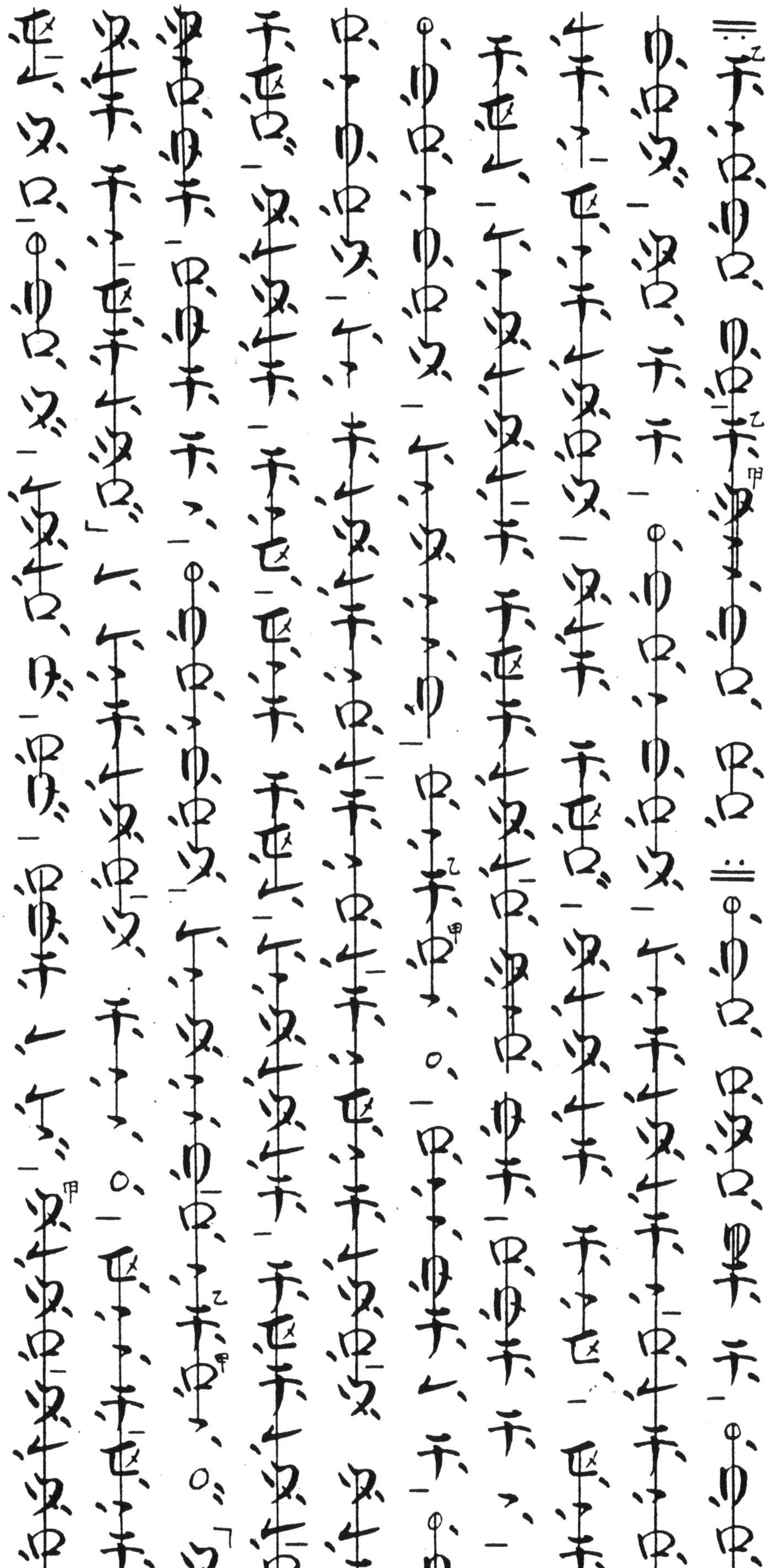

稗搗節

越後獅子

春雨

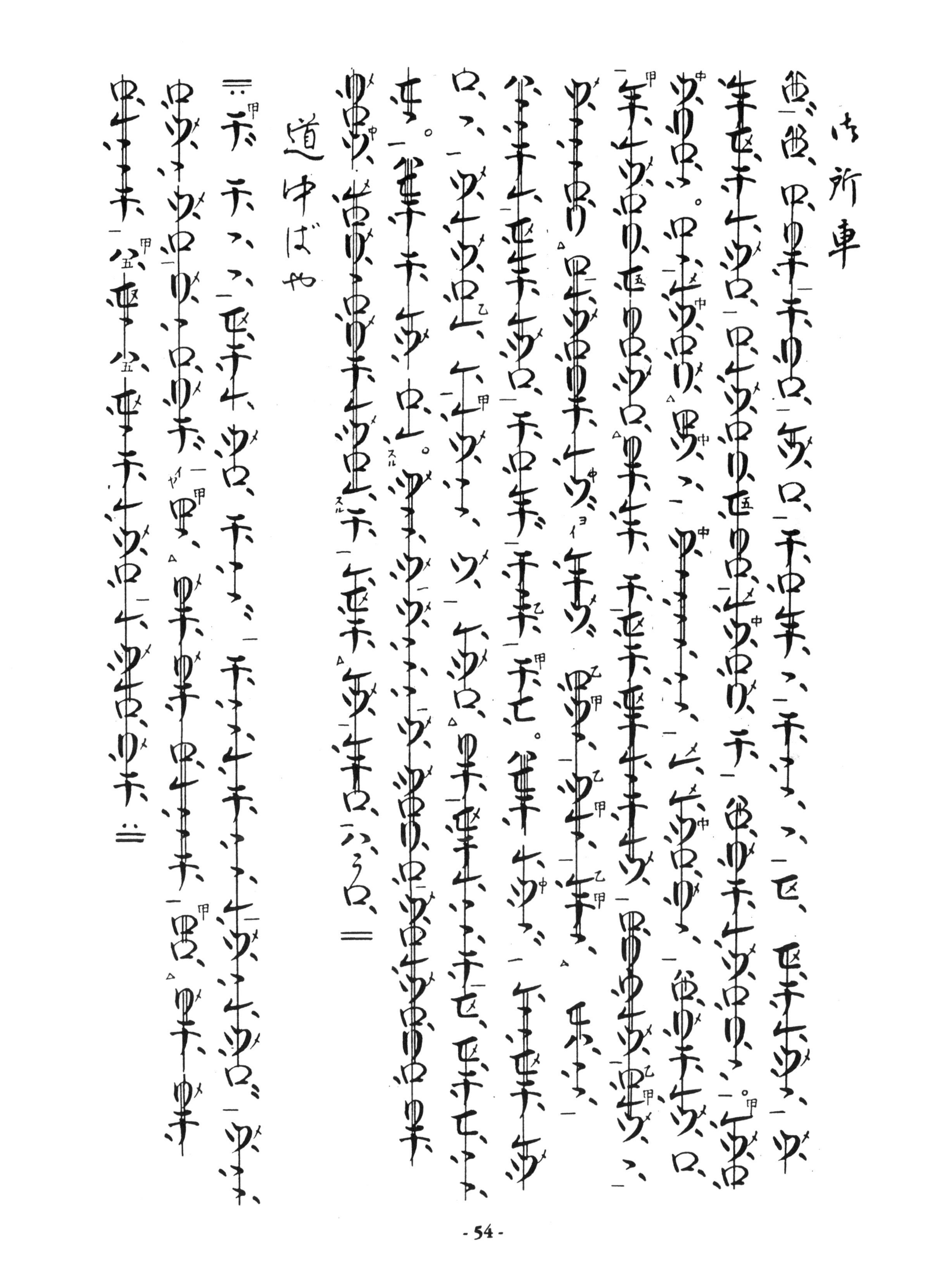

御所車

道中ばや

7905264R00085

Made in the USA
San Bernardino, CA
21 January 2014